THE BITTERSWEET SCIENCE

THE BITTERSWEET SCIENCE

Fifteen Writers in the Gym,
in the Corner, and at Ringside

EDITED BY CARLO ROTELLA
AND MICHAEL EZRA

The University of Chicago Press
Chicago and London

The University of Chicago Press, Chicago 60637
The University of Chicago Press, Ltd., London
© 2017 by The University of Chicago
Published 2017
Printed in the United States of America

26 25 24 23 22 21 20 19 18 17   1 2 3 4 5

ISBN-13: 978-0-226-34620-5 (paper)
ISBN-13: 978-0-226-34634-2 (e-book)
DOI: 10.7208/chicago/9780226346342.001.0001

Library of Congress Cataloging-in-Publication Data
Names: Rotella, Carlo, 1964– editor. | Ezra, Michael, 1972– editor.
Title: The bittersweet science : fifteen writers in the gym, in the corner, and at ringside / edited by Carlo Rotella and Michael Ezra.
Description: Chicago ; Illinois : The University of Chicago Press, 2017.
Identifiers: LCCN 2016037105 | ISBN 9780226346205 (pbk. : alk. paper) | ISBN 9780226346342 (e-book)
Subjects: LCSH: Boxing. | Boxers (Sports)—United States.
Classification: LCC GV1133 .B58 2017 | DDC 796.83—dc23 LC record available at https://lccn.loc.gov/2016037105

♾ This paper meets the requirements of ANSI/NISO Z39.48-1992 (Permanence of Paper).

CONTENTS

Introduction

BITTERSWEETNESS

Carlo Rotella and Michael Ezra

The more you know about boxing, the more you discover that you never truly know what's going on. Even if you have the best ringside seat and the best-placed inside sources at your disposal, even if you're a fighter or a trainer or manager, even if you're Don King in 1990 and you control the prime Mike Tyson and the world heavyweight title and the lion's share of the boxing business (but not Buster Douglas), you still confront an infinite sequence of unknowns and mysteries. Even if you can watch enough of a fighter's training sessions and bouts to arrive at a reliable assessment of his ability, there are still crucial considerations that don't yield so easily to observation: What did he learn from previous bouts? What else has happened to him, perhaps far beyond the ring, that affects him as a boxer? Where's the money behind his next fight coming from and going to, and what outcome would serve those interests? You encounter such questions, and their answers matter, even if all you care about is the usual sports-page concern with winners, losers, and athletic drama. The mysteries multiply, of course, when you push past the prosaic *who, what, where, when,* and *how* of boxing and into the analytical *why* and the interpretive *what did it mean?* The compelling spectacle of boxing inspires the impulse to plumb its significance and understand the workings of the machinery that produces it, to see what goes on inside and behind the violent whirlwind of man-made force. But it's never a good idea to get cocky about what you think you've figured out.

Boxing has always attracted writers because it issues a standing challenge to their powers of description and imagination, and also a warning—really, a promise—that no matter how many layers of meaning you peel away there will always be others beneath them. In assembling the essays that make up this book, we started from the premise that because we can't get to the bottom of boxing we should instead try to surround it. Our contributors come at their shared subject from several different directions and perspectives. There are profiles of characters ranging from marquee attractions (Brin-Jonathan Butler on Roy Jones Jr., Rafael Garcia on Antonio Margarito, Carlo Rotella on Bernard Hopkins) to a rising star (Sarah Deming on Claressa Shields) to compelling sidemen (Gabe Oppenheim on Emanuel Augustus, Hamilton Nolan on Darius Ford). Most of these portraits are made from a ringsider's point of view, but the book also features first-person, hands-on accounts written from a fighter's: Donovan Craig, Sam Sheridan, and Hamilton Nolan bring us to the gym to spar and learn, and Robert Anasi revisits his debut bout to dissect its chaotic scramble of action and emotion. From the backstage point of view, speaking from sometimes-painful experience in the business of boxing, Charles Farrell explains why and how to fix a fight, and Gordon Marino explores what it means to stop one by throwing in the towel. Looking back from the historian's point of view, Michael Ezra and Gary Moser go inside the records of all-time greats and would-be greats, teaching us how to distinguish between the two, and Louis Moore and Carl Weingarten take us back to earlier eras to trace the warping effects of the color line on fighters' careers and lives.

Juxtaposing and alternating these perspectives, we set out to produce a composite picture-in-depth of boxing. A thread of technical ring craft runs through the book, a series of lessons in the art and science of boxing that begins with Donovan Craig trying to be a competent sparring partner in the gym and takes us all the way through the advanced fight-night virtuosity of Emanuel Augustus and Roy Jones Jr. Its complement is a thread of boxing-as-business that begins with a trainer's and a manager's accounts of handling fighters, moves on to consider how the careers of Antonio Margarito and Bernard Hopkins were shaped by the encounter of style and money, and digs into the past to investigate just how badly Jimmy Bivins and Harry Wills got screwed. We tried as much as possible to set up such complementarities. The historical essays balance the immediacy of ringside and in-the-ring reports; for every scene under the lights on fight night, there's another in the gym or in a back room or some other place where the nuts and bolts get put together; for every champion, there's a regiment of journeymen, cornermen, dabblers, and anglers for advantage; for every aspirant struggling toward a hoped-for prime, there's a Roy Jones Jr. in steep decline.

Jones, a one-man thematic motif in his own right, takes the prize for the book's most ubiquitous character, appearing in the first and last essays and repeatedly in between. He commands our attention as one of the extraordinary talents of our era and also one of its leading cautionary tales. A star who was widely regarded as one of the greatest fighters of all time until a series of brutal knockout losses revealed his deficiencies, he achieved the rare feat of seizing control of his own career but then couldn't seem to stop fighting even if it killed him. Jones features in Donovan Craig's account of being good enough to get hurt, Michael Ezra's inquiry into the significance of fighters' post-prime bouts, Gary Moser's parsing of the cases for recent stars as all-time greats, Gabe Oppenheim's meditation on stylishness, and Brin-Jonathan Butler's profile of the former champion sliding with terrible momentum down the blood-slick slope of the years.

*

Now, about the title of this book. Pierce Egan, the early nineteenth-century chronicler of England's bare-knuckle fight scene, called boxing "the sweet science," and the name stuck despite being at best a partially apt epithet for such a punishing trade. Yes, the world of hurt in which boxers move makes their technique and strategy all the sweeter to behold. It's one thing to sink a twenty-foot putt to win the Masters and another thing entirely to rally with a picture-perfect combination after being battered so badly that not only your career but your physical well-being and possibly your life are on the line. But that same lethal context, extending beyond the ring to include the ungloved savagery that characterizes the business side of boxing, appends a dark, smoky aftertaste to even the sweetest display of style or heart. "Bittersweet" strikes us as the more fitting adjective.

All worthwhile fight writing is bittersweet because boxing, like war, is both a magnificent subject and a cruel, morally indefensible one. The recognition that fighters are hurt and exploited not as a side effect of boxing but as part of its compromised essence gives boxing writing a melancholy undertone, a brooding quality deepened by the fight world's autumnal obsession with its own past glories. Using it in our title inevitably raises echoes of A. J. Liebling's *The Sweet Science*, published in 1956 and still widely regarded as the GOAT, as they say (for Greatest of All Time), of boxing books. Why call on—or call out—Liebling's masterpiece?

First, Liebling left plenty of room for successors. Egan may be his only peer when it comes to narrating the buildup to a big fight and bringing you ringside to see how it came out, and Liebling may have no equal in the art of the labyrinthian digression, but there were significant gaps in his treatment of boxing that this book aims to address. For instance, he didn't get far into the details of the business, he wrote exclusively from a ringsider's point of view, he had little interest in amateur boxing, and his breezy style shied from sustained analytical argument. Then there's the plain fact that a lot has happened for us to talk about in the more than half a century since Liebling's last fight piece ran in the *New Yorker*. In addition to some of the most celebrated ring careers of all time—almost all of Muhammad Ali's, for instance, not to mention those of Sugar Ray Leonard, Roberto Duran, Mike Tyson, and many other major figures—there's the heavyweight boom of the 1970s and the middleweight cycle of the 1980s, the rise of women's boxing and white-collar boxing, the Eastern European invasion, the simultaneous global expansion and street-level contraction of the fight world, and the rise of mixed martial arts as a competing blood sport.

Second, *The Bittersweet Science* might have been a better title for Liebling's book than the one it bears. He wrote in a moment when boxing was already leaving behind its golden age of cultural primacy, the period from the 1920s to the 1950s when it was woven most deeply into the fabric of neighborhood life and mainstream culture, when baseball was its only peer as a popular sport in America, when on any given Friday night there were fight cards at union and church halls as well as stadiums in cities across the land. Liebling could see the signs of boxing's ongoing long-term decline into a niche sport. While brilliant talents were still entering the fight world, the numbers of competent trainers and boxers were already shrinking under pressure from deindustrialization, suburbanization, the coming of TV, universal secondary education, and the rise of football and basketball and other school-based games. Liebling delivered this news self-mockingly, his way of steering around the trap of sounding like yet another fight-world crab lamenting that everything used to be better. Sorrowing over the loss of manly prowess is a habit as old as Homer, the original fight writer, who took a little time-out from the action to note whenever one of his heroes picked up a stone that two strong men of his own sadly degenerate era could not lift together.

We don't want to force our composite portrait of boxing into a rote decline narrative. The pages that follow show that some aspects of the contemporary fight world haven't changed much at all since Liebling's time — or Homer's, for that matter. Styles still make fights, speed is still power, and a good big man still beats a good little man except when he doesn't. Some aspects of the fight world have grown, like women's boxing or the global flow of fighters and money, or at least gotten more interesting. But it's a bittersweet fact of life that, like a former champ pushing forty — still potent, in some ways trickier and more compelling than ever, but also clearly no longer what he was — boxing in the twenty-first century is well into its post-prime.

Though it's now a niche sport dreaming of a past heyday, boxing still pervades our culture, soaked into life and language like the stink of sweat into old hand wraps. Hollywood keeps making box-ing movies—or the same one, over and over—as if boxing was still one of the two most popular sports in America. Characters based on Ali, Tyson, and other fighters have been all over Broadway and Off-Broadway stages in recent years. As the previous year has demon-strated yet again, the reporting of elections abounds with candidates on the ropes, getting off the canvas, going for the knockout, and otherwise enacting boxing-derived clichés (including wrongheaded ones, like dismissing a trifler as "a lightweight," which should really be a compliment, since pound for pound a good lightweight is superior to a good heavyweight). And the old-school cachet of boxing still attracts actors, pop stars, athletes in other sports, and miscellaneous big shots, who mime boxers' training and show up for big fights. The mainstream action heroes in attendance at the showdown in 2015 between Floyd Mayweather Jr. and Manny Pacquiao included Tom Brady, LeBron James, Michael Jordan, Jay Z, Beyoncé, Mark Wahl-berg, Robert De Niro, Clint Eastwood, and four different men who played Batman, all basking in the reflected glow of two fading welter-weights.

*

When we set out to recruit contributors to create this book's com-posite portrait of boxing, we sought out the writers we would turn to in the aftermath of a confusingly messy bout that needs explaining, the writers we most want to tag along with when they investigate form and meaning in boxing. There are a number of former amateur boxers and other fight-world insiders among them, and also nine reporters and five professors (some are both), a former accountant, a former stockbroker, a recovering gangster, a couple of professional musicians, a New York Golden Gloves champion, a retired basement-and-backyard boxer, and writers of essays, scholarship, novels, short stories, poetry, screenplays, erotica, and children's literature. We asked them for new work, not reprints; with the exception of a couple of recently published pieces that fit too perfectly to pass up, the essays in the book are published here for the first time. That they gave so freely of their talent, time, and enthusiasm is a testament to the force of their passion for boxing and to their respect for the tradition of writing about boxing.

It's a long tradition, going back to the one-punch KO of the hopelessly outclassed Euryalus by the champion Epeus during the funeral games for Patroclus in Book 23 of Homer's *Iliad*. Euryalus, knocked out of time by the decisive blow — or, if you prefer, dropped, stopped, starched, stretched, nailed, drilled, crushed, felled, flattened, waxed, iced, smoked, dumped, decked, laid out, poleaxed, coldcocked, KTFO, put to sleep . . . the lexicon of boxing has more ways to say it than the proverbial Eskimos have for snow — has been falling for the better part of three thousand years:

> the way a leaping fish
> falls backward in the offshore sea when north wind
> ruffles it down a beach littered with seawrack:
> black waves hide him.

The fundamental unfairness of this obvious mismatch doesn't interfere with appreciating the craft of either Epeus or Homer. The opposite, in fact. Seeing the mismatch for what it is, recognizing a prizefight as both a heroic athletic contest and a bruisingly asymmetrical transaction, only adds more layers to the richness of the passage, a subtly enhanced complexity of flavor that we might as well call bittersweet.

GOOD ENOUGH TO GET HURT

Donovan Craig

People will tell you that fear and pain are the worst things you have to deal with in life, but this is wrong. Fear is energy. Fear can sharpen you, and people even get addicted to it. Pain also has its uses. It's the easiest thing in the world to understand, and because it's so clear, it's a powerful teacher. Sometimes, because people mistake pain for the valuable things it reveals, they will begin to look for it, especially if they think there's not enough of it in their lives.

The main danger, the most implacable adversary you face in this world, is not fear or pain but confusion. Nobody ever got addicted to being confused or sought it out for its own sake. But part of the danger of confusion is that people get used to being confused and eventually they forget what it feels like to be unconfused or if, in fact, they've ever seen clearly at all.

Confusion was my vocation for many years. I was a stockbroker, and back in 2000, during the last gasps of the dot-com bubble, I had a penthouse in downtown Atlanta that I couldn't afford, a wife I shouldn't have married, and a job I couldn't stand. Most people might once or twice in their lives become grimly aware that large impersonal forces control their destiny. I was reminded of this all day, every day, by the dozens of red, white, and green stock symbols blinking on the screen in my office. In addition, the business skewed all communication toward closing the sale, which means that it didn't matter what I said, just that I said it in the right tone of voice and to enough people.

I was a pretty good closer back in the day, but I began to realize that, although I spent most of my waking hours on the phone, I never talked to anybody *about* anything. I just kept going around and around with them. "Blah, blah, blah, fear and greed, yada yada," ask for the sale, "blah, blah, blah, you're going to miss it, yada yada," ask for the sale, etc. Over and over. The object was to keep them in a specific frame of mind until enough hot buttons got pushed or enough little bells rang that a switch in their mind flipped and they bought.

You could make a lot of money doing this, and it could also drive you a little crazy, make you a kind of highly functioning psychotic; that's what happened to me, at least. Eventually, I began to recognize the same manipulative games of persuasion I was playing on the phone at work were everywhere, pushing and pulling me the way I was pushing and pulling everybody else. In my heart of hearts, I considered myself a con man, and eventually the world felt like one huge con, a jabbering cloud of half-assed rhetoric, brute propaganda, and the lies and low cunning of the marketplace. All of it was for the sole purpose of chasing money, with that game being the biggest bamboozle of them all.

Thankfully, I lived within walking distance of the only honest place I knew, the boxing ring. There was a small gym run by a man named Johnny Gant, whose claim to fame was that he had once gone eight rounds with Sugar Ray Leonard. Atlanta was a hotbed for boxing, and Johnny's gym was where everybody came to train. When I found out about it, I started going in after work and on Saturday mornings, and, although I had boxed during college, it was at Johnny's gym where I really learned what the sport of boxing was all about.

I started boxing late. I was almost eighteen when I had my first amateur match, but I'd been a fan my whole life. As a kid my great hero was Jack Dempsey; later I liked Marvin Hagler, Mike Tyson, and

Julio Cesar Chavez. I always liked the fighters who were aggressive and indomitable. I grew up in a small town in South Georgia where nobody else cared about the sport and only a few people even had cable, so I followed boxing mainly by reading about it in books, magazines, and newspapers. It was easier to mythologize the sport back in those days and project what you wanted or needed onto your idols. While my friends wanted to throw touchdowns, hit home runs, or play in a band, I always looked up to boxers. I wanted to be tough, like the fighters I read about in *The Ring* magazine or *An Illustrated History of Boxing*, a beautiful, oversized book with giant photographs from all the great old fights. My most prized possession back in those days was a well-used paperback copy of Jack Dempsey's book *Championship Fighting: Explosive Punching and Aggressive Defense* in which Dempsey explained the mechanics of punching, how to train your body to get the most power out of it, and how to always be on the attack, looking for the finish, even when defending. I read this book so many times that this last part became the closest thing I had to a worldview.

*

When the bell rings, anxiety disappears and you experience a sense of relief, a denouement long delayed, as societal constraints come off and you meet, maybe for the first time, your basic self. You get a similar sensation in a street fight, but usually a street fight is over so quickly that you don't have time to appreciate it. In a boxing match, and even more so in the many hours of sparring that fighters go through in the gym, you have time to appreciate what's going on and to understand the nature of physical violence and your reactions to it. I drank up my time in the gym. Outside the gym, I was an onlooker to my own life, swallowed up by the world. Inside Johnny's, it was different. There, I could see a clear and direct line between what I did and what was going on around me. Like Hamlet in reverse, when I boxed, the barriers between thought and action disappeared.

A good sparring partner is rugged and tough, has good stamina, and is just dangerous enough to keep the other fighter on his toes, but not so dangerous as to represent a real threat. I fit the bill, so I always got a lot of work when I hung around Johnny's gym. Over the years, I sparred with a lot of really good boxers and a few who were actually world class.

Two of the best fighters I trained with were rising stars when we started working together in the ring. O'Neil Bell was a cruiserweight with ten knockout wins in his ten pro fights. Steve Cunningham was the 178-pound national amateur champion who was about to turn pro. Because all of us were about the same weight, and I had a reputation around the gym as being a good worker, we three trained together frequently. It was hard keeping up with them, of course, but it made me feel good after a long day of self-imposed moral emasculations (guys in the gym would ask me what I did for a living and I would tell them, "Lie") to be able to hang in there with two legitimate up-and-comers. Plus, I took pride in feeling that I had pushed them a little, which I tried to do every time we were in the ring.

Bell fought like a miniature George Foreman, throwing heavy, clubbing punches that got harder to take the longer you were in there with him. Steve, by contrast, was all technique and physical grace. The trick with O'Neil was to keep him on his heels, because once he warmed up, he'd start killing you. With Steve, I always tried to keep him hemmed in a corner and crowd him in order to make it an infight, where I had an advantage with my shorter arms and propensity to throw lots of hooks.

When they sparred each other, it was better than half the matches on TV. I'd tell people that I could see O'Neil and Steve fighting each other for a title one day. Although that never happened, they both became world champions. O'Neil even unified the cruiserweight title when he stopped Jean-Marc Mormeck, becoming only the only second man besides Evander Holyfield to hold all of the division's belts.

Sometimes people would see me working with the pros and ask me why I didn't go pro myself. I was making good money at the time and couldn't bring myself to stop just to box professionally, but I would fantasize about the idea, especially if I had just done well against somebody I knew was a good pro. An ancient trainer named

Pops set me straight one day. I asked him after a particularly violent session with O'Neil whether or not he really thought I was any good. "Boy," he said, "you're good enough to get yourself hurt."

*

The most famous boxer I was ever up against in the ring is Roy Jones Jr., in 2006 as he was gearing up for a comeback fight against Prince Badi Ajamu. After dominating boxing and barely losing a round or even getting hit cleanly for fourteen years, Roy suffered two devastating one-punch knockouts in a row, first to Antonio Tarver, and then to Glen Johnson. Roy lost his reputation for being invulnerable, and now people were asking whether he was shot. It was one of the quickest turnarounds in the public perception of a fighter I can ever remember and offers a cautionary tale about what happens when people fetishize your talent.

I was surprised by how hard he hit. His punches were so crisp and sharp they felt like electric jolts, zzt, zzt, zzt, even when they landed on my arms. He never threw the jab and worked pretty much everything off the lead right hand; maybe one fighter in a thousand is able to pull this off. By the time I was in the ring with him, Roy's defensive reflexes had started to slow, but he still had supernatural offensive hand speed. He was so fast that I usually couldn't even see him start his punches and could only pick them up after he was pulling back his fist after he'd thrown a punch. It was useless to try to slip or dodge his shots, so all there was to do was keep a tight defense and try to block as many as I could with my arms and gloves. It was clear to me that Roy was a different animal than what I was used to and that I had no business in the ring with him. That's the only time I ever felt that way. Roy had a bad habit of letting himself get caught along the ropes, and with me it was no exception. Whenever I'd get him in the corner or along the ropes, I'd whale away with hooks to the body. One time he chortled out to the gym in his best Muhammad Ali impression, "Joe Frazier! This boy thinks he's a white Joe Frazier!" "Man," I thought, "I just got trash talked by Roy Jones Junior. Pretty cool."

Roy and I sparred on two separate days, and something very

strange happened during those sessions. About three years before-hand, I had slipped a disk, and my lower back had bothered me off and on ever since. I'd gotten it under control by doing lots of core exercises and being sure to warm up whenever I did any kind of physical activity, but it would occasionally go out and really give me problems. About a minute into the first round, Roy hit me with a left hook to the body that was so sharp and accurate it made me do a quick, half-wincing semi-convulsion as I involuntarily jerked my upper body over to one side before recomposing my defense. After three rounds, when our sparring was done and I got out of the ring, I realized that Roy's body shot had thrown my back out again. The next time we sparred, I warmed up well and dosed up on Tylenol, but my back was still tricky. About a minute into the first round, he hit me with the same punch in the same place, and I had basically the same reaction. Except this time, when I got out of the ring, I realized that for the first time in three years my back didn't hurt at all, and it has never hurt since.

*

There's an old myth that some boxers like to get hit. I don't think this is the case. What they like is the ancient rush that one animal gets when it kills another. And this is so intense that they don't notice getting hit. Once someone experiences this, he becomes secure in his ability to take the other guy's best shot. Of course, it is a dangerous delusion, to feel that you can't be hurt. But it's an easy one to fall into when you've had a big strong man, a trained athlete, try as hard as he can to hurt you, and you realize that he hasn't.

Of course, as any fighter who hangs around long enough finds out, everyone can get caught. In twenty years, I've been hurt by three punches, and they were all the result of being overconfident. One was against a fighter named Walter. You hear about boxers who feel like they have bricks in their gloves? That was Walter, but he was very methodical and I could beat him to the punch all day long. One time, though, I got careless with Walter and walked into a right hand. My legs went stiff, and I toppled over like a statue forward into the ropes.

I instantly bounced right back up, embarrassed and completely alert (sometimes a shot like that will actually wake you up). This was the only time I ever got dropped in sparring, and at the time it felt like the hardest punch I ever took.

Years ago, when I was a middleweight, I was sparring with a crude beginner named T. J. Wilson, who was about six feet five and 240 pounds, young and athletic. I was having my way with him when he suddenly did something I never expected: he switched his stance and hit me flush with a left. My knees buckled, which surprised me because it had never happened before.

The next thing I remember was hitting the heavy bag. I found out later that I hadn't gone down, that I had sparred another round with T. J., and that nobody in the gym had any idea I was even hurt. I'd gotten out of my sparring gear, into my bag gloves, and hit the bag for I don't know how many rounds before waking up. I never let my trainer know what had happened, but I did stop sparring with fighters who outweighed me by eighty pounds.

The third of the hardest punches I ever took was against a fighter named Ronald Cobb, who, like me, was an amateur light heavyweight out of Georgia. He had a reputation for knocking everybody out with a poleax of a right hand he threw with a shrug straight from the shoulder. When I fought him the first time, he hit me with everything he had and I didn't blink. In the fight, I was aggressive and had him hurt a time or two, but I was impatient, defaulting to brawl mode, and lost a close decision. After the fight, I was unimpressed with Cobb and his dreaded right. I didn't see what the big deal was about him. I felt like I should have knocked him out when I had him hurt and was disappointed that I hadn't. The next time we fought, I was even more determined to blow through him. During an exchange, I caught him with a clipping little hook, and he took a short stutter step back to the ropes. Here's what happened next as it went through my mind:

"He's hurt! Get this motherfucker . . . Wow, what a nice pool. I love swimming. The sun feels so nice and warm and the water is wonderful. So crystal clear. Maybe I'll do a backstroke or even swim down to the bottom. How nice that I can do whichever one I want. I'm so free.

Happy, happy, happy, yum, yum. Perfection. Life is wonderful. Hold on, something's not quite right. How did I get here? This is all beautiful, but wasn't I just doing something else? What was it? OH SHIT!"

I came to as the referee was standing over me waving the fight off. I said that Walter's *felt* like the hardest punch I ever took. The really hard ones, the ones like Ronald Cobb's right hand, you don't feel at all.

*

Here is some of what I learned about how to fight over the years. The three basic principles of effective punching are deception, effective weight transference, and placement. Ideally, a blow will utilize all three, but any one of these is enough to knock somebody out.

If a man is expecting to get hit, if he can see the punch coming and steel himself to its impact, then it's unlikely the blow will knock him out. It's better to hit a man with a lighter punch that he doesn't see coming than a heavier shot that he's prepared for.

A good way of deceiving your opponent as to the timing and placement of a blow is to "hide" the punch inside a series of lighter shots. Keep your hands up and chin down, tucked behind the lead shoulder, and commit to starting and finishing exchanges with your opponent. It's within these exchanges that most damage is done in the ring, especially if you are the shorter man. Tall or short, whether you have reach or not, the great nullifier of an opponent's superior hand speed is a consistent and steady jab.

By feinting to one part of the body and throwing to another you can catch your opponent unaware or make him defend the wrong part of himself. Feinting should be done with the shoulders and head and not just the arms.

Body punching both drains your opponent and makes feints more effective. In addition to setting up a knockout blow to the chin with a sustained body attack, a rarer and more elegant knockout technique is to feint to the head and deliver a well-placed and accurate left hook to the opponent's liver when he doesn't expect it. It's also effective to throw a light combination to the head, getting your opponent to raise his guard, and then shoot a quick, precise left hook touching the short ribs just under the chest, as Bernard Hopkins did to finish

Oscar De La Hoya. This shot, when landed correctly, is the single most unpleasant blow to take and is the only punch that I know of that is so incapacitating it will make a trained professional quit.

Through the correct transference of your body weight, your punches can generate tremendous force over very short distances with little visible movement. This is the secret to infighting. The weight of the body should move up from the feet through the legs, hips, and then the shoulders and arms, finishing at the end of the fist with a snap. The movement is akin to the way one shifts his weight from one foot to another when dancing in place. Fluidity and commitment are essential, and punching power has more to do with coordination than bodily strength.

From O'Neil, I learned how to catch punches out in front, with your gloves and forearms, and tire out your opponent by doing so. From watching Vernon Forrest, I learned how to beat speed with a jab and also the difference between offensive speed and defensive speed. I once saw Evander Holyfield demonstrate how to subtly extend the distance on your jab by extending your left foot only. This is a good trick with which to keep your opponent confused about your range. I learned how to avoid a southpaw's left hand by pivoting to my left on the inside while sparring with Robert Allen, a former top middleweight contender who once got so infuriated while fighting Bernard Hopkins that he threw him out of the ring. From Ronald Cobb, I learned that a wide looping right hook to the head or body is a good way to set up a straight one. Also how, if it's straight enough and hard enough, a punch doesn't have to be fast. There's more, some other things here and there. For instance, I could tell you exactly how to throw a sneaky left hook to the head, a real good shot, and a KO punch if it lands, but I won't, because a true fighter will never show you how to throw his best punch until he's an old, old man.

*

When you find truth, things start to flow. Everything becomes easier to deal with. This makes it that much more difficult to stomach the lies and half-truths in which we all have to swim for most of our lives. Once you've seen what it's like to live without the bullshit, your tolerance for it evaporates. The gym also hones your capacity for violence (violence being a kind of truth), but at the same time cleanses you of viciousness, a psychological trait of the weak that is, unlike violence, always a bad thing. But the noble mindset a fighter develops in the gym can be a mixed blessing on the outside. If he doesn't watch out, disasters will come from odd angles. You'd hear stories occasionally.

Like the time O'Neil apparently lost his mind for a little while after making it to the top. One day, while in training camp, he was doing roadwork in the woods with one of his sparring partners. For some reason, he pulled a hatchet from his jogging suit and chased the guy, who fled hysterically and escaped. The first warning sign was probably when he changed his ring name from O'Neil "Give 'em Hell" Bell, which was awesome, to O'Neil "Supernova" Bell, which made no sense.

One time, Johnny Gant had words with a guy in his gym, another old-timer who had also been a boxer, and they went outside to the parking lot to settle it. The guy threw one punch and knocked Johnny out cold. The ambulance came and carried him away. It turns out the guy had a piece of metal in his hand. He never showed up again. People were worried Johnny would find him and kill him when he got out of the hospital, but he never did, and it blew over. The gym is still in Atlanta, although it has moved and is now called The Atlanta Art of Boxing.

Vernon Forrest, who I first met as an amateur in Augusta and later knew at Johnny's gym, was murdered on the streets of Atlanta. He got into a foot chase and shootout with a guy who tried to carjack him, and when Vernon ran out of bullets, the man's accomplice, who snuck up on Vernon from behind, shot him dead. A sad incident, but still, it's not the worst way to go out, Old West panache and all.

O'Neil also met his end on the streets of Atlanta late one night not long ago. Unlike Vernon, he wasn't armed and there apparently wasn't much of a fight. Two guys just drove up and shot him as he was getting off the train.

Walter, the only guy to ever drop me in sparring, died in the dressing room after an amateur fight. It was some kind of heart attack, they say.

Roy beat Prince Badi Ajamu in his comeback fight and then par-layed that brief career resurgence into a big-money match with Joe Calzaghe, to whom he lost badly. Roy and I became friends, and I even went down to Biloxi to watch him stop Jeff Lacy in what I bet was the last bout in which Roy had anything left. He still fights over in Europe from time to time, a shell of himself.

Steve, who fights as the "USS" Cunningham, is still a top con-tender although he's getting long in the tooth. He'd be a lot more famous if it weren't for Tomasz Adamek, to whom he has twice lost.

As for me, I ended up having two pro fights, both of which I lost by decision. They were four-round club fights, and neither of the two guys were anywhere near as good as what I was used to facing in train-ing. I felt and still feel that if they had been six- or eight-round fights, I would have knocked both guys out, but this may or may not be true.

The last time I did any training at all was a few years back when I was in Los Angeles. A friend of mine had an apartment a few blocks from Freddie Roach's Wild Card Gym. Roach is the best boxing trainer alive, and he might end up being the last great one. Although it was a business trip and I was on a tight schedule, I made time to visit the gym. Michael Moorer was behind the front desk. Moorer was on the wrong end of one of the great punches in the history of boxing, the right hand that made George Foreman the oldest heavy-weight champ ever in the sport. That day I also saw Manny Pacquiao come in with his entourage of handlers. This was right when the world was starting to catch on that he might be more than just a star and could end up an all-time great. My friend told me that a lot of the time Pacquiao worked out with everyone else in the gym, but on this day a gaggle of tiny Pinoy hustled him to an area of the gym behind a closed door. I paid Freddie's brother, Pepper Roach, five dollars a round to work the punch mitts with me and then I hit the bag. Seeing me out of the corner of his eye, Freddie said, "I can see you've been in a gym before." An offhand remark, to be sure, and slight praise, but when I heard him I felt a giddy jolt of elation. I still consider the experience the closest thing to glory I ever achieved in boxing.

THROWING IN THE TOWEL

Gordon Marino

While boxing may have seeped to the bottom of the back pages of the sports section, it still provides some of the most potent metaphors for capturing the hurly-burly of life. We encourage those who have absorbed a blow "to get up off the canvas" and praise them for refusing to "throw in the towel." A symbol of surrender in the stylized war that is the prize ring, throwing in the towel is a gesture that goes back to mid-nineteenth-century days of bare-knuckle fighting when a combatant's corner, judging their man to be beaten and in danger, conceded defeat by flinging in the sponge used to wipe a fighter's face.

One of the last and most famous of the bare-knuckle fights took place in July 1889 in Mississippi, when John L. Sullivan and Jake Kilrain beat each other about the head and body for over two hours in 108-degree heat. Sullivan began vomiting in the forty-fourth round, but he somehow regained control of fight. A ringside doctor informed Kilrain's seconds that their man might perish if he continued, so his trainer tossed in the sponge. In time, the towel would come to replace the sponge as the flag of surrender. After watching his man being humiliated and unmercifully thrashed by Jack Johnson for fourteen rounds in their 1910 bout, Bob Armstrong, trainer of "Great White

Hope" Jim Jeffries, flung in the towel. Max Schmeling's trainer, Max Machon, did the same when Joe Louis knocked his fighter down for the third time in the first frame of their historic 1938 rematch. At the time, throwing in the towel was not a recognized way of stopping a contest, so referee Art Donovan kicked the towel away and continued counting before recognizing that Schmeling was, indeed, done.

Even outside the ring, as a mentor in a world that constantly prattles about the all-importance of "having a dream" and "never giving up," it sometimes happens that the caring course of action is to help someone throw in the towel, even when that person is on a quest at the core of his or her identity. As a very slow Division I receiver, I was nailed to the dream of making it to the Elysian fields of the NFL. When that, of course, didn't happen, I felt distraught and worthless, and many disturbing behaviors ensued. I wish I had had someone in my corner to sit me down for a talk.

Few people have had the experience of *literally* throwing in the towel. Unfortunately I have. It felt like a left hook to the liver when I threw in the towel on Vicente Alfaro.

*

"Don't do it, Gordon. They'll break your heart!" That was the counsel Angelo Dundee offered when I confided to him that I was going to manage and train a professional fighter. Angelo had a prodigious capacity for friendship. After I interviewed him for a fitness magazine piece, we started chatting a few times a week about boxing, family, old times, our Italian heritage, good restaurants, whatever. He was always jabbing and japing; it was rare for him to take on a somber tone, but there was nothing jocular when he told me to stick with the Golden Gloves amateurs I had been coaching for decades and stay away from the pros.

One October afternoon, when I was teaching a boxing basics class to middle schoolers at the Y, a diminutive, athletically built Latino guy in his twenties pushed through the heavy armory door. Hands in his jacket pockets, he stood off to the side, his eyes fixed on us as we worked through jab drills on the mitts. He looked like a fighter, but I figured he was there to tell me about a cousin who wanted, or more probably, *imagined* he wanted to get in the ring.

At the end of the session, the twenty-something guy slid through the gaggle of kids and with a thick Mexican accent blurted, "Hey. You want to train me? I am Vicente Alfaro." Huh? At the time, his English was as feeble and as halting as my Spanish, but he managed to explain that he'd had a lot of amateur fights in Mexico and that he had a 4–0 record as professional.

Because of my exotic boxing/professor mix, I had received some local ink, enough so that my heavyweight ego would have liked to imagine that it was my reputation that lured Vicente to the Y. But it is more likely that he was just frustrated with his largely absent manager-trainer, Oscar Ortega (as I will call him), who lived about fifty miles away and worked on the railroad. Vicente complained that he never saw Ortega until a few days before his fights, and that Ortega was taking more than his fair share of Vicente's purses.

The next day, we started working together in the half-finished basement of a local Mexican deli. We lived in rural Minnesota, an hour from the boxing dens in the Twin Cities of Minneapolis and Saint Paul. From the first bell of our relationship, then, I knew that between our location and work schedules, getting sparring was going to be a major problem. Nobody in town was in Vicente's universe of boxing abilities.

Day by day, pieces of Vicente's fistic history emerged. I learned that his father, a former pro, had trained him back in Mexico City since the age of six. I also came to understand that upon coming to the states he took an eight-year layoff from the ring, which ended when Ortega just happened to walk by and catch sight of Vicente in a garage hitting the heavy bag. Ortega could see that Vicente knew how to use his hands and convinced him to compete again. In his first and only amateur competition in the United States, Vicente won the bantamweight belt at the Ringside Tournament, a national competition.

Ortega immediately convinced him to begin punching for dollars. For his pro debut, Vicente traveled to Detroit on a week's notice to take on former Olympian Ron Silas. As would become the rule,

Vicente was fighting in the other guy's hometown. He was supposed to lose. He dropped jaws ringside by putting Silas on the canvas and copping a unanimous decision.

I used to sneer when I watched someone fighting on television who hadn't been in the ring in a couple of years. "Must be laziness or fear," I used to think. But that was before I personally learned how hard it was to get reasonable matchups; unless, of course, you are a manager with pockets sufficiently deep to get your man on a card by paying the purses and expenses for both your fighter and his opponent. Tyson's team did just that when Iron Mike was clambering up the boxing ladder.

I couldn't bankroll Vicente's career. All I could do was beg and make nice with local promoters. But that was no abracadabra. Vicente's best fighting weight was 118. There were not a lot of small guys in Minnesota, and by the time that we hooked up, he had already muted the marketability of three local stars. No one below 126 pounds wanted anything to do with him.

After a year with only one bout, Vicente was offered a fight in California with Golden Boy prospect Manuel "Tino" Avila. Usually such tenders came with only a week or maybe ten days' notice, but this time he would have a month to prepare. We, or rather Vicente, would be exchanging leather with "Tino" in his hometown of Fairfield, California. Avila was 8–0, but he had yet to match up against anyone with a winning record. More importantly, he didn't seem to be a big banger. Even against weak opposition, he had notched only one knockout. The rule that I established with myself and we agreed upon was that I would never put Vicente in a bout I didn't think he could win. In his most recent tussle, he had beaten Gary Eyer, who was also 8–0, in his hometown of Duluth. Judging from the YouTube videos, it seemed plausible to think that he could pull off another surprise with Avila.

Although boxing was in Vicente's DNA, he was not one to fight for glory or fun. He was always in good condition, but he had no interest in working out until he had a contract. He took pride in his craft. He didn't drink or even have a sweet tooth; he husbanded his energies and the money mattered. He was trying to raise a family on a nine-dollar-an-hour wage as a factory worker. The promoter was offering $2,500 plus expenses, including the cost of the numerous medical exams demanded by the California State Athletic Commission. There was one more perk. The fight would be aired on Telemundo. Vicente's father, whom he had not seen in almost a decade, and in all likelihood might never see again, would be able to watch his son box on the tube. So, there we were on a late August night in a small-but-packed arena in central California.

*

On the circuit in professional boxing there are two dressing rooms: one for the favorites, the "A side" fighters, and another for the "B siders," those who, like Vicente, were brought in as fodder. We were stationed a floor below the ring level in a men's room turned locker room. It was like being in the anteroom of the Roman Colosseum. The building was vibrating from the noise. You could hear the mad roar of the crowd, fans erupting and stomping their feet, as some near-decapitating blow landed. One after another, our dressing room comrades came skulking back panting and in sullen defeat.

A lanky welterweight with a long angry gash over his eye pushed through the door and dropped into a folding chair. Shaking his head, he repeated, "I have to train harder, have to get back to work." He was already a veteran of two dozen fights. It didn't matter how much he trained; he was never going beyond opponent status.

The next victim, a short, stocky light heavyweight who also competed in mixed martial arts (MMA), returned with a huge welt on his side. Relieved to be done with his work, he was laughing, "I think that *motherfucker* broke my rib!" He and his trainer had packed some Coors in their ice bucket and were popping them open. They laughed the beating off and talked of getting an MMA booking when his rib healed.

At least at the local level, there are a lot of MMA fighters who cross over into boxing these days. In general, they are as comfortable in violence as they are on their living room couches. And unlike

boxers, they don't have their ego eggs in the basket of staying undefeated. They are not haunted by the terror of a loss. Perhaps as a result
of the trickle-down effects of Floyd Mayweather's mentality, many
professional boxers begin with an obsession about maintaining an
unblemished record. Instead of thinking of each bout as a session
in which they will learn something new about themselves and their
craft, boxers imagine that a defeat will detract from their paydays. But
in the cage, even the best fighters have losses and often a number of
them. Also, while a boxer can't really quit when he is getting throttled
and is hopelessly behind, MMA combatants can tap out honorably
rather than endure the indignity of being counted out. The relaxed
mindset of MMA fighters on boxing cards can sometimes translate
into a big punch and an upset, but not on this night. It hadn't worked
out that way for the jovial gladiator who had just pushed through the
door and plopped down next to Vicente.

We were about forty-five minutes out from fight time. Vicente was
playing with his iPod, joking with the other boxers. I was grinding my
teeth. To me, he seemed too loose. I was waiting for him to become
alert, to confront his fears and get his fight face on. But I was not
about to begin playing Cus D'Amato in the hour before a big bout.

Vicente did not cut easily, but it did not take much to get the faucet
of his nose pouring. Even during sparring, when his nose gushed, he
would panic because he felt like he couldn't breathe. Angelo, who was
an expert cutman, had tried to pass on some of his first-aid knowledge to me. Use pressure. Hold one nostril closed. Apply Adrenalin.
But my confidence in my EMT abilities was nil. When we signed the
contracts, I had insisted that the promoter provide a cutman who
would also wrap Vicente's hands. The guy was an old pro whom I
vaguely recognized from television, Jessie Estrella (as I will call him).

Maybe in his mid-fifties, Jessie was a short, powerfully built Mex-
ican with steely hair. For years, he had been running a local gym.
I had spent a good deal of the day before with him as we shuttled
Vicente from one medical test to the next. Almost the entire time,
Jessie blustered about his George Foreman–like punching prowess.
He boasted about having knocked this guy out in the ring and that

gang leader out in the street. When Jessie was looking the other way, Vicente rolled his dark eyes, shook his head, and suppressed a laugh. On edge as I was, Jessie jangled my nerves enough that there was a part of me that had an impulse to test him. But he was my partner for this night, and he knew his boxing.

About forty minutes before we were scheduled for the lion's den, Jessie came in to wrap Vicente's hands. For many fighters, this is when their nerves bubble up. I once had a 147-pounder in a Golden Gloves tournament who had me wrap the same hand three times. I became exasperated and pulled some faces. He fractured his thumb in the fight. A few weeks later, one of my other fighters confided that my welterweight thought I had left his thumb exposed on purpose because I was mad at him. Vicente, who à la Manny Pacquiao usually wrapped his own paws, was happy with Jessie's handiwork.

*

When we stepped into the ring, Avila, who was four inches taller and seven years younger than my fighter, now looked to be about ten pounds heavier. Boxers weigh in the day before a bout but in the next twenty-four hours can easily pack on pounds. The ring seemed as small as a closet, which should have been to our advantage, at least based on my mistaken assumption that Vicente would be the physically stronger of the two and the harder puncher.

Whenever I worked the corner in the amateurs, I was always clad in a black Fifth Street Gym T-shirt that Angelo bequeathed to me. I wore it only for fights. I also kept a boxing glove keychain in my pocket that Angelo had inscribed, "To my good friend Gordon, Angelo." It was like a diluted form of ancestor worship. Years ago, students were wearing bracelets with the letters WWJD—what would Jesus do? On fight nights, I was mentally wearing an amulet with the initials WWAD—what would Angelo do? As the minutes slowed and jerked toward fight time, I tried to channel my late friend, praying and thinking, "I can handle anything, but please don't put me in a position where I have to think about stopping the action, about 'throwing in the towel.'"

Just when Vicente was getting gloved up, I had gone to ask the promoter about something. While I was gone, the commission guy gave my second the wrong-sized gloves. Because I was as nervous as a fighter in his debut, I hadn't checked them. Worse yet, I hadn't even glimpsed the extra heft when we were warming up on the mitts. Only after we climbed into the ring did one of the judges notice that Vicente's mitts were ten ounces instead of the appointed eight ounces for weights below 147 pounds.

When the glove glitch was discovered, we were already in the ring and on the air. We remained under the klieg lights for the five minutes it took to exchange gloves and re-tape. The television crew was irate. Vicente, who was wearing a ridiculously oversized sombrero that kept falling off, was embarrassed but kibitzing and taking pictures with ringside fans. He was driving me crazy. I wanted him to stay focused, but it wasn't his fault that his trainer couldn't tell the difference between ten- and eight-ounce gloves. Tino was glaring with irritation, and I was giving myself instructions not to torture myself about the mishap. Silently, I kept repeating, "This is not about you. This is not about you. It is about Vicente." It may have been the best advice I gave all night.

Vicente was tight in the first stanza. He was backing straight up, and when he moved forward he was squared. He bent so far forward that he was pushing his punches. He wasn't snapping his left. Meanwhile, Tino was sticking him with hard jabs down the middle. About two minutes in, Tino connected with a short left hook to the head that knocked Vicente off balance and shook him out of attack mode for the rest of the round. When he came back to the corner, I asked Vicente how he was feeling.

"Fine . . . fine," he assured me. "I'm fine." I toweled him off a little, bent in low, and said, "Listen. We only have six rounds. This is his hometown. You know what that means. Pick it up. Let your hands go. When you get inside, stay there."

It is elementary. The shorter opponent has the advantage at close quarters. After all, it is hard for the taller opponent to get leverage and punch down. And when you tower above your opponent, you can't go to the body without exposing your chin. I was prodding Vicente to move his head, like Joe Frazier against Muhammad Ali. I wanted him to come in behind his jab, break the perimeter, and get underneath Tino's long arms. At the same time, he needed to keep that little bit of cushion, that little bit of space required for punching room. In order to do this, Vicente had to keep from pitching forward, and also to prevent Tino from doing the octopus move—grabbing him and tying him up.

In round two, there were some rays of hope, even though Vicente suffered a flash knockdown on what looked to be a slip. He caught a jab at the same time his feet got tangled up, and his knee hit the canvas. He wasn't hurt, but it meant at least a 10–8 round for Tino, which quickly sparked a sense of desperation in our corner. Vicente needed to put some pain in Tino's in-box fast.

Boxers practice different moves and combinations in the gym, but what works on the bag or in sparring does not always make it past the rehearsal phase. For example, Wladimir Klitschko is an NBA-sized six feet seven. Almost all of his opponents get low and try to get inside on him. One of the ways to checkmate that strategy is to bend that back knee and zing a right uppercut as the opponent is leaning in. Klitschko's trainer, Emanuel Steward, once told me that Wladimir had been working on that punch for years and had no trouble letting it fly in sparring sessions. But come fight night, he invariably left the uppercut in the tool chest.

In training, Vicente and I had been working on a fistic concoction. The plan was to stab a couple of hard jabs to the solar plexus then go low, load up the legs, feint the jab to the body, and snap a hard right to the head and punctuate it with a left hook. Ideally, your opponent should be trying to step in with a right hand to counter against the jab to the body, and then, at least theoretically speaking, you have the combined force of your right hand and his forward momentum.

Vicente possessed a straight and hard jab to the body. Tino had a high guard, and in the second stanza Vicente was able to lance him with the body jab. Then, as planned, he dipped, feinted the jab, and caught Tino square with the right on the chin. With renewed hope,

I flew off the stool, yelling *eso, eso!* The bad news: Vicente failed to bring the hook behind it. The worse news: it was Vicente's best right, and, while Tino acknowledged the shot with an annoyed look and a step backward, he was neither wobbled nor flustered.

Despite all the conditioning, the sixty rounds of sparring, the hundreds of uphill sprints, adrenaline was taking a big bite out of Vicente's stamina. In the corner, after the second round, I put my hand on his legs, looked intently into his eyes, and exhorted, "Use the jab. Get inside and let your hands go. Two combinations in a row! This is the opportunity of a lifetime. Give me everything for the next twelve minutes." "OK. OK," he answered with quiet purpose. But it wasn't OK. This wasn't the movies. Tino was gaining the momentum of confidence and starting to time solid rights. The stress of being on television and having to cope with this bigger and younger fighter was steadily wearing Vicente down. He was breathing hard, pushing his blows, feather punching. That wasn't the fighter I knew.

A minute into the third, Tino landed a left-right combination. It was a classic. Silver beads of perspiration flew, the crowd exploded with glee, and as Vicente's body recoiled his knees hit the canvas. He took some deep breaths as the referee gave him an eight count. I swung around the ring post to catch a glimpse of his eyes. He looked alert and in something less than deep distress. He stood up, the ref wiped off his gloves, and Vicente was back in the fray, bravely trying to work to Tino's body, but there was nothing on his shots.

Amid the din, Jessie came over and whispered, "Throw in the towel; this kid is too strong and he is too tired." I was shocked. Vicente was losing, but he was making a fight of it. "He can make it to the end of the round. I'll see how he is," I said without looking away. But just then another shot thudded against Vicente's forehead. I could see that both his eyes were swollen and he was breathing through his mouth, a sure sign of exhaustion. Like sweat, the thought was starting to drip, "There are three rounds to go—and no chance of winning." In the world of the ring, there is endless chatter about never quitting. Throwing in the towel is a radical move, almost taboo. Boxers are encouraged to think of themselves as warriors, and warriors don't surrender or have someone surrender for them. After Eddie Futch, who had seen four fighters die in the ring, stopped the third Ali versus Frazier fight, Frazier was so irate that he barely spoke to Futch for the next twenty years. If only to shield his ego, you want your fighter to finish on his feet, no matter how mangled his face might be.

Jessie was emphatic, "I worked with the other kid. I'm telling you. He's too strong. Your guy has nothing tonight. Don't let him get hurt." Jessie's last sentence grabbed me by the Adam's apple. As though I was getting ready to pull the lever on the electric chair, I stood up and clutched the white towel, watching, waiting, hoping that I could put it down. Then another gloved fist came crashing through the gate. Sentences, like news bulletins, were lighting up behind my brows: "He doesn't have health insurance. He has a family." Robot-like I stood up and tossed the white cloth into the night and over the ropes. Just as I let it go Vicente landed a hard jab. It took about a half-second for that towel to shift the scene, but fast as a dream, the third man jumped between them and the frenzied action screeched to a halt. There was a moment of perplexed silence in the arena, and then the howls and boos cascaded down toward the ring. The crowd was in a collective dudgeon for being cheated out of the coup de grâce. Vicente was puzzled and seemed to be asking the ref what happened. When he figured out that I stopped the fight, he came back to the corner with his arms extended as though crucified. His face squinched up like a ten-year-old boy's. He yelled, "What? What are you doing? I can't believe it!" He kept shaking his head in disappointment as though the man who had been with him five to six days a week for the last two years had suddenly put a shiv in his back. Maybe I had; I really didn't know.

Tino, who was broody to begin with, felt so cheated that he wouldn't even come over to shake hands. While I was pulling Vicente's gloves off, the ref slid over and quietly told me, "Brilliant stoppage." A few minutes later, the doctor echoed the same. Easy for them to say. Right or wrong, I would never have halted the fight at that point had it not been for Jessie's voice in my ear.

As soon as he finished cutting the tape off Vicente's hands, Jessie vanished. His son was in the next fight, the main event. Weeks later, I started wondering whether Jessie had pressured me to stop the fight simply because he wanted to get back to the dressing room to warm up his kid. Also, Jessie was working for the promoter. Tino was a prospect without many knockouts on his resume. Thanks in part to Jessie, Tino got one that night. Did the philosophy professor/cornerman get jobbed? Maybe so, but it wasn't about me.

*

In boxing, at least in this country, whenever a fighter gets trounced but takes a brutal beating, people slap him on the shoulder and offer praise for having a certain part of the male anatomy. It is as though the crowd gets its red badge of courage with the fighter's blood. Oddly enough, boxing people love to quote Nietzsche: "What doesn't kill you makes you stronger." Not always so. I have been around boxing long enough to know that those hurricane blows can shake the hinges off the world behind the brows. Muhammad Ali is a monument to the human spirit and the perils of the gloved game, but he is not a rarity. Go to the annual reunion at the International Boxing Hall of Fame and it can seem like a kindergarten; so many of the old fighters with brains and memories short-circuited, a pocketful of mumbles.

Mike Tyson once told me that when things get really bad, it is better for the corner to throw in the towel. As Tyson explained, you not only save your fighter's health but his ego. And the ego is essential in boxing. Tyson said, "After a few days, your fighter will be blaming you for the stoppage. He'll be telling himself and everyone else that he could have won, if it hadn't been for you. And that's what you want him to think." Maybe so, but on this Saturday night, we were a few days away from those few days.

After a quick check-in with the doctor, we were alone and I was holding ice packs to both of Vicente's swollen eyes. He wasn't looking at me. He was fuming. There were not many chances at being center stage for Vicente. What dreams there were drifted around the brightly lit squared circle to which he had been faithfully married for twenty-plus years. And now?

I winced as I thought of Vicente's father in Mexico watching the fight in disgust, the father who was so proud that his son in the States was fighting on television. There was a long uncomfortable silence, and then I all but whispered, "I love you, man, you're family. I couldn't let you get hurt." At first Vicente remained stiff and wordless. Then his shoulders relaxed and, choking back tears, he muttered, "*Entiendo, entiendo,* I know, I know."

THE REAL MILLION DOLLAR BABY

Sarah Deming

Claressa Shields was born in Flint, Michigan, the middleweight champion of hard-luck towns. Her dad was an underground fighter called Cannonball who went to prison when she was two. Her mother was an imperfect protector. When Cannonball got out, Claressa was nine years old and already a survivor.

Father and daughter drove around Flint in his big burgundy van, trying to make up for lost time. Cannonball told Claressa it was a shame nobody else in the family boxed. All the Shieldses could fight; most of the men had gone to jail, and some of the women, too. He said prison was a cycle somebody had to break. He said it was sad how Muhammad Ali had all those sons and none of them followed him into the ring.

"Laila did," said Claressa.

"She's a bad girl," said Cannonball.

Claressa thought he was telling her to box. Her favorite cartoon was *The Powerpuff Girls*, about three little superheroines who flew around smashing things and defeating evil. She loved how they were each a different color and they could all fight. One time at school, Claressa threw a chair at a teacher. They made her take anger management classes, which helped a lot, but sometimes she still felt like smashing things.

She was eleven when she walked into Berston Field House, the small community center that had already produced two Olympic medalists at middleweight, Chris Byrd and Andre Dirrell. The coaches worked her out the first day but would not let her return without written permission. She knew her mother would never sign, so she took the paper to Cannonball.

"Hell, no," he said.

When Claressa asked why not, he said she was too pretty to box.

Claressa had never thought of herself as pretty. Her father's words pleased her a tiny bit, even as they made her furious. She would not speak to him for several days. When he showed up after school one day to pick her up, she refused to get in the van.

"Shut up, little girl," said Cannonball. "We're going to my house."

Her father's entire family was arrayed in the living room: his wife, Lisa Allen; Claressa's sisters Tiffany and Kaya Gray; her brother Tray.

"We took a vote, and you won," said Cannonball, handing her the permission slip. He was the only one who had voted against her.

The workouts at Berston were hard but fun. Jason Crutchfield taught her to throw the right cross. He made her do it over and over, turning her knuckles every time. Jason's tubby belly and gentle smile belied his perfectionism. He had gone 8–1–1 as a pro lightweight at Kronk before life got in the way. He was especially strict about Claressa's balance. He taught her to step out to the side, shift her body weight, know good position so she was always ready to punch. He taught her straight shots and classic combinations. She had that strength of will that cannot be taught.

Claressa left her mother's house and went to live with Jason, because boxers need order in their lives. He made the most delicious barbecued chicken, but Claressa always told him it was bad, just to mess with him. Jason had a wife and kids and no room to spare in his house, but he could not turn 'Ress away. She was the best boxer he had ever trained.

She burned her way through the junior ranks. Her father didn't see her fight until her fourth match. Claressa was warming up in her street clothes when the opponent, a twelve-year-old named Chloe Kinsley, walked past with her mother and remarked, "I'm gonna stop her."

She was the first of Claressa's opponents to go the distance. Claressa almost had her. In the final round, Chloe was backed up against the ropes, crying. The ref jumped between them to stop it, but the bell rang. After that, Chloe Kinsley switched to soccer.

Cannonball told his daughter he had never seen a girl fight like that.

Claressa made the age cutoff for the London Olympics by two months and four days. She qualified for the US Trials by winning the Police Athletic League National Championships, the first tournament she entered as an adult. She was sixteen years old and had a record of 19–0.

She flew out to New York City for an event hosted by the public radio station WNYC. She didn't know what to expect, just that it had to do with boxing. A crowd of local media and boxing fans turned out to celebrate the sport's new Olympic status and hear Rosie Perez tease Claressa gently about dieting and boys.

Claressa knew she had seen Rosie's face before, but it wasn't until later that she remembered *Do the Right Thing*. When Rosie asked if she ever worried about head injuries, Claressa said no, but that got her thinking. Sometimes she got headaches, especially when Jason doubled up her workouts, which meant she would spar twice a day against men who hit hard. Claressa didn't like to complain, but after Rosie asked her that, she cut back on sparring.

There were lots of women boxers in the audience who stood up and asked questions. One of them was forty-two years old! She could have passed for twenty-five in Flint. Claressa supposed that was what happened when you lived a good and happy life.

Claressa did not know how deceptive her own appearance was. From where I lurked in the back of the crowd, trying to avoid ex-boyfriends and score free drinks, the gawky teen with the huge grin did not look like my sport's future. I had just turned thirty-eight and given my mother a kidney. Mixed in with my happiness about the Olympics was bitterness that it had not come sooner. Not that I was good enough to qualify, but it would have been nice to try. Like Cannonball and Jason Crutchfield and anyone else who has ever quit boxing, I will always look back with longing.

When I won the New York City Golden Gloves in 2001, women's boxing was enjoying its brief televised heyday. Christy "The Coal Miner's Daughter" Martin had been the first marquee name, brawling on Tyson undercards in blood-spattered pink trunks. Trainers were eager to make the next star, but Laila Ali and Mia St. John rode a wave of popularity that was already dying. My girlfriends who went pro faced an indifferent marketplace.

Sadly, these days most people's reference point for women's boxing is the 2004 Oscar-winner *Million Dollar Baby*. Based on the short-story collection *Rope Burns* by F. X. Toole, the film tells the story of Maggie Fitzgerald, a plucky girl who climbs the pro ranks only to be maimed in her title shot by Billy the Blue Bear. From the short story:

> Billy "the Blue Bear" Astrakhov was a big-busted, masculine-looking Russian girl living in Hamburg, who grew a faint mustache and dated fashion models. A former Moscow prostitute, she paraded herself in white tuxedos and lavender ties. . . . She was a big draw in Germany. Her favorite trick was to get inside and jam the palm of her glove into her opponent's nose, breaking it. That she might kill them didn't worry her. She promised to knock Maggie out.
>
> "After I vip her," she said at the weigh-in, grinning and winking at Maggie, "I take her to my room. On a leash."

Their foul-ridden fight leaves Maggie paralyzed. From her hospital bed, she then fends off venal relatives, bedsores, and gangrene; has her leg amputated; and is finally euthanized by her trainer.

Oh, was that a spoiler? Good. If I can save a single person from watching this misogynist melodrama expecting a feel-good sports story, my work in this essay is done. (And if you think Toole is sexist, you should read how he writes about black people and Mexicans.)

Even the muse hated it. Juli Crockett is a former pro welterweight from Alabama. When she met Jerry Boyd, the Los Angeles cutman who wrote under the porny pseudonym F. X. Toole, he pronounced her the incarnation of Maggie Fitzgerald. She was less than flattered.

"Jerry was against women boxing," she says. "His fear was that they would get hurt and he would go to hell. There's a way in which the story is all about him. The men are in control all the time. They decide when Maggie fights, who she fights, and whether she wins or dies."

"Why can't there be a female *Rocky*?" Crockett wonders. "Why can't she just win? Why can't she live?"

She can't win or live because *Million Dollar Baby* is a women's boxing story told by people who don't much care for either women or boxing. Jerry Boyd's epigraph for his collection tells us all we need to know: "Boxing is for men, and is about men, and is men. A celebration of the lost religion of masculinity all the more trenchant for being lost."

That's Joyce Carol Oates, of course. The most famous female boxing writer is also among the most virulent opponents of women in the sport. In *On Boxing*, Oates denigrates ring-card girls and female national anthem singers en route to proclaiming that the female boxer "cannot be taken seriously. She is parody, she is cartoon, she is monstrous."

When I first encountered Oates's mercifully slim volume, I was still boxing and took her words like a right hand to the solar plexus. Now I take them as seriously as the rest of what she wrote about boxing, which is to say, not very. Like Jerry Boyd, Oates uses fighters for her own peculiar project: in her case, one of establishing a position for herself alongside such serious, masculine names as Mailer and Hemingway. As a woman writer, she must have been particularly anxious to distance herself from the female flesh on display in the ring. All women, even intellectual heavyweights, are subject to being reduced to mere bodies. Oates watches the action from very far away and very high up. Empathy is risky in a game of pain.

Boxing is a sport of the poor, and all fighters are prizefighters. Male boxers fight for real prizes like money and belts, because real prizes exist for them, and because the poverty they come from is real poverty. Women fight for imaginary prizes like the right to be taken seriously as athletes, because there is little money in our game, and because—although plenty of women boxers come from economically disadvantaged backgrounds—we have all endured a more insidious kind of deprivation: poverty of the imagination.

Poverty of the imagination prevented Joyce Carol Oates from stepping outside of herself to see the crude women boxers of her day for what they were: pioneers. Those who go first are seldom the best, and the early women professionals were notable more for their bravery than their refinement. This remains somewhat true of women's boxing today, but young women like Claressa Shields are proof that it is changing.

Poverty of the imagination keeps sportswriters fixated on women boxers' physical appearance or their history of sexual abuse, as though these things had any currency at all inside the ring, as though they were the only stories to tell.

Poverty of the imagination led AIBA, the international governing body for amateur boxing, to propose that skirts be the official uniform for women's Olympics debut. They were quickly made optional after the ensuing uproar, but Poland still made its women wear them. They were incongruous and not even vaguely hot.

Poverty of the imagination is why—no joke—the most common question men ask me about my boxing career is, "What happens when you get punched in the breasts?" And surely it was poverty of the imagination that made Jerry Boyd and screenwriter Paul Haggis look down the road of their million-dollar heroine and see only a dead end.

The real Million Dollar Baby is Claressa "T-Rex" Shields, the most inspiring athlete I have ever known. She is Elizabeth Andiego of Kenya, who went without food while training for the London Olympics so her son could eat. She is bronze medalist Mary Kom, who runs a camp for youth boxers in strife-torn Manipur; silver medalist Sofya Ochigava, who reads Dostoyevsky between bouts; and gold medalist Katie Taylor, who bore Ireland's flag.

She is Juli Crockett, who retired undefeated, sings in a band called the Evangenitals, and describes her recently published dissertation as being "about the space that creating creates." She is Mia St. John, who posed naked for *Playboy* and doesn't care what you think. She is Michelle Cook, a Mohawk who fought in the USA Nationals while breast-feeding, and whose daughter's name, Konwanihara, means "gives words of thanks."

She is Stella Nijhof, my old sparring partner and four-time national champ, an awkward southpaw who wore her strawberry-blonde hair braided beneath her headgear and gave me many bloody noses but many more good times. Stella tends bar now in a former beauty parlor. We drink margaritas in pint glasses and reminisce about our brutal golden age.

Stella knows something about me no one else knows. She was my companion in that sweaty hell that I like better than heaven, and she saw me more naked than any lover. I never had much defense, in boxing or in life. Sometimes when Stella clocked me with her looping left I thought I might fall, but I'm still standing. Most Million Dollar Babies never make a dime, but we still have happy endings.

The day after I saw Claressa Shields speak, I followed her to Spokane. Twenty-four contenders would meet there for the first-ever US Women's Boxing Olympic Trials. Since the action in London was limited to three classes—flyweight (112 lbs.), lightweight (132 lbs.), and middleweight (165 lbs.)—many of the boxers were fighting outside of their natural weights. Claressa was a natural 154-pounder, so she would be giving up size as well as age. She still had a sixteen-year-old's soft body, lacking that nebulous thing called "woman strength."

On the flight to Spokane, Franchon Crews and her people were already celebrating. The five-time national champion at middleweight, the "Heavy-Hitting Diva" threw her haymaker right with bad intentions born in Baltimore and educated through trips to the World Championships and Pan-American Games. Crews had beaten most of the other middleweights before. She didn't know about Claressa Shields, fresh up from the juniors.

In the casino ballroom, the unranked boxers pulled marked ping-pong balls out of a basket to determine their draw in the double-elimination tournament. Claressa rooted through the bucket like a kid fishing for a prize in Crackerjacks. When she drew Crews, she pumped her fist in triumph. That was the moment I realized Claressa was special. When I fought, I was so scared of losing that I used to hope for the weakest possible opponent, but Claressa already knew she was going to win the whole tournament.

Before their bout, Crews's trainers were saying, "She trash already."

Claressa didn't mind. She looked serene as she climbed through the ring ropes, trotted over to Crews's corner, and initiated an extracurricular stare down that the referee hastened to break. That was just to let Crews know she wasn't afraid.

Jason made a show of admonishing Claressa, but few trainers really disapprove of that kind of thing. Claressa was already in her battle trance. She was about to hurt Franchon Crews.

Claressa knew that USA Boxing was political. When you fought their number one, you really had to beat her. You couldn't let her breathe. Right off the opening bell, Crews tried to hit Claressa with her big right hand, but Claressa just slipped it and jabbed. Almost immediately, she felt Crews give way.

Elite women amateurs fight four two-minute rounds. When Claressa came back to her stool at the end of the first, Jason read her the point score that the runners had brought from the judges' table. She was ahead, as always. Not only had she never lost a fight, she had never even lost a round.

In the second, Claressa started moving forward, taking the old champion to the ropes and launching tight hooks inside the wide haymaker rights. Every novice knows that a straighter punch beats a more looping one, but it takes conviction to stand toe to toe with someone stronger and draw tight lines inside her curves. Claressa was doing something very few women boxers were able to do.

She was no pioneer; Claressa was the ring's native daughter. She spoke the language of boxing with such fluency that she could say just what she liked at any given moment. And because she was so delightful and had so much to say, her fights were an emotional transmission.

To watch Claressa box was to believe that women did belong in the ring after all: not because it was sexist to exclude them, but because they could be so damn good.

The final score was a crushing 31–19. Crews walked numbly down the ring stairs and straight past her corner, her faith in the haymaker gone. She lost her next bout to a newcomer named Raquel Miller who fought with Bible verses written in ballpoint on the skin of her palms.

Claressa blew through the rest of the field with ease. Only one woman gave her any trouble: Tika Hemmingway, a crafty fighter out of DC with good timing and the wherewithal to tie Claressa up on the inside.

Claressa had beaten Hemmingway at the Police Athletic League Nationals 32–18 and almost stopped her, but Hemmingway was experienced enough to take a new approach. In the clinches, she put her head in the middle of Claressa's chest and leaned in with all 165 pounds. It was hard to adjust. Tika Hemmingway had woman strength, and Claressa still hadn't found hers.

Claressa grabbed the openings when they came, catching Hemmingway coming in and going out. She was so tired from pushing the bigger woman off her that she started panting, and her mouthpiece fell to the canvas twice. Claressa looked at Hemmingway's eyes, which teared every time she got hit, and thought, "She's tired too."

Claressa beat Hemmingway twice at the Trials, once in the winner's bracket and once after Hemmingway had battled back through the losers. Although Claressa was now the Trials champion, she spent the postfight interviews pouting about her low scores. She was used to scoring at least thirty points per match and didn't want Tika to brag about the fights being close.

Jason Crutchfield rolled his eyes and said, "Teenagers!"

Reigning national champions won both of the other divisions: flyweight Marlen Esparza of Houston and lightweight Queen Underwood of Seattle. Underwood had survived strong challenges from Mikaela Mayer, N'yteeyah Sherman, and Tiara Brown, while Esparza fended off Christina Cruz and Virginia Fuchs. After these top women, the talent level dropped off considerably. If it was disappointing to see relative novices contending for spots on our national team, it bore remembering that USA Boxing banned women from competition until 1993, when Dallas Molloy sued for the right to compete. Of all twenty-four competitors at the Trials, only Claressa Shields was young enough to have been born into a country in which girls could legally box.

Underwood and Esparza took their new teammate under their wings. When Claressa was named the Most Outstanding Boxer of the Tournament, Queen Underwood lifted her up in the air. Esparza gave her a rosary of red beads.

The losing boxers hit the casino disco to drink away concerns about their grim financial futures while the winners ate steak with USA Boxing's president, Hal Adonis, who mugged for the camera, his arms draped over the shoulders of the new young champions. The next day there was a press event in the hotel spa to "pamper the winners and show off their feminine side." Claressa was a little intimidated by the array of nail polish, but Marlen Esparza helped her choose something pink. It was the first time Claressa ever had a real massage. Boxing was so hard that it was almost unreal when the relaxation came. It made her feel like a queen.

Press row at the Trials was stocked with feminists in a party mood: Sue Jaye Johnson, the photographer of record for women's boxing; Christy Halbert, sociologist and champion of women boxers' inclusion in the Olympics; and independent journalist Raquel Ruiz, a dashing Colombian grandmother in four-inch heels. With their help, I learned that blogging about boxing gave me almost the same high as fighting but with less neck pain and more drinking.

Greg Beacham covered for the Associated Press, bringing a professional sportswriter's eye. The *Atlantic* sent a glossy culture reporter to follow Esparza. The *New York Times* published an exposé on Queen Underwood's childhood sexual abuse that made USA Boxing oddly proud. Ariel Levy, who was profiling Claressa for the *New Yorker*, got Hal Adonis on record outing sexual abuse survivors, bragging about slapping boxers, and fretting about lesbianism among the membership. He stepped down as president soon thereafter.

Even Joyce Carol Oates backpedaled in response to Levy's excellent piece. In a letter to the *New Yorker*, she generously allowed, "It is not unnatural or unreasonable that a gifted young woman athlete chooses to take up amateur boxing in 2012. I was writing about an era of boxing now past." She went on to claim that modern amateur bouts have more in common with fencing than with the brutal battles of boxing's golden age and concluded with a remarkable assertion from someone who has gained so much from the work of professional boxers: "In an ideal society, professional boxing would not exist." I would enjoy watching her say that in person to Claressa Shields.

At the training camp for Trials champions in Colorado Springs, Claressa felt like the main attraction. All the coaches had their eyes on her, trying to gain her trust, trying to fix things. Jason had told her how to handle that. She would obey while they were looking, but then she would go back to boxing her way.

The national coaches acted like she was some raw girl fighting on pure aggression. They kept trying to get her to jab and move, but Claressa was a puncher who used head movement as defense. At just five feet eight, she knew she would be the shorter combatant against full-grown middleweights. She needed to stay in the pocket. Claressa didn't need people to come in and fix what wasn't broken. If they took that as arrogance, let them.

Her next tournament would be a big step up. The American Continentals was not a qualifying tournament for the Olympics, but it would show how she measured up to the best female boxers from North, Central, and South America. Olympic gold medal favorite and three-time world champion Mary Spencer would be there, fighting on her home turf. The twenty-six-year-old Spencer was a proud member of the Cape Croker First Nation and, with her glowing skin and chestnut hair, a Canadian Cover Girl.

The US team settled into its bunks in the NAV Centre, an airy white complex in Cornwall, Ontario, that looked like a beached cruise ship. The best of the contenders from the Trials had fanned out into the non-Olympic classes, making this the strongest US women's boxing team in history. Franchon Crews, Mikaela Mayer, and Christina Cruz chowed down to maintain their higher weights, while Raquel Miller, Tiara Brown, and Alex Love radiated quiet martyrdom as they carried half-empty trays through the cafeteria. These women had weathered the death of their Olympic dream and were fighting on, without media attention, without sponsorships, purely for the love of the game. Sometimes I ate at their table, trying not to stare at their bright eyes and smooth skin, and once I trained alongside them in a little Cornwall gym, where Coach Izzy gave me two rounds of pads.

"Everybody wanted to beat you up until they saw you on the pads," Claressa told me later. "Then they stopped talking shit. You hit kinda hard."

I knew I shouldn't ask, but I did: "Why didn't they like me?"

She shrugged. "They said you were always hanging around, asking annoying questions and writing stupid things. I told them, 'It's not stupid!'"

"Thanks."

I can understand why the fighters were suspicious of me. I didn't have business cards, a byline, or much of a plan. All I knew was that the longer I stayed in the rooms with them, the better the work would be. When the going got hard, I thought of my role model, Lady Godiva, who—if my memory of the after-school special serves—rode naked through Coventry on a white pony because it would somehow save the poor. Everyone laughed at Lady Godiva, but she knew she was doing the right thing, and now she had eponymous chocolates. Sometimes you have to expose yourself for the sake of history.

Claressa's opening opponent in Canada was Roseli Feitosa of Brazil, the world light heavyweight champion: another bigger, older, more experienced woman who was ranked number three in the world. Going in, Claressa noticed Feitosa had barely warmed up. She was taking Claressa lightly, but Claressa had looked up Feitosa's fights and knew the Brazilian had nothing for her.

The old-timers say, "Never give up speed," and no other girl had hand speed like Claressa Shields. She was faster than the light fly-weights.

When the bell rang marking the end of the brutal first round, Claressa saw a look in Feitosa's eyes that said, "Coach, I wasn't ready for this." Claressa had broken her spirit. The rest of the bout was easy.

Afterward Claressa sat in the stands and watched Mary Spencer outclass the Mexican champion Alma Nora Ibarra. Claressa had to give credit where it was due. Spencer was slick and fast. She had good timing and saw things. But she made mistakes, too: she kept her hands too low, her head was open, her body was open. Mary Spencer couldn't beat her.

After she cooled down, Spencer took questions. When I asked what she thought about Claressa Shields, her dark eyes flashed with anger.

"Why should I think *any*thing about her?" she said.

The punch you don't see coming is the one that knocks you out. Nobody in the world could beat Mary Spencer before she met Claressa Shields. I repeated Spencer's words to Claressa, who rolled her eyes.

"I'm not worried about Mary Spencer," she said. "She can go home tonight and Google some information about me."

Jason Crutchfield arrived on fight day after a nine-hour drive from Flint. He and his crew prowled around the NAV Centre, eating chicken wings and speculating loudly about knockouts. They were not allowed in Claressa's corner for the bout but sat in the stands, degrading international relations.

From the opening moments of the fight, Claressa dominated Mary Spencer just as easily as she had Roseli Feitosa and Franchon Crews. The relaxed confidence with which Spencer had handled the Mexican champion now seemed like lack of explosiveness. The low left hand, which had looked so knowing, was now an open door for Claressa's lead right. Spencer was soft and lost and undertrained. Claressa worried she would have to fight both boxer and judges, until the first round scoring came back 5–2 in her favor.

The Berston Field House crew got rowdy. The Canadian and American teams fought to outscream each other.

"She ain't seen *nothing* like you, 'Ress!" Jason cried.

The atmosphere in the ring grew equally ugly. Spencer talked trash whenever the two got close. Claressa was thrown at first, but then she realized this was a sign of weakness.

"I got her," she told herself.

Toward the end of the bout, Spencer fouled with a hard body shot off the break. Claressa was still looking at the ref, and the punch damn near dropped her, but she held on.

When they announced the 27–14 decision for Claressa, the two women hugged and said, "Good fight," but there was no warmth between them. This was the first time Claressa had experienced a dirty fighter. Even Franchon Crews, for all her swagger, had kept it clean.

On the gold medal podium, the new Americas middleweight champion texted during "The Star-Spangled Banner," oblivious to the umbrage of her hosts. Claressa still thought the work should be over after the final bell. There might be a documentary crew following her now, but she was still just a kid from Flint. She still cursed on Twitter. She still believed nobody could beat her.

Although a big win, the Americas title meant nothing when it came to qualifying for the Olympics. Claressa's true test came in May in Qinhuangdao, an industrial seaport a few hours' drive from Beijing. The AIBA World Championships was the sole Olympic qualifier, determining which thirty-six women would box in the London Games.

AIBA released an obscure document about the qualification process that read like a Zen koan. Claressa would need to finish as one of the top two middleweights from North, Central, and South America combined. In theory, this was an easy task, since she had already won the continental gold. Yet in China her name would be thrown in the hat with all the other middleweights in the world. She would be unseeded for the random draw, and it was single elimination.

Claressa had fun while she waited to fight, even though eating in China was a challenge. The team had been warned that Chinese meat contained hormones that might make them fail the doping tests, so they were all on vegetarian diets. Claressa survived on rice, eggs, soy sauce, watermelon, oranges, and honeydew melon. It was hard to keep weight on. When she had the time, she devoured vegetarian pies at the Qinhuangdao Pizza Hut.

I was staying with photographer Sue Jaye Johnson at the official media hotel cum prison, where the modest cost of our room included censored Internet, complimentary round-the-clock surveillance by chain-smoking guards, and three meals a day at a restaurant whose staggering amounts of MSG and sodium left me so swollen I looked embalmed. I was a little worried about my single kidney, so I stopped eating entirely, and by the time we escaped to the Holiday Inn, I was a bantamweight for the first time in thirteen years.

Claressa thought the Chinese were the nicest people ever. When she got lost inside one of the vast, strange grocery stores, a tiny lady who spoke English helped her find deodorant and pay for it.

"I love Americans," the lady said. "I love you."

Jason wasn't there, although Claressa Skyped him every night. She was skeptical of the national coaches, who kept changing as a result of the infighting in the wake of Hal Adonis's dismissal. The head coach who had watched the action in Spokane was different from the one who had accompanied them to Cornwall, who was different from the one in Qinhuangdao, who would, in turn, be barred from the London corners for an AIBA rule infraction. This disarray would produce the only medal-less performance in Olympic history for the US men's team.

A press pass normally opens doors, but in China it functioned more like a biohazard sign. Only the most toxic, bunker-like areas were judged fit for media containment. I could sometimes sneak into the athlete bleachers by hiding my credentials, but soon I would be herded back with much shaming by the chain-smoking guards, all of whom were male and some of whom spent their free time—it is unclear whether for fun or as an intimidation tactic—reading brochures about missiles.

The Irish media had turned out in force to support their great lightweight Katie Taylor, who would win Most Outstanding Woman Boxer of the tournament and, later on, of the London Olympic Games. A gang of hard-drinking Liverpudlians was following Natasha "Laughing Assassin" Jonas. The Canadian Broadcasting people were after Mary Spencer for a comeback that never came, and two other Canadians filmed the Indian team for their documentary *With This Ring*. Al Jazeera noted the headscarved Afghans, whose inclusion represented a symbolic victory for women's rights but who were crushingly ill prepared as athletes. The Thai newsmen hadn't gotten the memo about journalistic objectivity and cheered in my ear at deafening volumes. The largest delegation by far was from Japan. The corps of listless Japanese men sat in the press room cum dungeon, eating muffins and radiating contempt for women's boxing in general and their subject in particular, middleweight Shizuyo Yamazaki, a famous comedian back home.

"Her technique does not go to international level," they told me.

"She is comedian, but maybe this will be tragedy."

When Yamazaki knocked out her first-round opponent, they all pulled out their cell phones and started texting Tokyo.

Claressa had an easy first-round outing against India's Pooja Rani, although she got overanxious and tired a bit in the closing rounds. She was still a little jet-lagged, but she did not worry too much about her next opponent, Great Britain's Savannah Marshall. Franchon Crews had dropped a 10–8 decision to Marshall in the Olympic test event and told Claressa that the lanky boxer would not be a problem. Claressa was now 26–0 with fourteen stoppages. It was her turn to be caught by surprise.

The British team knew how to take care of its boxers. Its three Olympic hopefuls trained year-round in a state-of-the-art sports center alongside the men. While Claressa was eating Jason's barbecued chicken, the Brits were eating five small meals a day prepared by sports nutritionists who kept tabs on their weight and hydration.

Savannah Rose Marshall was blonde and pale and long limbed. Outside the ring, she was painfully shy, with the look of an overgrown schoolgirl. Inside it, she was a dogged worker who understood how to maximize her assets. Marshall's coaches had done their homework and knew from the Tika Hemmingway tapes that Claressa could be frustrated by movement and tied up on the inside. They knew their girl was taller, more experienced, and in better condition. If she could weather Claressa's power early, she could win.

When Claressa looked across the ring at Marshall, she thought, "Oh my God, she's a giant." The British Amateur Boxing Association website had listed Marshall's height at five feet eleven, but Claressa swore she was over six feet tall.

Right from the start, Marshall kept moving. Claressa did what she always did, but whenever she got inside, Marshall would grab and hold. It was frustrating. When she came back to the corner after the first round, the coaches told her it was tied at 2–2.

"OK," Claressa thought, "I'm gonna step on the gas."

For her part, Savannah Marshall thought she had never fought a woman with such heavy hands. After the first round, she was afraid Claressa had broken her nose, but Marshall bit down on her mouthpiece. Of all the skills she had, her greatest was the stubborn ability to stick to a game plan.

Claressa tried harder in the second and the third, but Marshall just kept on turning and holding. It was like Tika Hemmingway, only worse, because Marshall was tall enough to catch Claressa on the outside. At one point, Claressa felt herself freeze and eat a big right hand.

She listened for Jason's voice telling her what to do, but Jason wasn't there. Claressa felt something cold in her belly. Later on, she would realize it was fear.

"I'm on my own," she thought.

Going into the final round, she was down by three.

"We're gonna get this," said coach Basheer Abdullah.

The words "be more aggressive" echoed in her head as she chased Marshall with a furious energy, but her legs were shot. The cold feeling would not leave her belly, and the ref wasn't doing anything about the holding. How was she supposed to fight Savannah Marshall and the referee, too?

Claressa didn't know what was happening because it had never happened before. She was losing. You have to learn how to lose. Claressa had always been a quick study, but this lesson would come hard, because she did not want to learn it. Even as she stood in center ring, awaiting the decision, she still thought she had won.

When the referee failed to raise her hand and the echoey loudspeakers broadcast the final score of 14–8, Claressa felt only shock. She looked at the lime-green canvas, then up into the stands at her teammates, then back down, shaking her head. When Marshall tried to embrace her, Claressa turned her back and walked out of the ring.

From the bleachers, Marlen Esparza yelled, "Whatever you do, Claressa, don't cry!"

She kept it in until she got to the locker room. The Nigerian coaches walked by and said they thought she won. Raquel Miller hugged her and said, "It's OK."

It wasn't. She had done her best, and her best wasn't good enough. She wasn't going to London after all.

She had been so *good* leading up to the tournament. She hadn't had sex. She didn't drink, didn't smoke, didn't cuss, went to church. She couldn't understand why God would do this to her. She wanted to wake up. She wanted to wake up and have it all be a bad dream.

The hardest part was when they told her Jason was on the phone. "What happened?" he asked.

"I don't know. I don't feel like I got outboxed."

Jason could be hard on the guys when they lost, and he had spent so much of his time on her back at Berston. She felt she had let him down. She had let so many people down. But all Jason said was that he was real sorry he hadn't been there. That maybe if he had, none of this would have happened.

Claressa said, "No, coach, it's my fault."

When she got back to her room, she wrote in her diary, which she had named Olympia, "Well, I really lost today. I'm not undefeated no more." Then she put down the pen and started crying for real.

That night Claressa talked to God for an hour. Ironically, her fate was now in the hands of Savannah Marshall. All of the middleweights from North, Central, and South America had lost in the preliminaries. Their final tournament rankings would now be determined by the rankings of the women who had eliminated them. Claressa could still finish in the top two for the continent if Marshall did well enough.

"God," Claressa prayed. "I know Savannah Marshall sucks, but I need to go to the Olympics. Please let her win. This is my dream."

When she woke up every morning, Claressa was in the habit of looking in the mirror and telling herself she would win an Olympic gold medal. The morning after she lost in China, she was surprised to find that nothing had changed. The face that stared back looked just the same. Somehow, she still believed she would win that gold.

When her teammates saw her at breakfast, they all started crying.

Alex Love, who had been eliminated on the first day from the 106-pound weight class and was now pushing 120, hugged her and said, "It's all right."

Claressa said, "I know."

"Wanna work out?"

"Yeah."

They went to the gym and hit the heavy bag, and Claressa sparred two Chinese girls: an aggressive one whom Claressa beat up and a slick one who outboxed her for a round until Claressa looked into her eyes and figured her out. They did not speak the same language, but they understood each other. It hurt, but she had to get right back to it. The next day, she followed along glumly as the group of international referees, boxers, and coaches took their scheduled field trip to the Great Wall of China. At the souvenir shop, she purchased a rubber "Shrieking Chicken," which let out a horrific wail when squeezed.

Savannah Marshall kept on winning. She beat Norway's Lotte Lien in the round of sixteen. She beat hometown hero Li Jinzi in the quarterfinals. She faced tough Russian Nadezda Torlopova in the semis.

Claressa squirmed in the bleachers as she watched the match that would determine her Olympic fate. Marshall was looking sharp, keeping Torlopova at the end of her jab. During the second round, everyone was congratulating her, but Claressa said, "Hush."

Marshall could still get knocked out. She could still get robbed. In the fourth round, Claressa got down on her knees in the stands and prayed. Who would have thought she would qualify for the Olympics on her knees?

Marshall won 18–10. Team USA leapt to its feet, screaming. Their baby was going to London.

Claressa wound her way out of the stands and down to where Savannah Marshall stood on the stadium floor, flanked by her coaches and teammates.

"Good fight," Claressa told her. "Thank you for helping me get to the Olympics."

She apologized to Savannah for not having congratulated her earlier. She admitted how scared she had felt during their fight, after that second round.

"She's a beautiful person, your Claressa," said one of the Liverpudlians, showing me a photo he had taken of this conversation. The two rivals stood very close together, both hands clasped: tall, blonde Savannah with the translucent skin and sleepy eyes; Claressa looking up at her, dark and solemn in her USA tracksuit.

"She don't even know," Coach Basheer told Claressa. "She just invited you to London to win the gold medal."

Claressa said, "She gonna find out."

She went home to Flint and trained like a dog. No days off. She told Jason everything that had happened, and he told her they were going to work on it all: getting out of the clinch, getting her legs stronger so she wouldn't tire, cutting off the ring, not freaking out. Claressa's sparring partner and prom date 'Rell was a tall, strong young man who did everything Marshall had done—moving, holding, jabbing—and sometimes Claressa would get so frustrated with him that she would rip off her gloves and throw them on the floor.

She got hold of a magazine in which Savannah Marshall bragged

THE REAL MILLION DOLLAR BABY 55

about beating her and said she had already defeated the best in the world. Claressa was outraged.

She told 'Rell, "This girl done lost her mind, bragging about me."

F. Scott Fitzgerald wrote that the test of a first-rate intelligence is the ability to hold two opposing ideas in the mind and still retain the ability to function. Claressa passed that test. She accepted her first defeat while still believing herself unbeaten. Perhaps this intelligence came easily to a champion from Flint. At the time of the London Games, Claressa's hometown would claim the number-one spot on the FBI's list of most dangerous cities with populations over one hundred thousand. Long before she walked into Berston Field House, Claressa already knew to protect herself at all times. She understood when to engage, when to keep her distance, and which corners were neutral. Jason had taught her to box, but Flint made her a fighter.

It wasn't like she didn't get mad when she thought about the things that had happened to her there, when she was very young. Her mother should have paid more attention. Her father should have been around. But Claressa believed in forgiveness. She came from a world of losses with victory in her mind. Everything was in God's plan.

When she did her morning roadwork past the boarded-up hood houses with their busted windows and wide-open doors, the drug addicts and alcoholics would wave at her and call her "Miss Shields." Everybody needs something to believe in, and Claressa could be that something for the people of Flint. When she would ask for donations for London and people would give her a dime because that was all they had, or a prayer because they didn't even have a dime, that made her strong. If she had a superpower, it was resilience.

The ancient Sumerians told a feel-good sports story about Inanna, the goddess of love and war. One day Inanna decided to leave heaven and confront her sister in hell. She adorned herself with gowns and jewels, but as she entered hell's gates everything was stripped away so she was naked when she faced her sister. Forcing her aside, Inanna sat for one proud moment on the throne of hell. Then the judges of the underworld killed her and hung her body from a hook.

But Inanna had a trick up her sleeve. Before she left heaven, she had told her best friend, "When I am gone, grieve for me and bang a drum. Beg the gods not to let me die."

The girlfriend went door to door, but the gods all said, "Inanna was wrong to crave hell as well as heaven," which is pretty much what Claressa Shields said when I told her this story. But Enki, god of wisdom, listened. With the dirt under his fingernails he created spirits who resurrected Inanna. She ascended back through the gates, reclaiming all her adornments, and resumed her rule of heaven.

I like this story because Inanna gets to have it both ways, as befits a goddess of love and war. She gets to experience victory and defeat. She gets to take her clothes off and put them back on again. She gets to go through hell and live.

In order to have an adventure, a heroine needs opposition. Inanna needed a sister in the underworld. The Powerpuff Girls needed the evil monkey Mojo Jojo. Claressa Shields needed Savannah Marshall, and she will need better opposition if she is to keep evolving. We won't see what women's boxing can really be until rivals of comparable weight emerge who can bring out the divine in each other, like Smokin' Joe and Ali, Holyfield and Bowe, Pryor and Arguello.

Maybe that will never happen, but we ought to at least give it space in our imagination. The most frustrating thing about *Million Dollar Baby* is the shallowness of the face-off, so that Maggie Fitzgerald becomes everything desirable in women and Billy the Blue Bear becomes everything the creators fear. It's a cheap substitute for the rich ambiguity of sisterhood.

"People don't understand why fighters hug," Juli Crockett told me. "When the final bell rang, I was always overwhelmed with gratitude toward the other person. I had just shared with her, in eight minutes, more experience than I'd had in all the rest of my life."

Worldly power can only open the gates to these naked confrontations. The fighter has to be willing to be judged and to die, because she will die eventually, and only the story will keep her alive. Because that's the other thing a heroine needs: Someone to bear witness.

Those of us who write the stories need to do the right thing, like Inanna's faithful girlfriend. We can't leave our heroines hanging.

Claressa wasn't the only one who grew up on the road to London. When I first set off for Spokane, I bristled at the phrase "women's boxing." I thought I could take gender out of this story. I wanted to write like A. J. Liebling did—as an insider, concerned with pure things like jabs and aesthetics—but I'm not in Liebling's weight class and I'm taking in the action from cheaper seats. I was lucky to catch Claressa. The aura of a great champion always pushes through to the back of the room.

I watched the London Games on the live feed at 30 Rock, where I had gotten a job at CNBC. Although it was disappointing to be across the pond from Claressa, the most dramatic part of her story was past. Her Olympic victory seemed written in advance.

She got a lucky draw: a first round bye left her fresh for her quarterfinal meeting with Sweden's Anna Laurell, the only boxer in the bracket who looked like she had to sweat down to the weight like a man. Laurell had won gold in 2001 in Scranton, Pennsylvania, at the very first Women's World Championships. Towering over Claressa, she ran around the ring's perimeter, popping out jabs and dropping rights on top.

Claressa was down by two points after the first round and one point after the second. In the third, Laurell stopped moving so much, and Claressa tied the score. She hammered it home in the fourth, handing Laurell a standing eight off a hard left hook and taking the bout by four points. This was the closest fight she had in London.

Savannah Marshall was upset in the quarterfinals by Kazakhstan's Marina Volnova, robbing Claressa of her rematch. Claressa couldn't believe Marshall had been eliminated. She had wanted so badly to erase the humiliation of her only loss.

The force of her frustration lent Claressa a manic energy for her semifinal against Volnova. As the two women made their ring walk, the stocky Kazakh flashed Claressa a look, as though she thought it would be easy because she had beaten the girl who had beaten her.

Claressa got her temper from Cannonball. When she first started boxing—even back when she had fought Franchon and Tika in the Trials—she had thought it was wrong to feel rage in the ring. Jason had always emphasized the importance of keeping her emotions under control.

Maybe her woman strength was finally coming in. Claressa now knew that she did not have to defeat her anger; she could distill it and let it flow out through her hands. Later, when she played back the tapes of her fights, she would feel the life inside of the work, the basic emotional rhythm. She liked to make a point, and she was eloquent with Volnova, twice handing her standing-eight counts en route to a brutal 29–15 victory that represented the highest point score of any boxer in London, male or female.

The gold medal bout looked like sparring. Nadezda Torlopova was Claressa's equal in height but her inferior in speed and strength. Claressa played it by the book, feeling the Russian out in an even first round, exploding in the second, and coasting home in the final two. She was having so much fun that she stuck out her tongue at Torlopova. The stern female ref told her to knock it off, but even she looked mildly amused.

Claressa tried to pay attention during the national anthem, but it was hard to stop laughing. Her legs were shaking so much she thought she might have a seizure. That night she wore her gold medal to bed, wrapped around her hand. She had this fear that when she woke up it would be silver.

CNBC's color commentator Laila Ali—who had spent the Olympics comparing herself favorably to the women boxers, complaining about makeup, and making our interns fetch complicated Starbucks beverages—finally gave it up to Claressa on air.

"She reminds me of my father," Laila said.

The national coaches would say Claressa won because of all the things they showed her in training camp. Claressa would say it was because of Berston Field House and Jason and 'Rell and because God wanted her to win.

Teddy Atlas said she won because she was too young to let it all get to her. At just seventeen years and 145 days, Claressa edged out Floyd Patterson to become the second-youngest US Olympic boxing champion in history after featherweight Jackie Fields of the 1924 Paris Games.

Coach Christy Halbert, whose tireless advocacy helped ensure the women boxers' inclusion in the Olympics, said that Claressa won because she had the most important quality for a fighter: the willingness to be vulnerable in the midst of explosiveness.

I think Claressa won because that's who she is.

I was talking to the venerable Hector Roca in his office at Gleason's Gym, beneath the photos of all the champions he has trained. He pointed to the one of Arturo Gatti and said, "He paid for my house." He pointed to the one of Hilary Swank in *Million Dollar Baby* and said, "She thanked me when she won the Oscar."

I told him he deserved it. Hector has a certain reputation with the ladies, but I'm sure he kept it professional with Hilary Swank. She looked pretty good hitting the heavy bag, better than Sylvester Stallone.

"Women learn quicker than men," he said.

When I asked what he thought about Claressa Shields, Hector Roca closed his eyes and smiled.

"Ah, that one. She's just a baby."

WHY I FIXED FIGHTS

Charles Farrell

I fixed a lot of fights over the years. In two I didn't fix but should have, people paid heavily for my carelessness. Even though I set up Mitch "Blood" Green and Leon Spinks cushion soft in their comeback fights, I managed to get one embarrassed and the other nearly killed. There had been opportunities for them, deals that came undone when they lost. It wasn't as if the winners benefited in any tangible way, either. At best their victories brought them smallish short-term bragging rights. Among boxing insiders, they were objects of scorn for having won, as incompetent at their jobs as Green, Spinks, and I were at ours.[1]

Writing about boxing sometimes adopts a heroic perspective on the sport. This seems especially common in a certain kind of popular journalism. When a boxer gets into the ring, he's seen as entering a magic theater of virtue and vice cut off from the rest of the world. For the fight's duration, his actions assume a kind of moral transparency, defining him as noble or ignoble. But when it's over and he steps outside the ring, becoming just a person again, the aura sticks.

---

1. An earlier version of this essay appeared on Deadspin.com on April 16, 2014.

To participate in fight fixing therefore defines him morally not only as a professional fighter, but as a person. Lost in this vision of things is any awareness of the way boxing actually works as a business, and the racially and economically inflected cultures within which that business is transacted.

Why did I fix fights? I fixed fights because it was the smart thing to do.

BLOOD

I started managing Mitch Green in late 1991, a little more than a year before his loss to Bruce Johnson. He'd been a high-profile contender—an imposing eccentric who'd famously fought Mike Tyson twice, once in the ring and once on a Harlem street, and who with a little work could be brought back into the title picture. Our first business meeting took place in Cambridge, Massachusetts, at a gimmicky penthouse restaurant that revolved slowly above the city. The first thing Mitch did was rise up from the table, peel down the top of his bright-orange jumpsuit, flex his pecs, kiss his biceps, and invite a roomful of sedate diners to "feast you eyes on what a real heavyweight is *supposed* to look like."

This bit of street theater made me optimistic: Mitch Green could still work a room. But no sooner had the ink on our contract dried than he got shot. While idling on the corner of 129th Street and Lenox Avenue in Harlem, Mitch slapped a man who'd been baiting him about his fights with Tyson. The guy bolted into his apartment and came back blasting. I still have the blood-stained sneaker, complete with bullet hole. I keep it as a kind of macabre reminder, though I'm not sure of what.

Mitch limped six blocks to Harlem Hospital. He was x-rayed, told the bullet had passed through his leg, given a clean bill of health, and sent home. The attending doctor missed the bullet lodged behind Mitch's knee. By the time Mitch called me a week later, he couldn't walk. His femur, further traumatized by running and jumping rope, had split like a tree branch. I flew him to Boston, picked him up at

Logan Airport, and took him straight to Beth Israel Hospital. The Celtics' orthopedic surgeon, Frank Bunch, had him on an operating table within two hours. If he'd waited another day, Mitch probably would have lost his leg.

During the six months of rehab that followed, Mitch lived at a house I owned near Boston. He regularly demanded cash; had two girlfriends flown in from different parts of the country for what turned into a nonconsensual threesome that ended only when my terrified downstairs tenants called the police; sent the "salary" he was getting home to his mother, who spent it on bingo trips to Atlantic City; and complained incessantly. I didn't get it: I was knocking myself out for him and he was doing nothing for me, yet he never stopped complaining.

Visions of Don King and Mike Tyson obsessed Mitch, along with those of a number of black civic leaders he believed to be in cahoots with them. It was generally assumed he was paranoid, crazy, and dangerous. But consider: When Mitch was a child in Georgia, his father had been shot dead at point-blank range by a man he was simultaneously shooting dead. The men's funerals were held in the same mortuary on the same afternoon, both families sweating through their Sunday best no more than a few feet apart. Or this: As a gang lord, Mitch had presided over New York's Black Spades, a gig that required him to maintain an aura of menace while fending off anyone insane enough to challenge him. Or this: As a young man who'd won the New York Golden Gloves heavyweight title four times in a row, he'd been given money, cars, and an assortment of flashy presents by some of boxing's white elite, like Shelly Finkel and Lou Duva.

After sleepwalking in 1986 through a ten-round decision loss to Tyson, held in Madison Square Garden and shown on HBO—for which he received $30,000—Mitch met his nemesis again on the street. Their brief, violent encounter made headlines. Afterward, Mitch dropped off the boxing map.

My job was to bring him back. Smarter men than I said it was impossible. Signing up Mitch Green even earned me 1993's "Sucker of the Year" award in *Boxing Illustrated*. The only money Mitch ever made me came from betting Al Braverman, Don King's director of boxing, that I'd be able to coax him back inside the ring.

I was sure I'd picked the right foil for Mitch's comeback match. A gangly, knock-kneed cruiserweight, Bruce Johnson came in with a record of 8–22–1. He'd been knocked out seventeen times and had never beaten a credible opponent. Johnson always arrived from out of town prepared to lose. His livelihood depended on his career going nowhere.

In the dressing room, Bruce told me he was afraid of Mitch, then held me up for $500 more than the price we'd agreed on. All I would have had to say for Mitch to win was: "You want five hundred more dollars? Get knocked out by the third round."

I didn't do that. I didn't think I needed to. Mitch was going to kill him.

But in a tiny arena in Woodbridge, Virginia, on a frigid winter night when a blizzard reduced the house to nearly nothing, Mitch Green, angry that he wasn't getting paid enough or being properly respected, got into the ring and refused to throw or block punches. Johnson was never on his radar. Mitch ignored his feeble jabs. He also ignored me, my partners Pat and Tony Petronelli, and everything but the private buzzing in his head, gazing stone-faced over Johnson's shoulder into the middle distance. After several warnings from the referee to start punching or risk having the fight stopped, the plug was pulled in the third round as the handful of spectators hooted. Mitch had thrown his future away in less than nine minutes.

I wouldn't talk to Mitch after that. I'd lost a year of my life and $80,000 on him.

THE FOOLPROOF OPPONENT

I never intended to manage Leon Spinks, the freewheeling heavyweight who'd upset Muhammad Ali in 1978. I was interested in his sons Darrell and Tommy and their fellow East Saint Louisan Freddie Norwood, and that interest required my looking out for Leon, too. It wasn't until he lost a decision in North Carolina to Eddie Curry, a dive artist who could fight a little if no one told him not to, that I got roped into actually managing him.

That night Leon and Curry quickly bogged down into a slow grind, their mutual lack of conditioning forcing them to drape themselves over each other in a sodden ring where the temperature was over a hundred. Leon hung in on heart; Eddie, with the dawning realization that he was going to get a win over a former heavyweight champion.

But Leon caught two lucky breaks: For one thing, Eddie Curry was being paid by the round; for another, I'd done previous business with Bobby Mitchell, the South Carolina commissioner brought in to oversee the card, who also happened to be Curry's manager. After eight rounds, under the impression that he'd gone the distance, Curry demanded that his gloves be cut off. Feeling a sense of responsibility to Leon, who was only fighting to help his sons, I climbed into the ring and told Mitchell the fight had to continue: The fight poster listed the main event as a ten-rounder.

Not even the judges were aware of the poster. The decision had already been announced for Curry, who refused to put his gloves back on. In the center of the ring, I made some noise: "It's a ten-round fight. You've got one minute before the next bell rings. Better get Eddie's gloves back on."

"The fight's over. The decision's been announced."

"It's been announced to three hundred people who'll never check the record book."

Mitchell conferred with Curry. "Eddie, this is your night. Spinks is an old man."

"No way. I ain't fightin' no more."

I butted in. "Thirty seconds before the next round. Let's go."

"OK, I see what you're doing. Can we talk about this in the office?"

"Absolutely," I said. "I just need it to go into the record books as a win for Spinks. Does Leon win the fight?"

"Shit, yeah. Leon wins the fight. But do we have to take care of it here?"

So Leon Spinks got his win, and I got stuck with Leon Spinks.

I had no idea what to do with him. He couldn't fight. The only interest promoters had in him was as a small notch on some young killer's belt. Then an unlikely offer to meet Larry Holmes in China popped up. It wouldn't pay by the standards of Leon's brief heyday, but it was a hundred times more than he was getting for his current bouts. I was sure I could get Holmes to listen to reason. Years earlier, in defense of his heavyweight title, he'd mercifully knocked out a much better Leon Spinks in three easy rounds.

But before the Holmes fight could be made—even as far away as China—I had to put Leon back in the public eye. That meant a high-profile venue where he could conspicuously knock someone out. I landed him a main event at the Washington, DC, Convention Center.

To get Leon on the cheap, the promoters, a small group of street-smart local hustlers raising money for Marion Barry's reelection, let me bring in my own opponent. But my fall guy came up with a bad CAT scan and the DC commission rejected him. I was stuck scrambling for a replacement.

John Carlo had never fought before. No commission would sanction a fight between an ex-champ, however diminished, and a debuting boxer who didn't have the equivalent of an Olympic pedigree. Online records had made it impossible to invent wins and losses in any commissioned state, so I had to falsify Carlo's entire professional career by staging his "fights" in nonsanctioned states. I imagined him as a journeyman with a respectable 13–2 record. For opponents I chose the names of real fighters, habitual losers who often fought in unregulated states. Even they wouldn't remember whether or not they'd lost to a John Carlo. But after these elaborate maneuvers to provide Leon with a foolproof opponent, I failed to take the one step needed to guarantee the result: I didn't fix the fight.

John himself brought it up. A couple of days before the fight, he asked, "What happens if I win?"

We both laughed about that.

"If you can beat him, beat him. If Leon can't handle a guy who's never been in the ring before, he has no business being there. You'd be doing him a favor."

A few seconds after the bell rang, Leon extended a brotherly right hand to John, intending to touch gloves. But John—intense fear producing the effect opposite of what I'd expected—was not in a collegial mood, first feinting and soon following through with a viciously professional left hook that felled the former champ as if he'd been nailed by a ten-pound mallet. Spinks dropped straight back, his head bouncing audibly off the canvas. He barely beat a very slow count, and John was on him in a delirium, dropping him again. A minute later the fight was over. So were any thoughts of Larry Holmes, China, or the $175,000 Spinks would have made fighting someone skillful enough not to hurt him.

THE ART OF THE FIX

No sport is romanticized more than boxing. Heroic writers use boxing to make moral sense of the world. Noble fighters, by their actions, stabilize chaos: their bravery in the face of untenable circumstances and violent hostility helps to restore value and security to a now-intelligible world, one inhabited by heroic journalists and their readers. Heroic journalism attaches a sentimental narrative to the rise of a titleholder, carving out a cinematic character arc wherein horrific circumstances are overcome through moral probity, grit, hard work, and determination, and climaxing with HBO viewers choking up a little as the victor tearfully accepts his championship belt after winning a brutal encounter at Caesars Palace.

Winning a world title is definitely hard, time-consuming work, so that kind of arc expresses some truth. What it obscures is the fact that most of the fights designed to get that fighter his title shot are fixed in one way or another. Anybody who spends his own money advancing a fighter and knows what he's doing engages in some form of fight fixing. And, wittingly or not, almost every titleholder has benefited from fixes.

A former president of the Boxing Writers Association of America once said, "When it comes to sports, all a writer needs to know is how wonderful it feels to win, how miserable it feels to lose, and how hard it is to try." If you get paid to write about boxing and believe this, the kindest thing that can be said about you is that you're a sucker.

I see boxing differently now than when I was managing fighters. Starting out, I assumed that an encyclopedic knowledge of the sport as art was all I'd need to handle the careers of professional fighters. I didn't manage opponents—my clientele was made up of champions, contenders, and prospects. I thought champions should be matched with contenders whom they'd beat, contenders should be matched with tough journeymen whom they'd beat, and prospects should be matched with lesser prospects or former champions or contenders whom they'd beat.

I could pick the winner of a fight more than 90 percent of the time, and I thought this was a unique talent. I didn't know that nearly everyone in boxing could do it; those who can't hire someone to do it for them. Boxing's political factions and complex, shifting hierarchies were also largely unknown to me.

In fights that aren't fixed, even well-informed mismatches can go awry. Personal problems, off nights, jealousies, injuries, internecine conflicts, double-crosses, hometown decisions, and promotional affiliations can all throw a monkey wrench into the most carefully laid plans.

Despite my cautious matchmaking for another fighter, Martin Foster, I watched him go from an undefeated heavyweight whose only real asset was his reliable chin to a sure KO victim whose knees would sag and whose eyes would roll into the back of his head whenever he was tagged solidly. This transformation took place over a matter of months. Finally, on a Don King card in Belfast, Ireland, Foster lost in a way that was chilling enough for me that I no longer wanted to be even partially responsible for his further participation in boxing.

Fighting the light-punching Frans Botha in a heavyweight title eliminator, Foster had his nose erased from his face by a bolo punch that everyone in King's Hall but he saw coming. It was such a sucker punch that Botha, who'd wound it up theatrically, started laughing. And then, still laughing, he did it again. And *it landed again*. As Foster began to sag to the canvas, the referee rushed in to save him. His cornermen, Tony Petronelli and Chuck Bodak, and I half-carried Martin down the ring steps and across the large auditorium to his dressing room. It took Chuck nearly a half hour to get Foster to spit all the blood from his broken nose into a bucket. By the time he was done, the bucket was fuller than it would've seemed possible.

Martin Foster owed me a lot of money at that point. But when we met at the airport the next morning to fly to different parts of the United States, I told him that I'd forget about the debt if he promised to retire from boxing. He had a wife and two young kids, and I was aware that somewhere down the line—in five or ten years—they were going to lose some of him even if he never took another punch. I was clear: If I found out that he'd returned to fighting, I would come after him and collect my money. We shook hands on it, then went to our separate planes. I never saw Martin Foster again. When I got Don King's paycheck for the fight, I kept all of it. After I stopped managing Martin, he was knocked out eleven times in twelve nonfixed losses, no doubt resulting in much additional damage.

Boxing managers have an obligation to minimize the amount of damage their fighters sustain. By the time any fighter gets a shot at a championship—usually his first opportunity to make real money—he will already have had very hard fights and been banged up in ways that will not yet be outwardly apparent to most people. His career is likely to be halfway over. If he becomes the champion, most of his title defenses during the next few years will be tough ones. If he fails in his title attempt, depending on the nature of his performance, he'll either get more chances or be demoted to the rank of "name" opponent. If he's lucky enough to get more title shots, none of them will be easy. The market demands that they not be: As a known loser, he's no longer entitled to have the path eased for him. Once he's slipped to the role of opponent, he'll get beaten up repeatedly, his purses and his health diminishing with each successive loss. And at this point, the fighter will most likely be looking at a postcareer future of neurological impairment. He may have four or five real earning years left to him.

These are hard facts, but they're almost unfailingly representative of what a "successful" fighter can expect. Why should any fighter take the punishment that this profession brings, if not for money?

The most responsible way to develop a new fighter is to combine easily winnable fights—albeit ones that require some of his attention and skill—with fixed fights that will move him quickly up the ratings. The goal is to earn a fighter as much money as possible without incurring unnecessary wear and tear. He'll have to be in enough tough fights when the time comes.

Fight fixing is such an accepted part of the boxing business that there's a standard way to do it. You call up or visit the gym of any trainer who represents "opponents" and have the following exchange:

"I've got a middleweight who could use a little work." (Read: *His fight shouldn't be more than a brisk sparring session.*)

"I got a good kid. But he ain't been in the gym much lately." (*He's out of shape.*)

"That's OK. I'm not looking for my guy to go too long." (*It's got to be a knockout win.*)

"My kid can give him maybe three good rounds."

And that's it. Your fighter's next bout will go into the record books as a third-round knockout victory.

Your guarantee that you'll get the result you want is simple: guys who deliver opponents have to earn a living. If their fighters win, they won't be able to do that. On occasions when an opponent realizes victory is within his grasp, his trainer reminds him that getting fresh will prevent him from being paid. If this doesn't work, the trainer stops the fight in the corner after the agreed-upon round. "I have to watch out for my kid," he laments. "He was taking too much punishment" or "His leg cramped up" or "Jeez, I can't explain it. The kid just quit on me. And he was doin' so good." He shakes his head sadly.

I've arranged for countless such endings. I've bought off referees and commissioners. I've simultaneously managed fighters from both corners. I've picked up the tab for entire fight cards, effectively guaranteeing that the judges were in my pocket. While standing a foot from ringside, I've had a KO'd opponent wink at me as he was being counted out.

UNFIXED

There was even an occasion when what was supposed to be a fixed fight turned into a real one. It was 1994. I was looking to bring former World Boxing Organization (WBO) cruiserweight champ Tyrone Booze back into contention as a heavyweight. To do this required his scoring a series of quick knockouts. I had a deal going in Raleigh, North Carolina, where every couple of months I would fly down with the winning half of the fight card. The local matchmaker would provide the homegrown losing half or I could bring one of my own.

This time around, Booze's intended victim was Marc Machain, a keg-shaped brawler from the trailer parks of rural Vermont. "The Rutland Bull" stood five feet seven and weighed 220 pounds—only a few of them fat. Machain was a sentimental, happy-go-lucky guy who loved to fight, whether he was landing or taking punches. His favorite type of fight was when he got to do both. In the past, he'd worked for me as sparring partner; I knew he'd never beat Tyrone Booze in a legitimate fight. But he might take him the distance, with the two guys banging heads and exchanging elbows and low blows for the whole ten rounds. Even in nothing fights, it's inevitable that heavyweights will do damage. If there's a way to minimize injuries, you're foolish not to use it.

I explained this to Marc Machain. "Have fun in there," I told him. "Give Tyrone five or six rounds, then I'll have Tony stop it in the corner." The Rutland Bull reluctantly agreed, and we had a deal. I *thought* we had a deal. At the time we made it, Machain undoubtedly thought so, too. He was an honorable man.

If you hadn't spent time around tough guys, you wouldn't peg Tyrone Booze as one. He had a round head, tiny amphibious eyes, sloping shoulders, and a layer of fat that no amount of training could remove. He smiled often and laughed easily. His voice was deep but

swooped up to a falsetto "whaaat?" when someone's behavior surprised him. When he was tired, he sometimes slurred his words.

Tyrone was an original thinker who knew everything there was
to know about the boxing business except how to make money in it.
He had spent his career losing competitive and occasionally unjust
decisions, one after another, to the monsters no one else would fight.
He had fought eight world champions, including Evander Holyfield,
Dwight Muhammad Qawi, and Eddie Mustafa Muhammad, without
having been off his feet against any of them.

Still, I had to be persuaded to manage him. He had too many losses,
and he almost never knocked people out. But Floyd Patterson, who
trained some of my fighters, thought something could be done with
him. And then later, when Booze went to Las Vegas to work as chief
sparring partner for Riddick Bowe, I got a surprise phone call from
Eddie Futch, asking if he could train him. He'd been impressed with
how Tyrone handled himself against the heavyweight champ. Bowe
had gotten a little out of line, so Booze had ducked his shoulders,
plowed into him, and tossed him over his head onto the canvas. You
didn't fuck around with Tyrone Booze.

In his dressing room before the Machain fight, Booze was queasy.
His last ring appearance had taken place seventeen months earlier
in front of over ten thousand people in Hamburg, Germany, where
he lost his WBO cruiserweight title to Markus Bott. He'd been char-
acteristically placid before and after the fight. It was nothing to him
to fight big-name opponents in hostile territory. When he fought
Evander Holyfield on NBC, he'd spent part of the fight laughing at
him, waving him on.

But here in Raleigh, fighting in front of four hundred people in
a dilapidated theater called the Ritz, Tyrone Booze was becoming
slightly unhinged. He couldn't settle down. He tried to lie down on
the couch, but wound up bolting from the dressing room, walking
the hall and back. We couldn't get him to work up a good sweat. He
suddenly had chills. His stomach was upset, and he thought he was
going to be sick.

"Man, I don't know why I feel like this," he said. "I can't get loose. I mean, I was cool when I fought Bert Cooper. *Bert Cooper*. Didn't *nobody* punch like Bert Cooper. And I got to worry about this fat little white boy? He ain't nobody to be afraid of."

Tyrone Booze wasn't afraid of anybody. Or anything. None of this came from fear. Tyrone Booze was unable to process getting back what he'd lost when he'd stepped away from boxing. If professional fighters really do fight primarily for money—and they do—it would still be naive to dismiss the existential elements that bring them back to the ring once their money is gone. Booze wouldn't have returned to boxing if there hadn't been a promise of big paydays soon, but what was knocking the shit out of his system was the inchoate elation of knowing he was able to get back in the ring.

More than almost any other activity, boxing forces and keeps you squarely in the center of each moment. To box requires you to be dynamically alive, to be alert to every possibility. Lapse for a moment and you'll get knocked out. Anything less than complete absorption might even get you killed. Once you've grown used to that degree of vitality, it's hard to withdraw from it.

As a rule, you don't tell the intended winner of a fixed fight that the outcome is rigged. It causes him to fight unnaturally, and the fix is easier to spot. But Booze was an old pro; I felt OK telling him to go easy. And I liked Machain. Durable as he was, I didn't want him to have to take too much of a pounding for his thousand dollars.

I brought in seven of the eight fights on that night's card. Besides Booze, future middleweight champ Keith Holmes and Olympic gold medalist Andrew Maynard got wins: pearls before swine. The Raleigh crowd, mostly drunken rednecks, was a universe away from seeing world-class fighters except when I brought them. They were yahooing with mayhem after a night of emphatic first- and second-round knockouts. For the main event, they were itching for something longer and more punishing; a decisive early knockout wouldn't do. They wanted to see a couple guys beat each other up in a slug-fest. Somehow this collective longing found its way up into the ring and imprinted itself on the two fighters waiting for the opening bell. Standing at ringside just below Booze's corner, I had an inkling that things might become unruly.

The fighters tried to do what was expected of them. At least for the first two minutes they followed the script. Then Booze caught Machain walking in and buckled his knees with a right uppercut. I don't think he intended to hit him so hard. It was a combination of training, muscle memory, and a sudden access of adrenaline. I could see Machain was badly rattled. He smiled at Booze. He said something through his mouthpiece; I couldn't make it out. He banged his gloves together. He threw a wild overhand right that missed by a mile. It sent a complex message: I'm still behaving, but don't try that shit again.

But it was more than that. There was an invitation in the punch. I could see it. The bell rang, and that's when I think the two of them decided to fight as hard as they could. They knocked gloves enthusiastically. Machain said something to Booze, who laughed.

In the second, I could see it was not going to be the sparring session I'd asked for. Machain pressed forward, fighting out of a crouch, trying to come in under Booze's headhunting shots, hoping to bang to the ribs, occasionally throwing haymakers at Tyrone's nicely tucked-in head. He succeeded just enough to keep himself in the fight, and keep the fight exciting.

Meanwhile, Tyrone was having a party. If you were going to make a real fight for him, it would be hard to pick a better opponent than Marc Machain, who constantly waded in with no concern for being hit, his gloves wide apart, his chin jutted defiantly forward. Booze teed off with uppercuts as the crowd oohed and "oh *shit!*"-ed. There was now an audible black contingent in the house. I started hearing the word "nigger" coming from both white and black voices, its meaning dependent on who was using it.

The first knockdown, predictably from a right uppercut, came late in round two. Booze placed it perfectly, nailing Machain under the chin as he came in, flooring him suddenly. Machain dropped in a heap at Booze's feet. I thought he was finished. He shook his head, trying to clear it, and worked his jaw.

Then, to my dismay, he got up.

At that point, I might have been able to signal to Tony Petronelli to throw in the towel. People would have bought it. I didn't do that. I looked at Tyrone Booze waiting in the neutral corner. He wanted to fight. Machain signaled to the ref that he was OK. He wanted to fight, too. The crowd wanted them to fight—rednecks and blacks alike. I thought, "Everyone wants the fight. Fuck it, let them fight."

For as long as it lasted it was a good fight, for the crowd. It had the appearance of give-and-take, although it was actually one-sided. Because Machain continued to come forward, except when he was being drilled with uppercuts, he gave untrained viewers hope for a miracle. They were true believers, as was Machain himself, who felt that if he landed just one haymaker, he could end things. Except that Marc Machain didn't actually punch very hard. And Tyrone Booze had absorbed, without flinching, the hardest punches of the hardest punchers of his era.

I settled in at ringside and allowed myself to become entertained by the fight. Booze was working off ring rust, getting his timing back, putting in some rounds. Machain was having the time of his life getting the shit kicked out of him. Toward the middle of round five my business sense returned. Even though the fight was one-sided, it had become predictably rough. Booze hadn't knocked Machain down again, so there hadn't been a "right" time to stop it. I started to worry whether Tyrone could score the knockout he needed.

I was about to walk to Machain's corner to let Tony know his fighter would need to be diagnosed with either a shoulder injury or a broken jaw (either one would require that the fight be stopped) when the end came. It was the same uppercut that caused the first knockdown. Booze's punch was just as perfect, but no harder. Machain, if anything, took it better than the first one, since he was now warmed up. But he again got dropped hard, and I only had to look over to his corner to get Tony Petronelli started into the ring.

"Oh no," Machain wailed, "I'm OK, I'm OK." He put his gloves up in fighting stance. Tony was leading him to his corner, pulling out the mouthpiece.

"Aw, Tony, why'd you stop it? I was having *fun*! Nobody wants it stopped."

He was right. Mostly right. *I* wanted it stopped.

After it was over, the two fighters sat at a table at a Denny's across from the Ritz. Machain was banged up a little. Not too badly. Booze was fine. Now ravenously hungry, wolfing down mountains of starchy, sugar-coated, butter- and oil-dripping fast food, they were still giddy from the fight. Effusively complimentary, talking with their mouths full, Booze and Machain relived every detail of what had just taken place.

"I couldn't believe you was gettin' up from them uppercuts, man." Booze shook his head in admiration.

"I couldn't believe how you kept catching me with them."

"That's 'cause you was walkin' straight in. You don't never move your head."

"I got a hard head."

"It's true! It's true. You do got a hard head. But I was timin' you, man."

"I know. You timed me good."

THE EIGHTY-NINTH SECOND

The best fixer I ever knew was Vin Vecchione. In the 1990s, we spent a lot of time together, making big plans, drinking bad coffee in cheap diners, laughing at our friends and enemies, forging boxers' medical records, and getting our fighters wins.

Vin died suddenly in 2009. I'd left boxing, and we'd lost touch. But I wanted to see how Peter McNeeley was doing, so I went to the memorial service. The embalmer had done a lousy job: Although still clutching a cigar, wearing his cap, and smiling his secretive half-smile, Vin didn't look like anyone I'd ever known or anyone who'd once been a person.

When I met Vin in 1993, I was managing an undefeated heavyweight I'd brought to Brockton from the Midwest. Vin handled McNeeley, also undefeated. I'd agitated on local radio shows and in newspapers for a showdown. Vecchione called to request a sit-down at a local luncheonette. When I arrived, he draped a hefty arm around my shoulder, walked me to a booth, helped me off with my overcoat, and sat down across from me. "My fighter ain't never going to fight your fighter," he said. "OK, we got that outta the way. Now we might as well get along."

Two years later McNeeley would last eighty-nine seconds against Mike Tyson in what was then the largest-grossing event in sports history. The fight ended when Vecchione nonchalantly slipped between the ropes to save his still-standing fighter.

There were two journalistic responses, both outraged. The first was based mainly on a perceived attack on the sanctity of the sport: People had paid big money to witness—depending on their temperament—a fight or a slaughter and had been euchred out of seeing either. McNeeley was still OK when referee Mills Lane waved things off. And though he was in some trouble when the fight had ended, it wasn't a sure thing he was finished. Boxing writers pointed out that McNeeley hadn't "gone out on his shield." Soon after the fight's conclusion, he could be seen walking around the ring with a goofy grin on his face, chatting with reporters, family, and friends, his distress wearing off by the second. Paid nearly a million dollars to serve as a human sacrifice, he'd escaped without a bruise.

The second response didn't show up until the fight narrative had passed through a series of plausibility tests and been green-lit as acceptable. This version featured McNeeley fighting valiantly ("He charged right at Tyson!") and being inexplicably robbed of glory by Vecchione. As Ferdie Pacheco stammered, "He doesn't belong in boxing if he's going to save his fighter." Vecchione had cheated both Peter and the public.

But Peter McNeeley, if not expertly maneuvered, would never have gotten nearly as far in boxing as he did. Vin earned McNeeley a $700,000 payday, pushing the figure to over a million by parlaying the fight's weird conclusion into two lucrative TV commercials and keeping the door open for Peter's ongoing viability as a high-priced opponent.

Granted, Vecchione wasn't thinking only of his fighter's welfare. Vin's payoff wasn't limited to the fight purse. The real money was in knowing exactly how Peter McNeeley would do fighting Mike Tyson. And Vin knew down to the second how his man would do. The night before Tyson-McNeeley, someone in Las Vegas placed a million-dollar bet on the fight not going a full ninety seconds. When Vecchione, seemingly unhurried, stepped between the ropes to force an automatic disqualification, eighty-nine seconds had elapsed.

I didn't know it was going to happen. Vin and I had gotten together in the dining room of a Braintree, Massachusetts, hotel just prior to his bringing McNeeley to Vegas and my heading back to my place in Puerto Rico. He'd said then that no one had approached him about having McNeeley take a dive. But later two strange things took place. I got a phone call from someone I didn't know well. This person mentioned that a private million-dollar bet had been made that the fight "wouldn't get past the first round." Soon after the fight, Vin called to ask if I'd come to his house to pick something up. I was still in Puerto Rico, so I asked if I could send someone. Vin said, "Send someone you trust." When my guy met with Vecchione, he was given an envelope that contained enough money to put my son through college (admittedly, an inexpensive one).

I've often thought about the kind of discipline that must have taken, the Zen-like calm of a small-timer who could wait and wait, during the biggest-money event in sports history, until there was literally not another second to wait. I've marveled at the ingenuity of Vecchione, planning ahead for years with no budget and no promise of good things to come, slowly and steadily bringing this move to its amazing conclusion.

He'd considered every angle. Vecchione knew that for all its posturing, the Nevada State Commission would have to pay him: Tyson was the biggest cash cow in the state's history, and any problem with the fight's outcome would gum up a billion dollars in future casino business. Vin had the state of Nevada, the casinos, the commission, pay-per-view boxing, and Don King by the balls, and he knew it.

A heroic narrative painted Tyson as a savage warrior from the mean streets of Brownsville and McNeeley as a soft white boy from suburban Medfield, Massachusetts, who hadn't earned his shot. But Tyson had been a multimillionaire for his entire adult life. McNeeley and Vecchione were a couple of hungry motherfuckers who didn't have a dime between them. Had McNeeley been a more accomplished fighter, he would have torn apart the easily discouraged Tyson. And Vecchione would have had to figure out some other reason to step into the ring early.

THE "WHAT WE GONNA DO NOW?" PRESENT

Even if they don't agree with it, almost anyone can understand the case for fixing a fight to keep a fighter from being unnecessarily hurt. Fixing one to get him paid might seem like a tougher sell.

According to the heroic ethic, boxers should fight only the toughest possible opponents, engage in fair play, maintain the moral integrity of the sport, perform courageously, make sure the fans get their money's worth, and not flaunt their successes unduly. From this perspective, figures like Roy Jones Jr. and Floyd Mayweather Jr.—or before them, Ray Robinson and the prehegemonic Muhammad Ali—are seen as agitators who have no business making rules for themselves.

In the same vein, there is the argument that boxers choose to participate in their matches, that they're aware of the chances they take every time they step into the ring. Well, yes and no. There's a difference between knowing that you can be maimed or killed in any particular fight and understanding how over a period of time you will in all likelihood sustain irreversible damage. The signs of this damage can be obvious, but they can also be subtle, invisible to boxing outsiders. Any punch-drunk professional fighter can still duck under the ropes and kick the shit out of you or me.

For managers, boxing is a business. The meter is running from the moment a fighter's contract is signed, if not sooner. Bankrolling a stable of winning fighters takes deep pockets. The sparring partners, as well as the winners, need to eat. They all need places to live. They have families to care for and bills to pay, whether or not they have promising futures.

My former business partner Pat Petronelli and his brother Goody became multimillionaires managing middleweight champion Marvin Hagler. Pat ran his stable like a feudal system. Fighters were told whom, when, and where they'd be fighting and what they'd be paid. Pocket cash was doled out in whatever increments he thought best. If a fighter needed to stay in Brockton between fights or while working as a sparring partner for Hagler, Pat would put him up at a rooming house run by Marvin's aunt Herbertine Walker. Herbertine rented out cheap, clean rooms, cooked healthy meals, and provided laundry services. She ran a tight ship; if you stayed at Herbertine's, you stayed in line.

Except for the conspicuous presence of crack users and dealers, walking from the gym to Herbertine's boarding house was like being in Birmingham or Mobile during the 1950s. The neighborhood was entirely self-contained. Barbershops, variety stores, bars, barbecue shacks, laundromats, and beauty salons crowded together. It was known to be a dangerous area, but walking through it—hearing talk and laughter, music pulsing from storefronts and boom boxes, smelling the competing scents of fried food wafting from the fast-food joints—didn't seem oppressive. In neighborhoods like this, where the only victories available are very small ones, victories show up everywhere. It was as if everyone in the neighborhood were operating under a different existential system than I was. Life was defined by the "What We Gonna Do Now?" present or the "After I Hit My Number Tomorrow" future. Those were the choices. The fighters lived on what some of them called "nigger time," an imprecise measure, a vague approximation of when an event might or might not take place. It was time largely outside the volition of those remanded to it.

Boxing is a business for boxers, too. They are born poor, and they usually die poor. For their short spell in the business, they inhabit a place in its professional hierarchy that all but guarantees they'll remain poor even during their active careers. Boxers often can't negotiate or even understand their own contracts. Of course, most contracts are unintelligible except to lawyers, but boxers typically have little education and are often functionally illiterate. Many fighters turn over the exclusive rights to sign their contracts to their managers. I'd never have managed a fighter whose contracts I couldn't sign or whose purse checks couldn't be made out to me.

All in all, it isn't surprising that boxers operate under a different system from the people who make money off of them or who watch and write about them. In the real world, boxers and their managers prearranging the outcome of fights, working collusively against a hostile system, makes sense. Fixing fights, even at the expense of the public, isn't just good business. It's a survival strategy for the disenfranchised class in boxing: the fighters themselves.

I got out of the business in the latter part of the 1990s. It would be a good story to say that I had a moral epiphany that lifted the veil from my eyes. That wouldn't be true, though. I got involved with some dangerous people, and some bad things happened. So I left. Over time, I've come to see boxing differently than when I earned my living from it. I've learned that, in boxing, damage isn't just possible or likely; it is nearly inevitable. I continue to love the art of boxing itself. But, nearly twenty years removed from it, I still find the works of the business—the larceny and the bullshit and the wheeling and dealing—the most difficult and absorbing thing I've done in my life.

INDIAN SUMMER

The day after the Spinks-Carlo fight was uncharacteristically hot for late October in DC. Indian summer, I guess. In the afternoon, I was sitting in the coffee shop of the Courtyard Marriott, directly across from the Convention Center, talking to someone I knew. The night before had been a fucked-up one for a number of people, myself included. None of us had lost money directly, but what had happened would keep us from making money.

Leon came across the lobby to where we were sitting. He kept himself at a slight distance, making his presence known, but not interrupting.

I said to my acquaintance, "Have you met Leon?"

"No, but I'd like to."

I introduced the two men. They shook hands. Once Leon had been introduced, he felt freer to talk to me.

"Mr. Farrell, I want a rematch. I do better next time. You get me a rematch?"

"No, Leon. No rematch. I'm sorry."

It was uncomfortable. Nobody knew what to say.

Leon, who'd taken a seat after being introduced, got up and started to move away.

"Can I get some money for something to eat?"

"The promotion is picking up the tab for the hotel expenses," I said. "Don't you want to eat in the hotel?"

Leon looked uneasy.

"OK, no problem. How much do you need?"

"I don't know. Can I get five bucks?"

I handed Leon some money, and we watched him go outside.

PLASTER OF TORRANCE

Unwrapping the Meaning of Antonio Margarito

Rafael Garcia

"The only sort of relationship worth having with boxing is one of love and hate at the same time."

"Is that so?"

"It could be all love, or it could be all hate. But neither would give you the whole picture. You'd be missing the forest for the trees and the trees for the forest. People say you don't want to miss the forest for the trees, but you've got to look at the trees too."

"OK."

"When it comes to boxing, all love makes you a savage."

"What about if you hate it?"

"All hate makes you a pompous ass."

We were surrounded by Puerto Ricans. Most of them had come from the East Coast, arriving one or two days before fight night. A fifty-something high school teacher and his early thirties nephew were sitting in the row in front of ours. While the older Puerto Rican philosophized, the younger one darted glances at a woman with a painted-on-tight scarlet dress who sat across the aisle. His careful timing guaranteed the woman's bulked-up male companion was always turned in the opposite direction when he looked at her.

The arena was halfway full with half a fight to go before the main event. My dad served the teacher his cue on a silver platter:

"What's the halfway point between a savage and a pompous ass?"

"The enlightened man, caballero."

The teacher smiled in self-satisfaction as he let the line sink in. My dad nodded in approval and went on, "You're obviously one of the enlightened. Why don't you tell me who's going to win tonight?"

"Cotto! Who else!" growled the teacher.

*

Fought in the summer of 2008, Cotto versus Margarito was billed as "The Battle," a riff by promoter Bob Arum on "The War," a fight he promoted back in 1985 between Marvin Hagler and Thomas Hearns that condensed into less than nine minutes more violence than featured in a dozen R-rated action movies from that decade. Or perhaps "The Battle" was simply stating what everyone expected on fight night: a vicious contest between Puerto Rico's biggest star—an overpowering combination puncher with a killer left hook—and an unassuming but extraordinarily tough fighter whose reputation for stopping punches with his chin matched the heaviness of his fists.

Although every reliable source lists his birthplace as Torrance, California, in the United States, Margarito occasionally tells interviewers he was born about 150 miles south of there, in Tijuana, Mexico. Why he does that is a matter of speculation. He may do it because he feels a keener connection to the land he lived in as a child than to the one his family abandoned when he was a toddler; perhaps it's a marketing move aimed at increasing his appeal to Latino fans; or maybe he just wants to eradicate every doubt as to the origin of his fighting style. In any case, Margarito grew up in Tijuana, selling newspapers on its infamously dangerous streets to supplement his family's income. Encouraged by his father, Margarito fell for boxing in Tijuana, a famous breeding ground for cliché-compliant Mexican boxers. When the family budget allowed it, Margarito's father would take him to boxing cards to check out the local talent; when not, television gave both of them their weekly dose. One time, at a boxing show at the Auditorio Municipal, nine-year-old Margarito watched from the nosebleeds a mob that formed quickly around a single person who slowly walked around the ring trying to find his seat. It took Margarito a moment to recognize who it was, but once he did, he couldn't believe it. His favorite fighter—the whole country's in fact—Julio Cesar Chavez, was right there within his sight. Margarito didn't hesitate in leaving his dad's side to reach Chavez, who shook his hand, sat him on his lap, and even took a picture with him.

Margarito joined a boxing gym around the time he was eight years old. But his amateur career was cut short—along with any dreams of finishing high school—when he started fighting for money at age fifteen. It was an unusually early age for someone to go pro, even by Mexico's standards, where fighters often get an early start in the racket for financial reasons. In practice, this guaranteed Margarito would be the younger guy in the ring every time he stepped between the ropes. The hardest part of his apprenticeship came as he faced older, more experienced fighters with longer amateur careers than his own. That's also when his reputation for being tough as nails began taking shape, and after he'd won enough fights and knocked out enough fellow Tijuanans, he stood out as a hard guy in a town filled with them.

Antonio Margarito was an avoided fighter, one of those cases where the financial reward for facing him and the potential brownie points for defeating him didn't quite compensate for the risk of losing to him. A relentless brawler who showed no fear of getting hit as he muscled his way inside to land crippling body punches and crashing uppercuts, Margarito didn't concern himself with winning fights as much as with beating up opponents. In a much-talked-about performance from 2005, Margarito's gloved fists did to Sebastian Lujan's left ear what Mike Tyson's teeth did to Evander Holyfield's right one almost eight years before. Months later, in his most impressive win yet, Margarito knocked out Kermit Cintron—not an elite talent by any means, but a strong, solid titleholder then regarded as Cotto's biggest threat in the battle for Boricuas' hearts and minds. Margarito continued facing ranked welterweights for a few more years, losing only to Paul Williams, a fighter with an otherworldly activity rate.

Floyd Mayweather, then king of the welterweights, famously refused an $8 million offer to face Margarito.

In 2008, it was Miguel Cotto who took on the Mexican's challenge, also granting him the largest payday of his career, with the bout coming to fruition largely thanks to the fact Bob Arum promoted both fighters. The promoter's decision to put Cotto's undefeated record at risk against Margarito was welcomed by the boxing public, but also inspired a degree of surprise. After all, Cotto was a much more valuable commodity than Margarito, a proven attraction in New York City and his native Puerto Rico, drawing crowds that Margarito could only dream of. There were even rumors that Oscar De La Hoya himself—fresh off a record-setting mega-fight with Mayweather—was interested in fighting Cotto. Margarito, unlike Cotto, couldn't count on a significant fan base to prop up his purses. Moreover, he lacked a signature win, and in fact carried around a record blemished with multiple losses, most of them inflicted in the early part of his career when he underwent harsh matchmaking as a teenage professional. Throw in a decidedly unflashy fighting style, his modest attitude and appearance, and a lack of marketing muscle behind him, and you can begin to understand why the proverbial break took so long to arrive for Margarito.

If Margarito, known as Margo, ever considered himself a boxing superstar-in-waiting, he never looked or acted the part. Topped by a hacked buzz cut, his long El Greco face evoked pious humility, with nary a trace of Cotto's self-assured gravitas, De La Hoya's boyish good looks, or Mayweather's cockiness to be found on it. His lanky frame doomed him to suffer to make the 147-pound limit, a potential missed-weight liability no promoter wanted to have to deal with on the eve of a big fight. The very attributes that garnered him something of a cult following were the same ones that made big names look the other way when he came up as a potential opponent. Being a true workingman who always showed up hungry and ready on fight night, and who could give anyone a tough fight, made him too dangerous for more popular boxers.

And perhaps, too, Margarito failed to amass a large fan base because he employed the wrong fighting style at the wrong time. Margarito usually moved and punched a couple of gears behind his rival, as if he alone of the two were fighting underwater. The heaviness of his fists, coupled with his busyness, made up for the disadvantage, but neither economy of attack nor elegance of form was ever in the cards. This anti-nuance, slow-motion stalking was too crude even for Mexican fans, striking them as both atavistic and vestigial. Throughout the first decade of the twenty-first century, Mexican fight fans became enamored with Erik Morales and Marco Antonio Barrera, featherweight superstars who offered a highly technical brand of brawling, as well as with Juan Manuel Marquez and his fearsome counterpunching. Those three names shared more than enough fighting talent to define an era in boxing, and they may have in some way contributed to the refinement of the Mexican public's tastes. If there's any truth to that theory, Margarito's plodding variety of boxing might have appeared to Mexican fight fans to be the comeback of an old, nasty habit that they had battled for years and outgrown. However, if they resented this old habit, those same fans were about to fall in love with it all over when they saw Margarito fight Cotto.

On fight night, Cotto entered the ring as a slight favorite, despite Margo's considerable size and reach advantage. It's not usual for the taller and physically stronger fighter to enter the ring an underdog, but in this case the odds reflected the adage that styles make fights: going against the advice even laymen would have quickly provided, Margarito refused to capitalize on the advantage his larger frame and considerably longer arms—he had a full six-inch reach advantage on Cotto—could potentially grant him. The Puerto Rican was undoubtedly the better boxer and the better mover, and it would be up to the lumbering Mexican to play catch-up. The opening round offered nothing to refute that storyline. Cotto took to managing the distance between himself and Margarito, dictating when and where shots would be exchanged. Margarito, on the other hand, seemed to wait until he was close enough to Cotto to count the hairs inside his nostrils before throwing any punches. The stocky, shorter Cotto moved around the ring like a light tank—constantly shifting direction, pivoting this way and that before planting himself to open fire and then moving quickly out of range again. His mark was so accommodating that even Cotto's straight right—usually a footnote in his plan of attack—arrived frequently and forcefully on Margarito's face. The Puerto Rican's confidence grew with every landed shot, so much so that by the end of the first stanza the stoicism that usually permeates his face dissolved just enough to show a faint hint of satisfaction.

What Cotto should've kept in mind was that hitting Margarito was always going to be the easy part, especially in the early going. Everyone touched Margarito a bit—manhandled him, even—in the early rounds. While the opening bell represents for most boxers a rude awakening, Margo always considered it his cue to press the snooze button. Proving his understanding that the fight with Cotto was indeed a big deal, this time Margarito allowed himself to doze only until the start of round two and not a second later. In the second stanza, he started landing his trademark left uppercuts, mixing in some left hooks and the occasional overhand right to bring the point home that the fight was officially on. The results were dramatic: at the end of that round, Cotto's cornermen frenetically swabbed his bleeding nose with Q-tips and similarly treated a subtle cut over the left eyelid that hinted at more trouble to come. From there on, in purely geographical terms, the fight was endlessly repetitive: Cotto retreated in clockwise fashion as Margarito stalked. The problem for the Puerto Rican, as the fight wore on, was that the concentric path he followed in the ring moved further and further away from ring center and by the end consisted of nothing more than continuous visits to the ropes. This played directly into Margarito's greatest tactical strength, his inside game. In the first half of the fight, Cotto outworked Margarito most of the time, scoring with both hands and landing plenty of eye-catching shots that snapped the Mexican's head sideways and elongated his neck to cartoonish proportions. But when Cotto stopped moving long enough for Margarito to plant his feet and swing away, the Puerto Rican's midsection absorbed a barrage of body punches. Cotto grew weaker and weaker with each passing round throughout the second half of the fight.

During the first six rounds, Margarito was consistently out-maneuvered and failed to match Cotto's punch output. But in round seven, he began throwing combinations the way a seasoned politician makes a speech, giving every blow enough oomph to leave a mark on its audience. Cotto's quickly decaying facial features attested to the fact that Margarito had taken command. In that round, Margo landed uppercut after uppercut, all of them malicious and powerful, the momentum of his swinging left arm lifting his whole body off the canvas. It was either brutal or thrilling to watch, depending on whom you were rooting for or what side of your brain was calling the shots. It was at this moment, also, that what had been billed as a fight became a rite, as there was little question from that point on as to who was the stronger fighter and who was the weaker, who was the one causing the damage and who was the one getting hurt. Cotto kept fighting, of course, after the turn of the tide in round seven, but for the rest of the night Margarito's most significant enemy was no longer Miguel Cotto but the timekeeper.

The contest was decided in that brutal round. As Margarito walked back to his corner at the end of the seventh, his face and torso and back splattered with Cotto's fresh blood, he nodded to the fans celebrating at ringside. It was clear that thereafter all Margarito had to do was keep hacking and chopping away at Cotto, keep grinding him down by pushing him back to the ropes and windmilling away with those long, awkward arms and keep hammering him with those heavy fists until Cotto couldn't take it anymore. And then at some point Cotto would just stop fighting, and that would be it.

That's exactly the path the contest took. Cotto went from sharp-shooter to prey, just as Margarito went from lumbering target to heartless hitman. Margarito's physicality took control over Cotto's. Incredibly, the Mexican's stamina seemed to improve as the fight progressed; he started chasing Cotto on his toes after the Puerto Rican backed away from yet another pummeling combination, while Cotto lay against the ropes more and more, his legs suffering the effects of Margarito's earlier body work. It all became too much: too much determination from Margarito; too much abuse endured by Cotto; in short, too much one-sided violence. Something had to give. In round eleven, after a minute-and-a-half of nonstop punishment, Cotto took a knee, and he did it because that's when the truth dawned on him, the same truth that had become evident to pretty much everyone else a few rounds before: taking a knee was the only way he could get a break. Margarito didn't display fire or rage or fury as he stalked, punched, and hurt Cotto—but rather a relentless and seemingly perverse sense of diligence about getting the job done, which was to drown Cotto in despair, wrap him up in self-doubt, and destroy his will to resist.

For all that, Cotto did get up after taking a knee. Unfortunately for him, Margarito welcomed him back to verticality with more crushing uppercuts. So Cotto did what anyone else in his situation would've done: he went back down on his knee again. This time, however, he wasn't looking for respite; this time his taking a knee signaled a cry for help. His uncle and trainer, Evangelista Cotto, obliged, throwing in the proverbial towel and ending the fight with fifty-five seconds left in the next-to-last round.

*

There are times when boxing matches resemble more a bullfight than they do a sports contest, and that happens when only a deus ex machina will do in changing the outcome of such a match. Bullfights are all about the journey, and not the destination, as the inevitable outcome is that of a bull lying dead somewhere, even though there are many ways to arrive at that outcome. Likewise, after round seven, the ending of the fight between Miguel Cotto and Antonio Margarito, like its beginning, was already inked. The only mystery left was how bad a beating Margarito was going to put on Cotto. But it didn't matter how certain the result of the fight became at that point, because you can't take shortcuts in boxing. You can't just jump to the end of a fight and skip everything that happens in between; to do that would be to miss everything that makes boxing boxing. More than in any other sport, how and why one fighter wins and the other loses is of the utmost importance, and can have massive consequences for each one's future. Of course, the in-between also has a significant impact on those who are watching the fights. How many who watched Cotto and Margarito fight struggled to repress a measure of horror at what they were watching? What does it say about us that we're willing participants—and paying customers—in this sort of blood spectacle, in which someone as hurt and helpless as Cotto was for a large part of the contest had to endure so much bullying and physical punishment from a man who was obviously going to defeat him that night, all for reasons no more laudable than sport and business?

The question is not novel in any way, but that doesn't take away from its sting. Fans of boxing have tried to deal with it for a long time, and all of us who enjoy the sport have learned that a corollary of our love for it is that we have to make peace with more than a few ugly truths. Each of us finds his own way of making this happen. For some the issue may have spiritual overtones; Norman Mailer called boxing "an old, primate religion of blood, a murderous and sensitive religion which mocks the effort of the understanding to approach it." If that seems like too much of a reach, maybe you'd like to consider Hemingway's take on the morality of bullfighting and apply it to boxing: "I know only that what is moral is what you feel good after and what is immoral is what you feel bad after; judged by these moral standards, the bullfight is very moral to me because I feel very fine while it is going on and have a feeling of life and death and mortality and immortality, and after it is over I feel very sad but very fine." If that also fails, I'm afraid we may have painted ourselves into a corner from which no rationalization can help us escape. Facing up to the facts, as Joyce Carol Oates does, is the only thing left to do: "all boxing fans know that boxing is sheerly madness, for all its occasional beauty; that knowledge is our common bond and sometimes our common shame."

Shame, indeed, is a feeling most of those familiar with the rest of Margarito's career remember vividly, especially those who cheered him on during his fight with Cotto.

*

Six months after leaving Miguel Cotto a bloody mess in front of a two-thirds-full arena in Las Vegas, Antonio Margarito went to Los

Angeles to fight Shane Mosley in front of a record-setting crowd at the Staples Center. The way Margarito defeated Cotto might have had a thing or two to do with his sudden boost in popularity. It's safe to say that, in the aftermath of the Cotto win, Latino fans realized the Mexican's style wasn't a bad habit at all but was in fact the synthesis of Mexican boxing, something timeless and precious, to be cherished and celebrated, not something to get rid of. So the guy got hit a lot, big deal. As long as he dished it out worse than he got, he'd be fine. More importantly, it made for great drama, like watching a horse race with a slow starter that's a great closer, that keeps you guessing as to whether he'll turn it on in time to catch up and win. If the Cotto fight proved all this, the Mosley fight would corroborate it, and make him the best welterweight in the world at the same time. At least, that was what all those ticket buyers were thinking when they forked over their cash. As it turned out, they were wrong.

Two things happened to Margarito the night he faced Shane Mosley. The first was that his longtime trainer Javier Capetillo got caught trying to insert plaster of paris in his hand wraps before the fight. The second was that Mosley beat the crap out of him. The event turned out to be a far cry from the coronation implied by the four-to-one odds in favor of the Tijuanan. To see why, let's look closer at both of those happenings, starting with the second.

The loss to Mosley has multiple possible explanations, and the real reason for it consists of a combination of them. Margarito's go-to explanation is that he suffered greatly to make weight for the Mosley engagement, his outsized frame having finally outgrown the welterweight division. But it's hard to imagine a scenario in which getting caught with an illegal substance on his wraps, whether or not he knew about it in advance, didn't affect Margarito's focus greatly during the fight. It also didn't help his case at all that Mosley was in great shape that night—especially considering the fact he was thirty-six years old at the time—and had the perfect stylistic antidote to Margarito's ruthless plodding. Mosley used his still considerable hand speed to get off first every time, landing strong, sharp punches in combinations before tying up and wrestling with Margarito. It's worth noting that in his prime Mosley was a very strong puncher, fleet of foot and possessing enviable hand speed, but at his advanced age—with the diminished reflexes and physical attributes to match—standing up to a fearsome pressure fighter like Margarito would've represented a death wish.

On fight night, clinching after attacking proved as brilliant a tactic for Mosley as it had in the past for many other cagey veterans seeking to frustrate younger, more powerful opponents. It also represented a creative variant of Miguel Cotto's game plan. Both Cotto and Mosley acknowledged, if reluctantly, that a toe-to-toe battle favored Margarito and so they both sought to outbox him. However, the two welterweights approached the same problem in different ways. Cotto attempted to outwork the Mexican and then get out of the line of fire—a game plan fully backed by Cotto's confidence in his own abilities and in line with the boxing aesthetics honored by the most successful Puerto Rican boxers, among them Wilfred Benitez and Hector Camacho. Alternatively, Mosley outworked Margarito and then smothered his attack with clinches. Cotto's approach yielded a furious debate with Margarito on the character of warfare, ultimately decided in favor of all-out battle over scattered, focused skirmishes; Mosley, for his part, turned his fight with Margarito into a droning monologue on the importance of efficiency, disallowing the Tijuanan the very capacity to rebut him. Naazim Richardson, a trainer known for helping former middleweight champion Bernard Hopkins extend his career to preternatural lengths by employing exactly that sort of trick, was the man behind Mosley's plan. Round after round, Mosley went to work, never deviating from his well-laid agenda, capping off his performance with a highlight-reel knockout that ultimately laid waste to any hopes of a comeback rally that Margarito's fans might still have held after nine terribly one-sided rounds.

The outcome shocked a large majority of observers, most of whom had no idea of what had happened in Margarito's dressing room before the fight. While the broadcast team mentioned the incident on air right before the start of the contest, it could've easily been missed by those watching. Those present in the arena had no way at all of learning about the plaster found in the wraps of the fighter they had paid good money to cheer. But everyone caught up to it soon enough, through websites and newspapers, turning the humiliation into a delayed double whammy: Margarito lost the fight that night and then had his reputation ripped to shreds the next day.

Shane Mosley must have experienced a mixed bag of emotions after the fight as well, as his own career had already gone through an arc similar to Margarito's. In 2003, Mosley, having already once defeated Oscar De La Hoya, scored a big win in their rematch in Vegas. That same year, as part of the federal investigation of the Bay Area Laboratory Co-operative (BALCO), the famed purveyor of anabolic steroids to professional athletes, Mosley admitted that in preparing for the second fight against De La Hoya he took steroids and other performance enhancers—some of them illegal but undetectable, others not even tested for at the time. Mosley, just like Margarito following the plaster incident, claimed ignorance of his wrongdoing, regretting only the blind trust he placed in his strength and conditioning coach, Darryl Hudson, who had introduced him to BALCO and its products. Just as Margarito's biggest win—his entire career, actually—was tarnished by the discovery of plaster in his wraps before the Mosley fight, Mosley saw his own reputation and the validity of his second victory over De La Hoya undermined by the BALCO revelations. For both the man whose fists were compared to rocks and the man whose speed was deemed borderline unnatural, admiring metaphors turned into scandalously literal truths.

The plaster incident raised questions regarding Margarito's career in general and about the fearsome display against Cotto in particular, as that was the performance that raised his profile and made his reputation as a stone killer. How could it be any other way? Margarito became the highest-ranked welterweight in the world based on the damage he caused his opponents with his fists and nothing else. He never showed the faintest notion of defense; his footwork was awkward at best; and even his punching technique was subpar. Margarito practiced the most physically taxing, most dangerous brand of fighting a boxer could practice, and everything the Mexican accomplished could be traced to three attributes alone: his apparently indestructible chin, his extraordinary punching output, and his fists' ability to hurt people. It remains up for debate—and it's probably a moot point now—how much of Mosley's success the night he faced Margarito was due to Richardson's fight plan and how much of it was due to his opponent being distracted by his imperiled reputation. Whether Margarito knew all along about the plaster in his wraps or only found out about it at the same time the officers of the California State Athletic Commission (CSAC) did, the discovery of the plaster had to affect his performance against Mosley. Not much will dent a fighter's self-confidence as badly as knowing his trainer feels he has to cheat—and if his trainer had done it without telling him, Margo had to realize that perhaps he had unwittingly been made to cheat on past occasions. Maybe he wasn't the puncher he thought he was. Regardless of how much he knew before the discovery, Margarito's mind would've been juggling the torpedoing of his reputation and the legal ramifications of what had just happened, perhaps even the prospect of doing jail time, at the very moment an extremely focused Mosley aimed and fired right cross after right cross squarely at his chin and then wrapped him up in a clinch before he could respond.

The revelation that a trainer inserted plaster of paris in his fighter's wraps, no matter the pugilist's fighting style, would never go unnoticed or dismissed as irrelevant. But the fact that Margarito was the fighter whose fists almost tore Sebastian Lujan's ear right off his head, the one whose fists turned Cotto's face into a morbid museum piece and left him a helpless victim in Las Vegas, made it all seem much, much worse. If the incident was a willful attempt at cheating, it made Margarito a double cheater, as inserting hardened plaster in his wraps would mean he not only competed on a grossly uneven playing field, but also that he tricked everyone into thinking he was a lot more fearsome than he really was. After Margarito left the ring of the Staples Center in disgrace, and after the legal proceedings were over and the trial by media had taken place, it was Javier Capetillo who took the fall for the plaster debacle. He declared it was all a mistake, that some other fighter he trained possibly threw the plastered wraps in his bag, and then he, Capetillo, mistakenly grabbed those altered wraps and inadvertently used them to wrap both of Margarito's fists before Mosley's trainer and the CSAC officers identified them and forced him to remove them. As far as Capetillo was concerned, it was all an honest and terrible mistake. Margarito, for his part, maintained he had no knowledge of anything illegal being hidden in his hand wraps, for the Mosley fight or for any other of his fights. He also proclaimed that he trusted his trainer fully, so much so that he didn't even look at what Javier wrapped around his knuckles before his fights. Those inclined to believe Margarito and Capetillo can surely find comfort in declarations obtained by the media from celebrity trainers—Freddie Roach, Emanuel Steward, Don Turner—shortly after the plaster incident stating they could, plausibly and hypothetically, get away with hiding an illegal substance between the wraps of their fighters without them becoming aware of it. Even Naazim Richardson, who first raised the issue of Margarito's wraps in the Mexican's dressing room that night in Los Angeles, admits that a trainer could get away with it if he wanted to.

Whether it was just a mistake or bald-faced cheating, the legal consequences for Margarito and Capetillo were concrete, although too mild in the eyes of many. Javier Capetillo—who had been in corners and trained fighters in the United States for years—was no longer allowed to work any bout that took place on American soil. As for Margarito, his fighting license was revoked for a year. If he wanted to box in the United States after the ban was lifted, he would have to apply for a new license.

Margarito cut off all ties—at least publicly—with Capetillo, the man who had trained him for over ten years and to this day considers himself a father figure in Margarito's life. Anything else to be said about the case is, unfortunately, pure speculation. There's no way to prove whether what Capetillo was caught trying to do was intentional or not, just as there's no way to prove whether Margarito knew about what Capetillo did—mistakenly or not—the night of the Mosley fight. It's even more difficult to prove whether Margarito had plaster hidden between his hand wraps for any of his previous fights. In several interviews he's given since, Capetillo has always denied any intention of cheating for the Mosley fight, for the Cotto fight, or for any other Margarito fight he worked. He has also always maintained his stance that Margarito should be exonerated of any blame, that what happened in Los Angeles was entirely his own fault.

Capetillo has never deviated from that story. We can't tell, of course, whether he's just sticking to the most plausible cover or genuinely contrite about an honest-to-God mistake. But if Capetillo inserting plaster into Margarito's wraps was done on purpose, and if Margarito had knowledge of this, it's at the very least interesting that Capetillo would keep defending Margarito and keep averring that he thinks of the fighter as his son even after Margarito and the rest of his team not only allowed Capetillo to become the sole scapegoat—something that had a direct bearing on his ability to make a living—but effectively cut him off completely, severing all financial, professional, and emotional bonds that existed between them. Under these circumstances, Capetillo would have little incentive to keep defending Margarito, and yet he continuously does so every time the issue comes up. Of course, a sense of honor can work in mysterious ways, and Capetillo could also be an intentional cheater who feels guilty enough to believe he has to take the fall for his misdeeds.

*

Every member of the madly dysfunctional family that is boxing— every fan, every member of the media, every blogger, every suit, everyone with skin in the game and many without—has his own opinion about Margarito's plaster debacle. They all have carefully and selectively built their own case for or against Margarito's innocence, collecting tidbits of information here and there, focusing on some apparently insignificant details while dismissing others, all of this based on individual preferences and biases. But the ultimate truth about the biggest questions regarding Antonio Margarito—Was there plaster in his hand wraps for any of his fights? Did Capetillo ever cheat for his fighter, and did Margarito know about it?—will in all probability never be known, and is in all likelihood irrelevant at this point, at least from the point of view of anyone who's interested in The Truth.

When Antonio Margarito says he was born in Mexico even if a hospital in Torrance begs to differ, maybe he's just seeking immunity from F. Scott Fitzgerald's dictum that there are no second acts in American lives. Just as the reputation of his fighting style made a major comeback following his overpowering of Cotto, Margarito himself, with no shortage of help from promoters, athletic commission officers, and network executives, staged a comeback that rendered irrelevant, even laughable, any attempt at finding The Truth regarding what happened that night in Los Angeles.

Throughout his year as a boxing pariah, Margarito never lost the desire to box again, and to do so on the grandest stages the sport could offer. Once his year was up, his promoter, Bob Arum, latched on to that desire, and on to Margarito's notoriety, to stage two huge bouts. The first was a money-grabber in Dallas against Arum's most prized asset, Manny Pacquiao. The marketing buildup promoting the fight presented a remarkably different Margarito from the one who was forced to walk away from the spotlight following the Mosley affair. Gone was his clean-cut image. Fans were instead served images of his heavily tattooed torso, a devilish goatee, and a mullet that made it look as if Margarito had indeed spent a year in jail. His demeanor had changed too: in interviews taped to promote his bout with Pacquiao he alternated between playfulness and remorse, also apologetically addressing the issues of the events in Los Angeles and his parting ways with Capetillo. If Margarito was to be rehabilitated as a good guy who had gotten mixed up in an unfortunate wrongdoing, he would have to offer at least a semblance of regret to HBO's cameras.

But that wouldn't be necessary if he was going to wear the black hat. After Margarito lost a unanimous decision by wide margins on all cards to Pacquiao, his second big comeback fight was a rematch against none other than Miguel Cotto, in New York City. The promotion for it included a staged face-off between the two fighters, with Cotto brandishing a tablet showing a picture of Margarito celebrating his victory over him, being carried around on someone's shoulders in the ring in Las Vegas. Then Cotto zoomed in on the picture, confronting Margarito with a close up of his ungloved but still wrapped right fist, which showed a peculiar tear that would be very difficult to explain without the presence of some foreign, hardened material hidden somewhere in the wraps. Margarito dismissed it nonchalantly, pretending not to understand Cotto's allegations (even though both were speaking Spanish) and ending the segment by stating, "I'll beat you up again!" It made for riveting television, something straight out of the WWE, and showed in its final form Margarito's newly adopted persona as ring villain. The mullet, the tattoos, the facial hair, the insolent attitude—they all amounted to a new character, one far removed from the humble, soft-spoken Margarito who beat Cotto and lost to Mosley. Margarito had finally realized that neither modesty nor self-effacement were valuable in the business of boxing, so he remodeled himself as a justifiably remorseless douche: if he had done nothing wrong—as he always maintained—then there was nothing to apologize about. The rest of his felonious persona was only to help sell tickets.

And sell it did. Over forty thousand tickets were bought for the Pacquiao fight in Dallas's enormous Cowboys Stadium. The rematch with Cotto packed New York's Madison Square Garden. Margarito earned more for the second fight with Cotto—over $2.5 million—than he did in what was supposed to be his coronation bout against Mosley. Not bad for a guy whose reputation had been in ruins only a short time before. Everyone seemed to come out a winner from Margarito's comeback. The Tijuanan squeezed a couple of juicy paychecks from his name and his newly crafted image while giving Miguel Cotto a chance at lucrative revenge, fans someone to root against, and the promoters and networks a chance to cash in. Moreover, Margarito played to perfection the role that had been handed him: not only did his malevolent reincarnation touch fans and the media in the right spots, this evil Margo also lost both big fights. And not only did he lose, he lost big. Pacquiao busted up his right eye so badly, breaking the orbital bone, that all Cotto had to do was throw some water at it for Margarito's eye to swell shut. Cotto went instead with a never-ending string of left hooks, which also got the job done.

Looking at all the money produced by Margarito's comeback for HBO and for Bob Arum's Top Rank, in retrospect it looks silly to suggest it never should have taken place. But with such an obvious financial imperative at play, it became a safe bet that there was little call for further investigation into Margarito's and Capetillo's behavior in Margo's previous fights. Nobody who mattered in the fight world needed to know The Truth about what happened to Lujan, Cintron, and Cotto at the hands of Margarito, not when promoters and networks could forge their own version of the truth, package it, and sell it for mass consumption. Still, if nothing else, two hard-hitting facts emerged from the Tijuana Tornado's comeback: 1) Antonio Margarito lost the two high-profile fights he had after Javier Capetillo was caught trying to insert plaster in his wraps; 2) Margarito lost the two high-profile fights he had after cutting his ties with Capetillo. Is there any way to make sense of the relationship between them?

Seen from a distance professional boxing is a deceptively simple spectacle: two men beating on each other until cunning, physical prowess, or a combination thereof produces a winner. But complexity increases as we zoom in, as the business side—nothing more than a manifestation of human nature—interferes in all sorts of ways with what most fans would rather believe is a purely athletic competition. Many who watch boxing never move past their romantic notion of the sport, constantly framing what they see in terms of platonic concepts such as courage, valor, honor, and pride. Yet those same notions are hammered into irrelevance by forces significantly more pressing to the fighters and the suits promoting and managing them, namely, money, power, and influence. Narratives we attach to fights and fighters differ from one viewer to the next depending on how much they care to learn about what they're watching, and—as both Cotto-Margarito and Margarito-Mosley abundantly demonstrated—the narratives can also change over time contingent on information that surfaces after the fact. The sport offers no truths, but only informed beliefs to subscribe to; each being valid to some extent, but each also flawed in its own ways. The Truth is there's no purity in boxing; there are no absolutes to rely on. Enlightenment is to be found in the ring only on occasion and fleetingly; outside it, there's only the insouciance of a Socratic paradox: not all we see is real, and we'll never see it all.

Joyce Carol Oates is right when she says boxing can offer us beauty in the ring, and the first fight between Cotto and Margarito—at least when we saw it live—certainly proved this. But if Margarito's comeback proved anything else, it's that she's wrong in calling boxing "sheerly madness," just as Norman Mailer was wrong about calling it a religion, and just as Ernest Hemingway would have been wrong to declare it moral because of how fine and alive it can make us feel. If boxing is anything more than a sport, it is business: rational in its pursuit of profit, passionless in dealing with its own consequences, and amoral in pursuing its goals. Margarito's becoming a boxer at age fifteen was entirely a business decision; his comeback in spite of all the disturbing circumstances and open questions surrounding it, questions that also threatened to undermine the validity of what those who love boxing think they see when two boxers go to war in the ring, was just business as usual.

DARIUS

Hamilton Nolan

"We're not on HBO," Darius will say. "Listen man: we're not on HBO." He'll warn new guys before they get in the ring. "Whoa, whoa. We're not on HBO." He'll stop guys who are trying to smash each other in sparring. "This is practice, man. We're not on HBO."

We are not on HBO. We're in Gleason's Gym, in Brooklyn. Darius Ford is not on HBO. He's on a folding chair, in front of his big black locker, in Gleason's Gym in Brooklyn. The locker is bigger than he is. He's five feet six, tops. At five feet nine, I tower over him. He's short and round. Not fat, but stout. His head is round, too. He's built like a snowman. When you spar him, and hit his head, it feels absurd, like punching a big rock the size of a pumpkin. Why even try?

Darius has been training me maybe five years now. "Training" with Darius is a loose concept. It's more of a falling into his orbit, and learning through osmosis. His training style tends to be relaxed to a fault, although if he decides to actually train you, he can train you. I had another trainer before Darius, who was more violence oriented. Darius is more technique oriented. He doesn't get alarmed by events around him. He drinks coconut water and spends hours absorbed in his phone. For a while, his Facebook bio read, in total, "I'm on the phone a lot." He knows we're not on HBO.

Even sitting in a rickety chair in front of his locker, silently, Darius has a lot of things going on. He has kids calling him and a wife calling him and students texting him and all the other trainers and fighters yelling all over the gym, and the Facebook. His attention can only be one place at a time. He's not the type to tell you to fuck off and leave him alone, though. Sometimes this means that Darius will lapse into an echo state. Everything you say to him, he'll simply say back to you, barely rephrased, because his mind is elsewhere.

"You see that Pacquiao fight last night, Darius?"

"Oh yeah man, Pacquiao."

"Pacquiao looked good though, you see that?"

"Yeah man, real good."

"He looks a little slow though, like he lost a step, you know?"

"Yeah man, definitely slow."

You could continue this conversation ad infinitum, stating things and then stating their exact opposites, and Darius would continue to agree. In a way, it's much nicer than having a trainer who tells you to fuck off and leave him alone.

Like Alcoholics Anonymous, Darius gets his students through attraction, not promotion. He watched me hitting the bag for a while, back when I was with the other trainer. "Some things you do good; some things not so good," he said. Darius does not believe in making boxing overly complicated. His instructions after sparring often amount to him, standing sideways to you, miming a lazy, poking jab with his fingers extended. "Body, head," he'll say. "Up, down." He'll mime poking your gut, then your temple. "Body, head. That's it, man." He ends these instruction sessions with an elaborate shrug. This shit could not be more simple.

Darius is almost fifty years old, though he doesn't look it. He still spars. Not championship-fight-training-type sparring, but we're-not-on-HBO-type sparring. Just moving. "You wanna move?" he'll say. "I just wanna get a sweat." When I spar with Darius, I just move. I only touch him to the body. No head shots. It's best to keep him genial.

"This is like chess," he often says. "Boxing is up here." He'll point to his temple. "This is a chess match." One of his signature sparring moves is to step on your front foot, pinning you in place, then hit you. Sometimes he does this several times in a single round. Sometimes you can catch him smiling a little after he does it.

If you hit Darius too hard, he might get mad. "I've been doing this so long that every punch hurts," he says. He's not interested in that. The only people who make the mistake of hitting him hard are new guys. They're too nervous. They think that sparring Darius means fighting Darius. They're tight and twitchy. So the round will start, and they'll run up and hit Darius in the head with something hard. If they continue down this route, then Darius will flash his power. He can really punch. He's short as hell. He bends down and throws these low, scooping underhanded body shots, and if you're a full grown man, I'll be damned if you can contort your midsection into a small enough shape to be able to block them. He just slips them right under your elbows. Right into your belly button. He never really cracks sparring partners in the face these days; that would be uncouth, somehow. But he's happy to dig in with a body shot. A couple years ago, the Esquire Network had a reality show called *White Collar Brawlers*, filmed at Gleason's, and the idea was that two office workers who'd never boxed before would train at the gym for six weeks, and then fight each other. Halfway through their training, they had the newbies spar someone from the gym. One of them sparred Darius. Because he had never sparred before, the guy on the show came out nervous and threw a few hard punches. Enough to get on Darius's nerves. So Darius leaned down and sunk an uppercut into this kid's gut that made the will to live absolutely drain out of his face, and he had to spend the next round and a half attempting to box while looking like he'd prefer to throw up. If you have the Esquire Network on your television, and you can find this episode, I highly recommend it. Darius himself has still never seen it. He wants to, though.

Most of the time when Darius spars, it seems like he barely moves. You can learn a lot about distance just by watching his feet. He'll stand in the middle of the ring, gloves high, because he's short, and just rotate on that front foot. Rotate, rotate, rotate. While you're getting tired circling around the entire ring, he's just moving in one tiny circle. He's great at slipping punches. He likes to slip a jab, bending all the way over to his left, and come back at the same time with a sort of looping overhand right that's almost impossible to pick up on, because it seems to come from behind his back, like the world's worst surprise. He'll usually pull back on this punch at the end so it just taps you. It's easy to imagine it taking your face off. If he's feeling feisty, or if he spots somebody watching him spar, he might spend half a round fighting how he did when he was younger: bouncing on his toes, juking left and right, putting his hands down and shimmying his shoulders and throwing flurries of crazy-angled shots from his waist. "Wooo," he'll say when the bell rings. Half a round of that makes him pour sweat. Every so often, he'll tell me he wants to go down the street and run sprints up the hill with me. "We gonna run that hill, man," he'll say, patting his belly. "Yeah, I'm gonna come out and run that hill." He's still never run the hill.

Darius is from Guyana. Georgetown. He comes from a boxing family, which is a boxing cliché. "Boxing was my way out," he says, which is a boxing cliché. "I turned pro because I wanted to support my family," he says, which is a boxing cliché. "Boxing is all I knew," he says, which is a boxing cliché. All these boxing clichés are also true. True enough to define a man's entire life.

Darius had two uncles, Patrick Ford and Reginald Ford. Both were boxers. Two of the best boxers in Guyana, when Darius was growing up. Darius followed them to the gym. He used to be their timekeeper, when he was a little kid. Darius says the gym they went to was "one of the top gyms in Guyana." How many rings did they have? "There was no ring." They just fought on a space marked out on the floor.

Reggie Ford was a middleweight. He lost to Marvin Hagler in 1977, and retired in the mid-1980s with a respectable 27–15 record. Patrick was a lightweight. In December of 1979, he knocked out Cecil Fernandez in the tenth round in a fight in Georgetown. Fernandez died after the fight. Nine months later, Patrick Ford became the first Guyanese boxer to fight for a world championship. In 1980, he lost a split decision to Salvador Sanchez for the featherweight belt. He was a national hero. The Guyanese government gave him a house and a car. In his later years, he became a trainer at Gleason's, along with Darius. He died in 2011.

These two men taught Darius how to box. From Patrick, who didn't like to go backward, he learned offense; from Reggie, he learned defense. "Your offense is your defense" is what Patrick used to tell him, and what Darius tells everyone he trains now. If you ask Darius, he'll say he was more of an offensive fighter. But he's a much more defense-oriented trainer. It's always move, move, catch, catch, slip, slip, then come back. Darius is dismissive of gladiator-style trainers. "Everyone know how to punch. The smallest kid know how to punch," he'll say. "*Defense.*"

In 1980, Darius started fighting in the amateurs. He traveled around the Caribbean competing. He fought in Cuba in front of Fidel Castro. He lost in the Olympic Trials to Michael Parris, who went on to win a bronze in the 1980 Olympics. To this day, that's the only Olympic medal Guyana has ever won. Four years later, Darius turned pro. He won his first fight, in Georgetown, with a first-round knockout. Over the next two years, he had eight pro fights in Guyana; he won all of them, except for two losses to his nemesis, Michael Parris.

In 1987, Darius came to New York City. You could say that he came to live the boxing dream, but the boxing dream was not so dreamy. "It wasn't an easy road," he says. He caught on with Top Rank for a while. He fought on a James Toney undercard. He was a sparring partner for a lot of fighters. He sparred Hector Camacho, for example. "He was fast. Smart. Very tricky," Darius says. If you ask him who the best fighter he ever sparred with is, though, he'll still tell you it was Patrick Ford.

The majority of people who make a living in boxing are like Darius. They are not world champions. They are not big-money fighters or celebrity trainers. They are the legions of people who grew up in boxing, who loved boxing, or perhaps who just held on to boxing, because they didn't have anything else to hang on to. They gave it a shot, and perhaps had a pro career for a while, and then had to figure out how to turn that into a livelihood. If you look up Darius in the record book, you'll see a professional record of 6–4 and a fighting career that ended in 1993. But in reality, Darius has been in boxing for more than forty years, in its edges and sidelines, squeezing a living from it in any way that presents itself. Darius has a boxing skill set that takes decades of pain and toil to learn. The market rate for that skill set is currently somewhere around thirty dollars an hour for his white-collar clients.

This kind of boxing work is a hustle. Some trainers get paid every time you work out with them, but Darius tends to just collect money in spurts, for a varying number of future sessions. He asks for money when he needs it—for his kids, for his gym fees, for rent, for whatever. It's a floating plan. It all evens out in the end. This bothers some of his more traditionalist students. But I view it as a fair, need-based system. Darius doesn't try to rip anyone off. He's a man with many responsibilities. You're just one of them. If you want to train with him, you try to look out for him as best you can afford. That's just how it is.

Darius is not a bitter man. Ask him about the boxing business, though, and bitterness comes out. "It's a cutthroat business," he says. His lip curls involuntarily when he talks about it, like he's just sampled something rotten. "You get next to nothing. Five hundred dollars. You're fighting for nothing. The sport is so corrupt." Twenty years after Darius's retirement as a fighter, Bob Arum is still doing quite well. The sport is still corrupt. And Darius still can't get the taste out of his mouth.

It's a different calculation, being a trainer versus being a fighter. Fighters have to be aggressive, and violent, and intense, because, as we know, your offense is your defense. A fighter can be the nicest guy in the world, and still a monster in the ring. Trainers, though, tend to manifest their own natural dispositions in their work. They don't have the pressure of direct combat. They can create their own methods. Some trainers are sadistic people, and they train their students sadistically. Darius is not that. He's a reflective sort. He thinks about things. So he trains defense. He lights up when he talks about teaching little kids how to defend themselves from bullies at school.

He's that kind of trainer. From the bottom to the top. "I've seen the effects of what boxing can do," he says. "I've seen it take a drastic toll. After a while . . ." he trails off. His uncle suffered severe boxing-related dementia, an ever-present reminder. "Get in, make money, and get out."

Still, if he's being honest, Darius loves boxing. He might hate the business, but he loves the game. "Boxing is the only sport you look forward to," he says. "Boxin the only spahht ya look fahward to," it sounds like, with his accent. "Other sports"—here he makes a dismissive motion with his hand, sweeping them away—"I take them or leave them. But this"—here he beams with a wide smile—"This ya look forward to." If you hang around the gym sparring long enough, Darius will start to call you "champ." Even if you're very far from a champ, objectively. It feels nice. "Hey champ," he'll say. "What's up, champ?" This alone makes his fee a bargain.

He'd like to find a young kid he could shape and mold into a champion. That's the classic daydream of every trainer. Darius is constantly training teenagers, hoping that one of them might pan out. But he's not mean enough to throw them to the sharks. He's not the trainer who will let a kid toughen up via beatings. I don't know if that hurts his chances of landing the future champ or not. It might all be totally random. It might just be a matter of being the guy sitting in that chair in front of the locker at the right hour of the right day when the future champion of the world walks into the door of Gleason's Gym and asks for a trainer. Until then, to make a living in this game he trains people who box for fitness, and amateurs, and a jumbled assortment of low-level pros from all over the world who come to him by word of mouth, and white-collar weekend boxers, and whoever else wants to train with him. He's in the gym five or six days a week, making thirty dollars at a time. The gym is his office. His base of operations. He's a grown man with kids. His daughter just recently graduated from college. "That was my American dream," Darius says. He smiles when he says it.

I don't know if the American dream is better than the boxing dream, for a fighter. But it is a dream, and it is the dream that Darius is living right now. The ones who get to live the boxing dream are outliers. Boxing is not one world champion. Boxing is a million—or, really, maybe a thousand—men like Darius Ford. On Saturday night, there will be fights on HBO. On Sunday morning, Darius will wake up and come in and unlock the locker and hand out gear and watch all of us spar and sweat and pay him for one more day. "Don't get reckless," he'll say, again and again. "We're not on HBO."

POST-PRIMES AND CAREER ARCS

Navigating Boxing's All-Time Rankings

Michael Ezra

Key information about many boxers rests in their post-primes: how they fought, and perhaps even how they lived, after their peak periods in the ring ended. Few fighters finish their careers on the high side; those that exit with both their finances and health in strong shape are miracle workers. Many of the greatest ever, from Sugar Ray Robinson to Muhammad Ali, left the sport broke and unwell. The trope of the pathetic post-prime prizefighter, penniless and punch drunk, has always served up nicely as part of a moral argument against boxing and for a long time was sports' most reliable cautionary tale, although it has recently been replaced by the suicidal ex-footballer or prematurely deceased professional wrestler.

Arguments about all-time greatness in boxing fixate on two subjective criteria, talent and achievement. How good was the fighter in his prime? What did the fighter accomplish overall? Both questions deserve discrete exploration, although the latter usually holds more weight than the former. When both were near their primes in 1993, for example, Roy Jones Jr. clearly beat Bernard Hopkins at middleweight. Hopkins, however, receives higher consideration as an all-time middleweight than Jones, with his career record making the difference. Both Hopkins and Jones exemplify how post-prime accomplishments and failures can define pugilistic legacies more than prime ones. In their 2010 rematch, Hopkins won as expected in a fight that had minimal effect on either man's historical value.

Post-prime bouts can have great significance. Boxing's biggest-money contest of all time featured two post-prime fighters, Floyd Mayweather Jr. and Manny Pacquiao. It was a long-delayed matchup, with the eventual victor, Mayweather, refusing to make it happen until years after his smaller rival had demonstrated definitively crippling ring wear, and even then only at a weight that would afford the larger man a major advantage. Career-defining prime-versus-prime matches are rare these days because fighters would rather stay undefeated. Zero losses in boxing is like zero miles on a car; market value evaporates once the number changes.

Aging gracefully in boxing is quite an achievement, a measure of character beyond mere ring accomplishments. The post-prime period, as much as any other aspect of a fighter's career, can define his essence; some of the greatest greats have had remarkably impressive post-primes, and some, like Hopkins, only became recognizable during their post-primes as the professors of boxing they had always been. Post-prime accomplishments sometimes corroborate prime ones, like Ali's wins over Sonny Liston gaining increased credibility after he beat George Foreman a decade later.

By a fighter's prime, I mean his speed and weight. A fighter is in his prime at the weight and time when he executes at his fastest without any significant loss of defensive technique, endurance, relative hitting power, footwork, or durability. The most definitive change that takes place during a fighter's post-prime is that he gets slower. A loss of speed characterizes the post-prime more than anything else. Speed is the most important quality in boxing. Speed is to boxing as youth is to beauty; it can hide a boxer's every flaw and make him look great. You can win with just speed. Once you lose your speed in the ring, though, the other qualities that make you a great fighter, or not, become all the more important. Weight often influences speed, but not always. Many of the greatest fighters in history have fought in multiple weight classes, and understanding how to value the bouts they had outside their prime weights is key to appreciating their significance.

Speed goes first and dissolves quickly, never to be regained or relearned or improved. Whatever the *Rocky* franchise might say about chasing chickens or running on the beach, a fighter cannot increase his speed, and he certainly cannot recapture what he has lost over time. Age, training, lifestyle, weight class, and ring damage all can influence how long a fighter retains peak speed. Boxers who rely solely upon speed have the toughest road to long-term post-prime success. Even the fastest speed merchants can wind up like Jones, knocked out and discredited, or Hector Camacho, who early on became obsessed with safety. Ali is the rare and extreme example of an all-time great whose most impressive post-prime accomplishments depended upon significantly different skills than the hand and foot speed that won him earlier bouts.

Ali's case illustrates how speed can make weaknesses appear as strengths, but also indicates the unsustainability of relying primarily upon speed. Nearly unhittable during his first championship run despite significant defensive limitations, including not holding his hands high enough and the reluctance to slip punches via side-to-side movement, Ali was more easily tagged in his post-prime, the longstanding defensive flaws later embodied by Parkinson's disease. Although it was Ali who beat up Foreman for eight straight rounds and not the other way around, the Rumble in the Jungle and the myth of the rope-a-dope still pay proper homage to the toughness that rests at the heart of Ali's consensus standing as the all-time-greatest heavyweight champion. The belief now taken for granted that Ali could convert his prime talent into wins against the division's all-time best solidified only after the full extent of his resourcefulness and will were revealed in his post-prime.

The sudden exposure of the post-prime moment can result in catastrophe for those who employ speed as the sole route to success; in the case of Jones, it struck seemingly out of nowhere. Before Antonio Tarver landed that decisive blow, Jones was considered by many to be one of the greatest fighters of all time. Afterward he became known as someone who couldn't take a punch. Jones's spectacular rise and fall reveals the illusory lure of speed and how it gets mistaken for greatness. Jones in his prime was perceived to be as close to Robinson as you could get these days. Unquestioned for nearly a decade as the best pound-for-pound fighter in the sport as a middleweight and then a light heavyweight, Jones controlled most every round he fought for nearly fifteen years, culminating with a victory over heavyweight champion John Ruiz, pitching shutouts in many of the title defenses he didn't win by knockout.

Despite this run, in nearly all aspects of the sport other than speed, and perhaps conditioning, Jones was not great. He had above-average power, but rarely took the risks to apply it, he didn't jab, and most importantly he had a glass jaw. However, because he had maybe the quickest hands, pound for pound, of any fighter in history, Jones never really got hit until his rematch with Tarver. Only in retrospect can most of us see the shortcomings that were hidden by Jones's transcendent reflexes; he probably ducked Nigel Benn, Gerald McClellan, and Dariusz Michalczewski over the years, knowing these fighters had a chance to overcome his major asset.

No moment in boxing ever had the credibility-destroying effect of Jones's knockout loss to Tarver, when an all-time-legendary fighter's pugilistic worth was so radically recalibrated by so many so quickly. Roberto Duran's No Mas versus Sugar Ray Leonard, or Liston's quitting in the corner against Ali, or Liston's rolling on the floor in their rematch, doesn't even come close. The odds were 9–1, and longer shots have come in, but Jones-Tarver 2 may well be the greatest upset in boxing history when we consider its shock value and almost-instantaneous effect on Jones's perceived historical value. Little credit is due Tarver, by the way, who proved to be no great shakes when shortly thereafter he lost the championship to Hopkins, who was still winning the big ones thirteen years after Jones took their middleweight title bout. Tarver was simply a man in his prime at his best weight, in the right place at the right time, against an overrated champion whose post-prime day of reckoning had finally come. The assertion that Jones's demise resulted from his losing too much weight too quickly after beating Ruiz is easily refuted. It was only eighteen pounds he had to shed; an older Archie Moore lost more in less time prior to a light heavyweight championship defense that came right after a nontitle match. Other light heavyweight kings have also moved up for heavyweight bouts and then have gone back down to successfully defend the crown; if Jones was so depleted by the process, he would have tired rather than finished strongly in his victory over Tarver in their first fight.

Hopkins enjoys a rarified status as one of the few pugilists whose post-prime accomplishments far outstrip his prime ones, and who truly got better over time, at an age when almost every fighter becomes irrelevant. Jones-Hopkins is the uncommon post-prime-versus-post-prime rematch that more accurately reflects the reality over a prime-versus-prime first bout. Most post-prime rematches either reinforce or fail to influence how fighters get remembered. It is significant that Jones no longer receives credit as Hopkins's superior, even though it was once a given because Jones had bested him in a prime-weight, no-excuses, at-their-seeming-physical-peaks, clear-cut decision. Even in his pre-prime Jones got recognition as an all-time great, but his post-prime proved him to be just another good champion. Hopkins went the other way, having been known as just another good champion in his prime, at last getting recognition as an all-time great deep into his post-prime run. Hopkins is in the most fundamental ways the ultimate post-prime fighter, and in this manner also unlike Jones, in that he left the sport with both his health and finances in fantastic shape, fit as a fiddle and rich as hell, with a bright future. His style—never reliant on speed but rather on slowing down the pace and even, if need be, on turning the bout into a grappling contest—served him well over the long haul.

Besides bounteous speed, the other variable that most often creates a false sense of a fighter's historical value is his career arc: when he fought, who he fought, and who he could or should have fought. When does he make his definitive fights, against whom, and in what weight classes? At what age and stage of his career does he leave the sport for the first time, and does he come back? Fighting on too long rarely influences the historical standing of an all-time great; of course we forgive Robinson's losing to Joey Archer and Ali for the Larry Holmes disaster. All-time worth gets boosted, however, when a fighter quits at or near his prime, even if he returns unsuccessfully years later. Not coming back, as in the case of Rocky Marciano, is a bonus, but rare is the boxer who retires with big fights ahead of him.

Leonard's career arc reveals the importance of quitting while ahead. Leonard's prime lasted only five years from debut to retirement, his peak potential seemingly gone when he returned to the ring after taking two years off as a result of a detached retina and looked lackluster against fringe contender Kevin Howard. Leonard then was inactive for three more years before beating Marvelous Marvin Hagler in one of the most celebrated post-prime-versus-prime victories in boxing history. The win was a narrow one with the result likely influenced by the critical advantages that Hagler stupidly gave away to Leonard in exchange for the lion's share of the purse, namely, a bigger ring, bigger gloves, and twelve rounds instead of fifteen. It nevertheless has cemented Leonard's bona fides as not only one of the best few welterweights of any era, but also one of history's best pound-for-pound fighters, having defeated the great middleweight champion Hagler, at the bigger man's prime weight and when the bigger man seemed near his peak. To most people, the win evidences Leonard's all-time superiority over Hagler, who was also one of the best-ever pound-for-pound fighters. Such thinking endures even though Leonard's margin of victory was thin at best and the bout was difficult to score. One of the most hotly disputed big-fight decisions in boxing history, the contest was so close that the reputation of the judge who tabbed Leonard the decisive winner was forever sullied.

Leonard's triumph against Hagler is overvalued as a post-prime-versus-prime win. People ignore Hagler's career arc, assuming him to have been near his prime when he faced Leonard, and they overestimate the negative impact that a five-year layoff had on the challenger. What made Hagler a bogus 3–1 favorite was not only the misinterpretation of his recent performances, which seemed impressive but were subpar, but most importantly that he appeared much closer to his prime than Sugar Ray. Looking back, though, Leonard was nearer his peak speed and skill than Hagler when they met. The bout was more a prime Leonard versus a post-prime Hagler, albeit at middleweight, than vice versa.

Hagler was in steeper decline than Leonard for their match, even though most observers perceived it the other way around. Leonard was thirty years old; Hagler claimed to be thirty-two, although there is talk that he fudged his age downward by as much as two years. Leonard had thirty-four bouts; Hagler had sixty-six. Hagler had been a pro about fourteen years, with no layoff. Leonard fought five years, retired, then had one bout in five more years. Leonard went on long after their encounter, but Hagler retired immediately. Also taking into account that both fighters partied in the years leading up to their meeting, the sabbatical did Leonard better than Hagler's activity against the division's best did him, ducking nobody in nearly seven years as champion. During Leonard's rest period, Hagler defended the title eight times against tough opposition. Hagler's post-prime title reign, which includes his definitive victory against Thomas Hearns in one of the sport's most-admired fights ever, nonetheless reveals that he struggled in the years leading up to Leonard, against Duran and John Mugabi. We should also not forget that Hagler was rocked and cut severely by the smaller Hearns, who broke his right hand in the first round and had a below-average chin. Hearns was an all-time-great pound-for-pound fighter on a level similar to Leonard and Hagler.

Career arc can have a drastic effect on a fighter's meaning. Foreman, like Leonard, benefited from a self-imposed layoff, taking ten years off while still near his prime. Had Foreman not retired initially, he would have likely become fodder for the next era's contenders, from Gerry Cooney (whom he would later destroy) to Tim Witherspoon to Mike Tyson. He would have taken a pounding, piled up brutal losses, and might even be dead by now: no recaptured heavyweight title, in one of the most celebrated post-prime victories ever, no grilling machine, no lucrative second life as a jolly pitchman.

Had they quit while they were ahead, some fighters would enjoy a reverence that now eludes them. If Donald Curry left the sport for good following his blowout of Milton McCrory, we'd still be wondering how it would've turned out between him and Leonard. If Jones had decided to hang it up rather than give Tarver a rematch, there would be plenty of people ranking him the very best middleweight of all time. Marciano retired undefeated and never had a post-prime period—never helplessly sprawled, dangling on the ring apron, in the way he left his predecessor Joe Louis that sad night in Madison Square Garden. Louis in his prime was far superior to Marciano, and it is worth stating the obvious here—the result itself sometimes fails to provide the information and perspective necessary to deconstruct what happened in a given bout.

Boxing enjoyed a post-prime renaissance during the 1980s due to the immense surplus of talent between 140 and 160 pounds, when unusual quality percolated through the middle ranks, led by Leonard. Normally, it is a charismatic heavyweight champion who carries the sport, as when Ali single-handedly resuscitated mass public interest in boxing in the United States during the 1960s and tapped emerging worldwide markets during the 1970s. During the reign of Holmes, however, smaller men became the sport's biggest draws. High-level fighters Aaron Pryor (at 140 pounds), Wilfred Benitez, and Curry were not even their era's best welterweights, even though at their peaks all might beat the best welterweight of the past decade, Mayweather.

Popularly regarded as the current era's greatest pound-for-pound fighter, Mayweather is no such thing. Ricardo Lopez, Guillermo Rigondeaux, and Pacquiao all deserve higher consideration than Mayweather, whose undefeated record has hoodwinked people into vastly overestimating his value. Although possessed of considerable speed, ring intelligence, and old-school defensive generalship, Mayweather would be hard-pressed to last the distance against Leonard or Hearns at welterweight or Duran at lightweight. Pacquiao was so far past his fastest and best when they met—not to mention twenty-plus pounds above his optimal weight—as to render the result unusable as a measure of supremacy. Pacquiao's devastating victories against much larger opponents across an unprecedented span—no fighter has romped through weight classes like him—favorably contrast Mayweather's lackluster performances against bigger men like Oscar De La Hoya. Mayweather's split-decision victory over a faded ODLH contrasts the work done to him by more complete fighters, whether Hopkins's left-hook-to-the-liver knockout over the Golden Boy or Pacquiao's beating Oscar into retirement.

Leonard, Hagler, Hearns, and Duran resonated most deeply with the public during the post-Ali, pre-Mike-Tyson period. One fought against another nine times. Only Leonard beat the other three; only Duran lost to the other three. Their win-loss-draw records during this series reveal the following order of dominance, if, as many people do, you let the record book tell the story: Leonard 4–1–1, Hagler 2–1, Hearns 1–2–1, Duran 1–4. Duran's ledger looks much the worst. Not only did he suffer a devastating knockout loss to Hearns, the most one-sided of all the nine fights, but he was also the man who quit during his rematch with Leonard, who simply walked away without a mark on him, in the middle of a round, no less, without injury, and said "no mas." A failure to understand career arc would prevent the casual fan from accepting that Duran is the greatest fighter of these four all-time legends, if not of the last fifty years altogether. Those who did not see him at his peak, before boxing's comeback in the 1980s, probably require an explanation of how Duran could be the pound-for-pound best of these immortals. Three factors establish Duran's superiority: the quality of his prime wins, his definitive post-prime bouts, and his overall career accomplishments.

Duran won the lightweight title twenty-nine fights into his career at twenty-one years of age. When he beat Leonard for the welterweight crown eight years later, he had defended the lightweight championship thirteen times, against stiff competition. By the time Duran entered into the series with Leonard, Hagler, and Hearns, he was a veteran of seventy-two fights, weighing twenty-five pounds more than in his debut twelve years earlier, and twelve pounds more than as lightweight champion. Duran, in other words, at age twenty-nine was past his prime when he bested the bigger, faster, prime Leonard in their first bout. Duran, past his prime and well over his peak weight, fought Leonard, Hagler, and Hearns when all three were nearer to their primes and at optimal weights. Thus his losing record against them is not in itself any indicator of his inferior quality. An observer trying to make sense of Duran's historical value must take this into account.

The savagery of Duran's prime wins while lightweight champion sets him apart from the other three great champions, all of whom could decimate a man. Each had their impressive knockouts, sometimes against very good fighters, whether Hagler's win over Hearns or Hearns's over Duran. Of all the devastation, however, only Leonard's one-punch starching of Dave Green came close to the heights of scariness that Duran's title defenses regularly reached, when you feared for the well-being of his opponent and after turning off the television were left wondering about the extent of the damage he had suffered. Would Ken Buchanan be able to procreate? Would Ray Lampkin live through the night? In the early and mid-1970s, the sport's most memorably harrowing moments happened in Duran's fights. His definitive post-prime victories also reinforce his superiority over the other three. The only man to defeat the prime Leonard, Duran also had late-career wins against Davey Moore and Iran Barkley that considerably outstrip anything Leonard, Hearns, or Hagler accomplished during the twilights of their careers. While Hearns's victory over undefeated light heavyweight champion Virgil Hill might seem the most impressive post-prime victory by any of the big four, Hill was vulnerable to a smaller and faster man, as demonstrated by his knockout loss to Jones, who dispatched him with a single body shot. The lifetime records tell much about their career accomplishments: Duran 103–16, Hagler 62–3–2, Hearns 61–5–1, Leonard 36–3–1.

Quitting against Leonard in their rematch hardly blemishes Duran's record because what he did was not all that out of the ordinary. Considering Duran's fearsome reputation and macho persona, the decision to fold in such a crucial bout was surprising and disappointing and significant at the time, but over the long haul it barely matters. Duran has never revealed his reasons for quitting in that match, even as Leonard continues to obsess over them. It wasn't because he was taking a bad beating, like Ali when his corner stopped the fight against Holmes with five rounds to go, or Alexis Arguello when he willingly took the ten count in his rematch against Pryor. Duran received a battering from Hearns, but he didn't quit. Even when hopelessly outgunned, he kept coming forward before being blasted into unconsciousness. It wasn't because he claimed an arm injury, as Liston did versus Ali, or Julio Cesar Chavez did in his bout against Grover Wiley. Fighters quit in all kinds of ways. Tyson and Bonecrusher Smith mutually agreed to stop fighting during their heavyweight title bout, both of them holding and clinching their way through twelve insufferable rounds, neither man trying his best. Besides, Duran's mettle figured significantly into his win over Barkley, not to mention other late-career matches, some of them losses.

Only a fool thinks that the most honorable way to lose a fight is to be carried out half-dead, never able to compete again. It's not heroic being Jess Willard—who had to quit anyway—against Jack Dempsey. One of the most-heralded examples of ring courage, the Thrilla in Manila featured a winner who admittedly almost quit and a loser whose trainer would not let him answer the bell for the fifteenth round. We do not hold it against Ali and Joe Frazier that it went this way, even though if it were up to him, had his trainer not forced him to continue, Ali would also have quit after being blinded in his first fight with Liston. Fighters as valued for their toughness as Duran, like Ali and Chavez, knew that it was sometimes appropriate to say no mas. Duran quit once, but he was no quitter. He lacked good reason to keep going against Leonard that night, just to be clowned. The prime Sugar Ray was too sharp for the smaller man, and Duran was astute enough to realize it long before most observers could. His going the distance would not have changed the outcome, except to make him look increasingly foolish, perhaps the one thing he could not stand to happen in the ring. Duran also assumed wrongly that he would soon get a rubber match, as he had granted Leonard a chance for redemption shortly after their first fight.

Boxing fans afford great respect to fighters who get needlessly hurt and criticize referees who stop matches too early. Nearly all MMA fans, on the other hand, understand that a fighter needs to tap out when necessary. MMA referees intervene quickly, before considerable damage can be done. Relatedly, MMA losses don't necessarily dull market value—fighters are expected to lose, unlike in boxing, where no less than a figure as big as Mayweather feared losing more than anything else.

While strong post-primes characterize the careers of many legends, there are those true greats who scale heights so monumental as to excuse their relatively short periods at the top, in boxing and other sports as well. Baseball has Sandy Koufax, good for six seasons only, but of unquestioned all-time quality. At twenty-five years old, John McEnroe had won seven grand slams, the same number he had to his credit upon retirement. Gale Sayers played only five full years but set the NFL season record for touchdowns as a rookie and racked up astonishing prime numbers. Leonard is boxing's avatar in this category, having established legendary status in the fewest number of fights. Only 32–1 when he first retired, Leonard by then had beaten formidable opposition: Benitez, Duran, and Hearns. Other notable such achievers are Pryor (36–0 before his drug-induced retirement), Frazier (29–0 before being crushed by Foreman), and James J. Jeffries (19–0–2 before his fight against Jack Johnson)—all recognized among their division's all-time best despite short peaks and ignominious comeback attempts that showcased dramatically their inability to sustain prime momentum.

Ali was one of the indispensable post-prime fighters, as already stated, not just because his loss of speed forced him to radically shift his style, and notwithstanding his debacle against Holmes, one of the most pathetic of all the post-prime-versus-prime spectacles in the sport's history, on a par with Louis-Marciano. Ali's true post-prime significance may very well rest beyond the ring, as someone who lived with Parkinson's disease. Although he no doubt touched millions as a race man and athlete, Ali's biggest impact on society might be that if ever there is a cure for Parkinson's, he could rightfully be credited as the person singly most responsible for it. Nobody raised awareness of this common and deadly affliction, and money to combat it, more than Ali did. Such a contribution would surely resonate with humankind as much as his draft resistance, racial consciousness, or in-ring artistry. Whereas the prime Ali was divisive, the post-prime Ali was perhaps the most beloved and respected figure in the entire world.

Boxing fans invest a lot of energy in comparing fighters from different eras and speculating about their relative worth. The wrangling over these fantasy rankings, mostly within a given weight class but also pound for pound across the divisions, figures prominently into how people make meaning of the sport. Explanations of who would win various what-if matches and who are the best fighters of all time hold great significance for the many fans who get more riled up talking about the top three heavyweights ever than talking about the top three heavyweights now. These conversations about all-time quality, which are ultimately exercises of the fictional imagination even when they have a veneer of analytical precision, nonetheless matter to the culture of boxing. They not only compel fans, but boxers, too, who agonize publicly over their supposed place in history and whether they would beat comparable fighters from bygone eras. Unlike other sports, boxing has proven resistant to statistical analysis. In this void, its observers devote considerable passion, sometimes even great knowledge and artistry, in cultivating a case for why, for instance, Louis would beat Liston.

That Ali was favored against Holmes even though he had no chance of winning illustrates just how woefully misinformed the public is about boxing, how sentiment trumps analytical clarity, and how important post-primes are in the marketing of the sport. No fan base knows less about its chosen pastime; even the most rabid consumers are mostly clueless. Thus bouts like Mayweather-Pacquiao, or Ali-Holmes, or any number of matches that should have been easily recognizable as rotten way past their expiration dates, instead become the sport's biggest blockbusters. The many resurrections of Tyson represent boxing's tendency to recycle its stars and the public's willingness to be conned into accepting an inferior product. In basketball, football, and baseball, talent is cycled out ruthlessly. With the exception of canny role players and aging stars, there is hardly such a thing as a post-prime. Even sedentary sports like golf recognize the need to segregate older players from younger ones in order to preserve the quality of the product. But in boxing, one's faded glory can linger for decades, just a few rigged fights and a promotional campaign away from another title bout.

Boxing itself seems mired in an eternal post-prime, never quite off the radar screen, but ever decreasingly of use, creating little interest beyond the core fan base, rarely covered except on specialized websites, and—as with all blood sports—always of questionable morality and purpose. Scary new data about head injuries and concussions make known to laypeople what boxing insiders have always accepted, that those who step into the prize ring will get damaged. In a sense, you enter the post-prime of your life the minute you get involved with the sport. Boxing, perhaps best characterized by its cockroach ability to survive any crisis, will one day have company in the sports gutter, joined by the NFL and WWE, both of which now tower economically and culturally over the fight game but are no less toxic. Boxing will never die, even as it remains permanently in its post-prime. The post-prime ethos in many ways is emblematic of the sport and its greatest fighters, representing the ability to survive under duress, and the character to press on—and produce revenue—in hard times. To those who love the bittersweet science, these qualities prove irresistible.

The author would like to thank Charles Farrell, Kurt Noltimier, and Gary Moser, whose unique ideas about boxing have influenced this essay.

BERNARD HOPKINS, PREFIGHT AND POSTFIGHT

Carlo Rotella

AUTHOR'S NOTE

In deciding how to time the publication of a story about a boxer, a magazine typically has to choose whether to preview his next big fight or report on its outcome. I wrote the former kind of profile of the light heavyweight champion Bernard Hopkins for the *New York Times Magazine* when he was approaching his fiftieth birthday and preparing to meet the formidable Sergey Kovalev. But Hopkins, to my mind the most sophisticated and accomplished boxer of our time, is not a subject whose measure I feel comfortable trying to take in a single pass. I've never liked the idea of updating an essay to uproot it from its moment of publication and replant it in a new one, and I wanted to write something original for this book, as the other contributors were doing. So I decided to write an entirely new postfight companion piece that, even though it begins months before the Kovalev bout, includes the fight and is written with the knowledge of its outcome. You have before you the resulting tandem entry. First up is "Prefight: The Baddest Forty-Nine-Year-Old on the Planet"; with only a few stylistic changes and my preferred title, it's the *New*

York Times Magazine story that ran on November 2, 2014, six days before Hopkins-Kovalev. Second comes "Postfight: Your Intelligence Come Up," written in the summer of 2015, when Hopkins had both Kovalev and his fiftieth birthday well behind him and was deciding whether to fight again.

PREFIGHT: THE BADDEST FORTY-NINE-YEAR-OLD ON THE PLANET

"There's a god of this world," Bernard Hopkins was saying. "Some say the mass media is the god of this world. It's like a song, like that 'Happy.' They shoved it down my throat. At first I hated it. Why I got to be happy? My dog died! But it ended up being one of my favorite songs. They put one of those songs out every twenty years. No matter how bad your life is, no matter how legitimate your reasons for being upset, they say, 'Don't worry, be happy.' Song's only three minutes, then you stop being happy. The way they control human beings, like cattle. How do a sheepdog keep fifty or one hundred sheeps in order? I'm watching a dog keep a herd on TV, and I'm thinking that's the way the system got most human beings: 'Eat this. Drink that.'"

I had at some point asked him a question about boxing, but I hadn't really expected a straight answer. Asking Hopkins a question is like trying to hit him. He won't let you, but the experience of being frustrated by him can be instructive. Among other things, it can help you understand how Hopkins, the oldest champion in the history of boxing, continues to hang on to the title, his money, and his considerable wits at the age of—this is not a typo—forty-nine. Hopkins currently holds two of the four major light heavyweight belts and will try to further unify the division's fragmented title on November 8, when he faces Sergey "Krusher" Kovalev, the unbeaten Russian knockout machine who holds one of the other two belts and who, though relatively untested, is widely considered one of the deadliest seek-and-destroy punchers of any size.

Unlike most other boxers, who train down to their fighting weight only when they have a bout coming up, Hopkins keeps himself right around the 175-pound light heavyweight limit. Fight people marvel at the ascetic rigor that has kept him perpetually in superb shape for almost three decades, his habit of returning to the gym first thing Monday morning after a Saturday-night fight, the list of pleasurable things he won't eat, drink, or do. But to fetishize the no-nonsense perfection of his body, which displays none of the extraneous defined muscular bulk that impresses fans but doesn't help win fights, is to miss what makes Hopkins an exemplar of sustaining and extending powers that are supposed to be in natural decline. He has no peer in the ability to strategize both the round-by-round conduct of a fight and also the shifts and adjustments entailed by an astonishingly long career in the hurt business. He has kept his body supple and fit enough to obey his fighting mind, but it's the continuing suppleness of that mind, as he strategizes, that has always constituted his principal advantage.

Opponents don't worry about facing his speed or power. They fear what's going on in his head.

*

On a hot summer afternoon, Hopkins was having his hands wrapped in preparation for a workout at Joe Hand Boxing Gym in North Philadelphia. I had asked if he ever felt tempted to dumb down his subtle and hyperefficient boxing style—if he ever throws more punches than his exquisite ring sense tells him is necessary to win a round (which would increase the risk of being hit in return)—for the benefit of ringside judges unequipped to appreciate its nuances.

"I understand and I don't understand human beings," Hopkins began, warming up for the filibuster to come. "In life—I'm gonna give you life and also sport, intertwined—in life, when you start being conscious of what people are thinking or judging, you're in trouble." From there, he took off on his disquisition on the hegemonic power of mass media. It's one of his favorite subjects, and also, he didn't want to talk about judges, in keeping with his disinclination to discuss any topic related to fighting or training that might give even the slightest advantage to the large subset of the human race he regards as potential enemies. From "Happy" and sheepdogs he segued into a critique of the prison-industrial complex, another frequently recurring subject for Hopkins, who learned to box in his early twenties while serving five years at Graterford Prison, outside his native Philadelphia, for assorted felonies. "It's *privatized,*" he said. "You can buy stock in prison! That means, when I do something"— illegal, he meant, that leads to imprisonment—"you can buy stock in *me.*" He's not shy about pointing out that both private and public interests invest heavily in the social failure of black men. All the more satisfying, then, to have beaten the odds: "But I flipped the script on the norm."

Hopkins is sure that "the shot-callers and string-pullers" yearn for his comeuppance. They and their pawns are always after him to quit, he said. "'You got enough money.' Now they counting my money! 'We don't want to see you get hurt.' Where were they when I was walking off nine?"—a reference to the nine years he spent on parole following his release from prison in 1988, a period of self-reform and toeing the line that he considers the hardest thing he ever did. It's part of a litany of youthful troubles and redemptive turns, a personal Stations of the Cross composed of vividly emblematic scenes from a life story that begins in the Raymond Rosen projects in North Philly and eventually arrives at the big home in suburban Delaware where he now lives. Along the way came three stab wounds collected before age fourteen, a prolific career as a violent street criminal culminating at seventeen in an eighteen-year prison sentence, jailhouse rapes and a murder he witnessed, the shooting death of his brother Michael, a Quran given to him by a fellow inmate that reawakened his faith, the bracing plunge via Graterford's boxing program into the icy clarity of the gym and the ring, the warden who supposedly said "You'll be back" when Hopkins was paroled.

Hopkins began playacting a scenario in which *They* look for a weakness with which to bring him down. "'We gotta discredit him. Do he drink? He don't drink. Do he run with whores? He don't. He lives clean. He don't party. He don't use drugs. Who cooks his food? He cook his own food. He stands in line at Whole Foods with everybody else.' So they try to find guys to beat me, and I beat them, and I get rich. They become part of my discipline." Then he was off on another of his regular topics: the conspiratorial failure of Whole Foods, Nike, and other corporations to make a "poster boy" of him, a bad boy who became a good citizen and the most potently healthy-living middle-aged man imaginable. How come the marketers, who ate up George Foreman's fuzzy-bunny routine and Lance Armstrong's lies, aren't lining up to pay for the celebrity-pitchman services of an outspoken Sunni ex-con who abjures alcohol, caffeine, refined sugar, processed grains, tap water, performance-enhancing drugs, weakness, and just about everything else other than winning fights and making money? This grievance is part of the eternal drama of Bernard Hopkins, a renewable energy source that helps keep him going strong in and out of the ring.

*

Hopkins climbed through the ropes and onto the canvas, stretched and shadowboxed for a while, and then spent a few rounds working on the mechanics of not being hit. A burly young man named Bear came after him with a blue foam wand in either hand, trying to tap him with simulated punches. Hopkins timed Bear's advances, shifting the range between them to forestall blows, then stepped in close to put his shoulder on the bigger man, driving him back by expertly shifting his own weight. When Pharrell Williams's "Happy" came on the gym's sound system midround, Hopkins gave me a significant look over Bear's shoulder: *They* never rest.

There are masters of defense who rely on will-o'-the-wisp elusiveness, making a spectacle of avoiding punches. Others build a fortress with their gloves, arms, and lead shoulder, deflecting incoming blows. Hopkins can slip and block punches with the best of them, but his defensive technique is founded on undoing the other man's leverage by making constant small adjustments in spacing and timing that anticipate and neutralize attacks before they begin. It's somehow never quite the right moment to hit Hopkins with a meaningful shot.

Boxers, especially big hitters, feel a kind of click when the necessary elements—range, balance, timing, angle—line up to create an opening to throw a hard punch with proper form. Hopkins doesn't run away, but an opponent can go for long stretches of a round without ever feeling that click.

Frank Lotierzo, a former boxer from Philadelphia who is one of the fight press's best analysts of ring style, broke down some of Hopkins's defensive habits for me: "You'll notice he's looking down a lot, watching the other guy's front foot to see when it comes up, which it does when you step into a punch, and that's when he makes his move. He ties up opponents' elbows on the inside; you control the elbows, you control the arms. He never backs straight up; he'll give you an angle every time. He will pick a side and go away from your power, isolate one side of your body, step over and fight you on your blind side." Drawing from that repertory, Hopkins went around and around with Bear in a state of tautly maintained détente, discouraging wand-blows but not throwing any punches himself.

Naazim Richardson, Hopkins's trainer (and Bear's father), took over for a while, wearing a glove on one hand and a pad on the other to catch punches. A steady skullcapped presence in Hopkins's corner, Brother Naazim, as he's known, is more coconspirator than mentor. At this point, Hopkins, who received advanced instruction in his craft from English "Bouie" Fisher, George Benton, and other wise men of Philadelphia's deep ring tradition, knows more about boxing than most trainers. Hopkins and the much larger Brother Naazim shoved and hauled in a series of messy tussles from which Hopkins would emerge to bang the pad with a clean shot or two. Hitting the pads, intended to ingrain accuracy and speed and precise punching form, has become for most boxers in training a largely empty exercise in self-affirmation. The trainer holds up the pads, and the fighter pop-pop-pops them with blisteringly impressive combinations in predictable rhythm, combinations that he's unlikely to throw in the give-and-take of a real fight. But Hopkins was rehearsing a more realistic struggle in which he would spend a lot of time shifting and mauling to denature an opponent's leverage, looking to create an opening in which to score with a sneaky inside shot.

*

Figuring out what the other guy wants to do and not letting him do it is a matter of policy for Hopkins. But it's also an expression of his inmost character and worldview. He's not so much a contrarian as a serial agonist who regards life as an unending train of struggles for the upper hand, and over the years he has come around to the premise that such a life is best lived through a relentlessly calculated managing of self rather than the self-destructive fury of all-out aggression. One key to his longevity at the top of the fight world is that he has come to consider it "barbaric" to exchange blows with an opponent. Hopkins, who listens to Sun Tzu's *Art of War* while he does roadwork, will employ any tactic at his disposal, fair or foul, to frustrate an adversary—fighter, manager, promoter, TV executive, conversational foil—while he applies his strategic acumen to the problem of divining that adversary's deepest intention and coming up with a scheme to nullify it while absorbing the absolute minimum of punishment.

After Hopkins's record-setting reign as middleweight champion from 1995 to 2005, it was widely assumed that he would retire and duly enter the International Boxing Hall of Fame. Instead, he retooled his body to move up two weight classes, straight to 175 pounds from 160 without pausing at 168 (super middleweight), an unheard-of leap in the modern era, and thrashed the light heavyweight champion, Antonio Tarver, who was heavily favored to beat him. In middle age, Hopkins has made a specialty of flummoxing and defeating younger men who were supposed to have too much power for him: Tarver, Felix Trinidad, Kelly Pavlik, Tavoris Cloud, Jean Pascal.

Hopkins, who used to be known as the Executioner but now styles himself as the Alien, has a record of 55–6 with two draws; he will turn fifty in January. Imagine, if you're looking for parallels in other sports, that the linebacker Ray Lewis did not retire at thirty-six last year and was still playing in the Pro Bowl and Super Bowl in 2026; or that Derek Jeter, who was fourteen when Hopkins had his first professional fight, decided to carry on past forty and was still playing in the All-Star Game and the World Series in 2023. But getting old in the ring is a far more brutal and unforgiving process than getting old on any playing field. Winning title fights is the highly visible part of a much larger spectrum of effort that includes giving and taking countless blows, weathering the grind of making weight, training more consistently and shrewdly than anyone else, guiding his own boxing and other business affairs, preserving the integrity of his fortune and brain function, and priming his seemingly inexhaustible motivational engine. Even great boxers tend over the long haul to lose the desire to do what it takes to win fights, but Hopkins's sense of purpose, like his fighting mind, shows no signs of flagging. If anything, it's getting sharper and stronger.

*

"To me, Bernard, he ain't no real gifted athlete," says Robert Allen, a former middleweight contender who was in his early thirties and already in decline when Hopkins (who is four years older than Allen) beat him in 1999 and 2004. "He's just a little of everything on the average: average punching power, average hand speed." Measured by the absurdly high standards of elite fighters, Hopkins's only outstanding physical attribute is his chin—the ability to take a punch—which in his case has less to do with natural gifts than with conditioning, technique, experience, and will. Hopkins's "ring generalship" is what sets him apart, Allen says. "The ring is like his home. It's like he's sittin' on the couch watchin' TV, relaxing. He's like a snake, not even breathin'." In 2011, Allen said of Hopkins: "He's not really a fighter. It's like something more political when you get in there with him."

Hopkins has changed his style over time to accommodate advancing age, moving the emphasis to efficiency over action. A mature-period Hopkins fight goes the distance—he has never been knocked out, and he hasn't knocked out an opponent since Oscar De La Hoya, ten years ago—and, considering they're boxing matches, they don't have that much hitting in them. His objective is to prevent the other man from doing much of anything at all so that Hopkins can win rounds with a few well-considered blows. Sometimes he shaves his margin of victory too fine, or the other man is just a little too active and strong, and Hopkins loses a close decision, but nobody ever gives him a beating. Louts who lust for blood may boo when Hopkins works his punch-expunging magic, but Sun Tzu, who taught that a wise general wins by attacking his opponent's strategy rather than by risking the contingencies of pitched battle, would approve.

Hopkins's former opponents describe fighting him as an ordeal and an education. First come the prefight head games. "He touched me, pushed me in my face at the weigh-in, and it worked," Winky Wright told me. "It made me want to hurt him and knock him out, instead of outbox him." Once in the ring, "he won't allow you to do what you want to do," as Allen put it; I heard versions of that phrase over and over from men who fought Hopkins. And when an opponent does sense an opening, that could well be a trap. "He's always five steps ahead of you," De La Hoya told me. Hopkins set him up for the diaphragm-paralyzing left hook to the body that ended their fight by letting De La Hoya delude himself into believing that he was coming on strong. "He let me throw some punches for a couple of rounds, let my confidence build up," De La Hoya said. "I got a little too confident, let my guard down, and that's when he hurt me with a punch I didn't see." Smiling ruefully, he added, "I really thought I was going to win the fight!"

A skilled fouler, Hopkins will also hold-and-hit, punch low, step on an opponent's instep, and follow through with his own smooth-shaved skull after a punch to initiate a clash of heads. And he shamelessly complains about the dastardly things supposedly being done to him by the other guy. "When he bent over like I'd hit him low, he looked so *wronged*," said the former super middleweight champion Joe Calzaghe, laughing. "But he was just buying some time."

Hopkins has hung around in boxing long enough to profit from the passage of time. (The same goes for his extensive real estate holdings in once-depressed and now-gentrifying neighborhoods in Philadelphia.) Sixty or eighty years ago, when the sport was more popular and more deeply embedded in day-to-day life in industrial America, there were several fighters in every weight class who knew all the little things that together add up to Hopkins's big edge in the ring. But no longer. Hopkins is an enduring atavism, a one-man history lesson in the boxer's craft.

The men he has fought, even much younger ones, have slipped away into retirement in his wake. The will to fight diminishes, and the once-peerlessly toned body follows. "Oh man, I'm done," Kelly Pavlik said when I asked him if Hopkins's longevity gave him ideas about a comeback. De la Hoya said, "More power to him, but I'm done." Winky Wright said: "I'm done. I play a *lot* of golf. It's easier."

*

Hopkins makes a habit of putting his hands on potential opponents to size them up, assessing their strength and feeling for weakness. In July, I watched him do roughly the same thing to a Showtime producer. Hopkins made a joke about being camera-shy—he's not—just so he could laugh and slap the man's shoulder, run a hand along his ribs, get a feel for whom he was dealing with. This habit can turn sitting and talking with him into a contact sport. He scoots his chair up to yours and bumps your knee with his own, as if striving for position. Leaning in so close that you can feel his hot breath on your face, he pokes and prods a shoulder, a forearm, jabs stiffened fingers into your torso just a little too hard, nominally to illustrate a point he's making about digestion or human frailty or whatever. When I asked him about it, he said: "Feeling for softness is important to my diagnosis. Sometimes you can see and look, but you gotta feel to really check."

At the time we were sitting face to face on folding chairs in the media room of the MGM Grand in Las Vegas. Hopkins, a minority partner in Golden Boy Promotions, Oscar De La Hoya's company, which he joined a couple of months after he knocked out De La Hoya in 2004, was in town to boost a fight promoted by Golden Boy. But we were talking instead about how he learned the business side of boxing. This part of his story is essential to understanding his longevity because it's about rigorous self-knowledge. A great strategist knows his enemy, Sun Tzu says, but he also knows himself. Hopkins performed his own diagnostic routine on himself as a young felon and didn't like the resulting self-portrait—that of a doom-seeking knucklehead—and so he found the discipline in boxing to go straight and make good. He examined himself again as a rising middleweight in his late twenties and, again, didn't like what he found: a patsy who dutifully did all the hard work at the behest of others who took more than their share of the money.

So, armed only with native smarts and a jailhouse GED, Hopkins set out to turn a weakness into strength. "I started asking questions, trying to figure out how everybody else was making more than me, and I'm taking the punches," he said. "I had to learn the business—international rights, marketing, license fees, the gate, concessions, merchandising, sponsors." He did it on the sly at first. "I didn't want to let people know I was trying to learn, or they would have tried to stop me, so I would ask questions about other fighters who set an example for me not to do."

By 1995 he felt ready to take over his own boxing affairs, and he has managed himself ever since, employing lawyers and other "soldiers who do the legal mumbo jumbo" to help negotiate deals that allow him to take home a much greater share of the money he makes in the ring. "I started getting mines late in the game, once I realized I should know this before I became another fucked-up fighter," he said. "If you don't know your own value, somebody will tell you your value, and it'll be less than you're worth."

Hopkins, who has put his ring earnings into a conservative business portfolio strong on real estate and bonds, resolved long ago not to end up punchy and cadging for handouts, as so many former fighters have. In addition to looking out for himself, he has a wife, Jeanette, and three children to provide for. He offers advice to younger fighters, like the undefeated super middleweight Andre Ward, who told me: "He's always hammering home: 'Nobody gets paid unless you get in the ring. So get what you've got coming, and save your money. Everybody likes nice things, but wait.'"

When I asked Hopkins about advising other fighters, he said, "I was perceived as a troublemaker" when he began managing himself, "because I was a slave who learned to read. Maybe I'm more of a troublemaker now—somebody trying to stand up for themselves and maybe influence others, teach the other slaves how to read."

*

Bernard Hopkins may well be the best old fighter ever. Sugar Ray Robinson and Muhammad Ali, whose names come up often in discussions of the greatest fighters of all time, were both over the hill by their late thirties. Even among the few greats who fought into their forties—Bob Fitzsimmons, Archie Moore, George Foreman—it's difficult to find parallels to Hopkins's late-career run of lucrative high-profile victories over top-flight competition. Others who fought into middle age have typically ended up taking a pounding that made them look pathetic, but Hopkins gets hit less than ever these days, and his post-forty-year-old losses have been by debatable decision. And of course, Hopkins and his few near-peers in long-term success are all exceptions to the fight world's Hobbesian norm of short primes followed by brutal declines. Consider Mike Tyson, who is a year younger than Hopkins. Tyson peaked in 1990 at twenty-four, and was effectively finished as a serious fighter by 1997.

Hopkins may be richer, more sophisticated, more patient, and (according to those who work with him) mellower and less abrasively paranoid than he used to be, but he's constitutionally unequipped to grow overcomfortable in success. When I asked if he had been concerned, back when he started managing himself, that he might be blacklisted by the powers that be, he said, "I feel like I was blacklisted in 1965"—at birth. "I don't get blinded by a few successful peoples, like Jay-Z or Oprah. I look at the people who didn't make it—the penitentiaries, the thousands." A handful of champions make serious money, but boxing remains fundamentally a sport for those who, like Hopkins as a young man, feel they have nothing to lose. While he had to outgrow that earlier version of himself in order to survive and prosper, he hasn't lost touch with it. He used a mug shot of him taken in 1984 as wallpaper for his phone. He looks older in it than he does now, he says.

I asked, "Are we talking about the motor that makes you go?" and he wrong-footed me by coming back with a straight answer. "Yes," he said. "Being the person I *became*, this is the person I *am*."

POSTFIGHT: YOUR INTELLIGENCE COME UP

Inspecting the shelves of the cosmetics and vitamins aisle of a Whole Foods Market in Las Vegas, lethally taut and hard amid products that vied to outdo one another in gentle harmlessness, Bernard Hopkins was the very embodiment of Raymond Chandler's tarantula on a slice of angel food cake. He was talking on the phone with his lawyer. "I'll fight whoever I can make more money with," Hopkins said. "Whoever step up, I'll fight him. Then the other one." When the call was over he put a series of searching questions to a young woman manning a display table loaded with designer soap, and came away with an aromatic armload of purple and white bars. "Two for six dollars," he said, grimacing with pleasure. Holding my gaze, he advanced his face to within inches of mine, as if inspecting me minutely for signs of insensitivity to a bargain. "Two for six! *Smell* this shit!" He waved a bar under my nose and went off around the corner into the next aisle, calling to Malik Chambers, a longtime member of his carefully chosen crew, "Get me some of that coconut water." To me, he said, "No tap water. Never. And no white rice. Worst thing for you."

It's a never-ending source of offense to Hopkins that people are surprised to discover he's so abstemious and measured in his habits, such a paragon of deferred gratification and fiscal prudence and other traditional Calvinist virtues of a capitalist society's model citizen. Yes, he's a miracle of longevity in a violently unforgiving trade and upward mobility from an extremely unpromising start in life, but at this point he's also exactly the abstemious and measured type: a fiftyish guy with plenty of money who lives in the suburbs, associates with similarly moneyed professionals, works long hours, manages his investments with care, works out obsessively, eats whole grains and kale and egg whites, and derives a certain quiet upper-middle-class joy from shopping at Whole Foods. Such guys don't often have the Raymond Rosen projects and Graterford Prison on their CVs, though.

We left the store and got back in the car—a black SUV, because if there's a fighter with a title involved, especially in Las Vegas, you can usually count on a black SUV. Chambers, who was driving, held up the World Boxing Association (WBA) championship belt with one hand and said, "It's a piece of junk and you can quote me. I don't answer to nobody but God, and everybody else can kiss my ass." Hopkins and his crew do not get sentimentally attached to titles, but belts do lead to bigger paydays, and the WBA light heavyweight title was one of two that he would be defending in his next fight. It was July, 2014, and he was in Las Vegas to help tout the Canelo Alvarez–Erislandy Lara bout for Golden Boy Promotions, but he was also negotiating to determine his own next opponent. Adonis Stevenson, a southpaw who loaded up big lefts, was moving out of the picture, and Sergey Kovalev, a colder-blooded two-handed hitter with a pressing style, was moving in.

We picked up Eric Melzer, Hopkins's lawyer. Hopkins said, "This thing we're going to," a publicity shoot for Showtime, "is my look and likeness going to be used for profit?" Melzer, who is considerably younger and more rounded in contour than his client, said, "I think we're good." Later, Melzer mentioned that he doesn't swim on the Sabbath, which led Hopkins down a circuitous path of associations to a vision of the afterlife of Jose Sulaiman, longtime head of the World Boxing Council (WBC), who had died a few months before. "Sulaiman up there charging God three percent," said Hopkins, looking out the window. "You ever been to Phoenix? It's hot, but they got lovely spas."

After the Showtime shoot, heading back to the MGM Grand in

the black SUV, Hopkins said, "My first rule in the game, I look to get fucked. I assume it. I *expect* to get fucked. Then it's 'How can I avoid getting fucked?'" He appeared to be addressing this lecture to Melzer, who represents other athletes in addition to handling details of Hopkins's negotiations with opponents, promoters, and television networks. "You got to be patient," said Hopkins. "In this business, if you don't be patient, you overplay your hand and you get killed. Don't commit to anything. A venue date is not a TV date." He had November 8 reserved on HBO; they would nail down venue and opponent next. "You get the TV date first, venue is second. You gotta play poker."

*

When I first went to see Hopkins on assignment for the *New York Times Magazine*, in Philadelphia in late June of 2014, I got little more from him than his stump speech—chunks of the recombinant verbal boilerplate he usually dispenses to reporters. His stump speech is of uniquely high quality, including as it does his homemade critiques of race in America, the hegemonic power of mass culture, and the prison-industrial complex, but it still consists of things he says all the time, even if sports reporters aren't often interested in listening to it. Getting the stump speech the first time out is par for the course when I'm working on a magazine profile. I often schedule a first encounter on the subject's home turf, a place where he or she is most comfortable and likely to present me with a preferred self. I met Hopkins at his regular gym, and what I got was Hopkins in declamatory character as The Fistic Sage of North Philly, playing not only to me but also to members of his crew who had heard it all many times before. When I got home I called Kelly Swanson, his high-powered publicist, and explained that I needed a second session somewhere other than the gym, and that in it he would have to extend himself beyond his stump speech. After checking with him, she promised that if I went to Las Vegas he would give me what I needed. That suited my purposes. I try to schedule at least one subsequent encounter somewhere other than on the subject's preferred ground. While Hopkins has fought in Las Vegas many times, that crawling hive of pandemic indiscipline, impatience, and excess is not his safe happy place.

I caught up with Hopkins there in the MGM Grand's media room. He was making the rounds of the morning radio shows set up at desks on raised platforms around the perimeter of the room. It was loud; overlapping radio voices chattered with forced energy in Spanish and English. Waiting to be called for his next radio appearance, Hopkins was telling a couple of guys a story about recently posing in the nude for ESPN's Body Issue. He said, "I was good for two hours," until a female photo assistant started applying body oil to him. "She was going up the back of my legs, and it's like . . ." He stuck out his stiffened arm and turned from side to side so that fist and forearm banged into his auditors. "'Oops. Excuse me.'"

While they were still laughing, he turned to me and hissed so that only I could hear, "I got up early and ran 880s on the track at UNLV. I'm not like these *idiots*." He gestured around at the room full of people talking and talking and laughing and laughing. "Time is *passing*. What's your *plan*?" The whiplash shift in tone made me feel like Frodo when he puts on the ring and enters a freakish ghost-space separate from whatever's going on around him. Was Hopkins merely registering impatience, asking if I had a plan to get the most out of my interview time with him? Or did he have a more general philosophical message to convey, something on the order of *Because life is short, it is good to have a plan for using your time wisely, so you don't waste it on trivial nonsense like what's going on in this room*?

Later, when I took him aside for an extended sit-down in a corner of the media room, he told me about his practice of feeling for softness in the bodies of opponents, and he told me the tale of how he learned the business of boxing. It wasn't his stump speech; I ended up putting a good deal of it in my story. We also talked about some other subjects that didn't make it into the story.

He wanted to talk more about time, for instance. "I pay attention to time," he said. "But the way I pay attention to time, it's not a boogeyman. I pay attention to it based on who I am and what I give time to. It's twenty-four hours in a day. Five of those hours you gonna be sleepin.' That leaves nineteen, eighteen hours. Gym time. Get dressed. Dealing with business." He gave me a characteristic look, the ecstatic and alarmed grimace of a guitar player drastically bending a string. "These things are magnified in my head," he went on. "I'm not a slave to the check. I respect the check. I respect time so much where that I know it's time to eat, not when it's too late. Your body talk to you. Your body even talk when you're dead."

I asked him to push past the usual discussion of age and retirement—people saying he should stop fighting before he gets hurt, Hopkins asking why they suddenly care about his welfare—and tell me how he would know when it was time to stop boxing. He rephrased the question, one of his favored rhetorical techniques: "Was there ever a time when you say to yourself, 'I'm tired. Let me get out. I made my point'?" He understood asking the question at all to constitute yet another attempt to undermine or undo his achievement. "But wouldn't that be what you want? To trick me amongst my labor and say, 'Go off and get fat, and take your medications, and start having diabetes and *enjoying* your life and don't help anybody else become the next champion, or the business or social side. Just go away. Don't team up with Oscar. Don't keep going.'" The essence of his defiance, he said, is "wanting a respect to force them to acknowledge that they can't dictate a thought. It's not up to them when I go. It's up to God and me. And I'm hoping He'd give me a sign." If how he lives, what he is, constitutes a perennial victory over his enemies, every day that he wakes up and is still recognizable to himself as Bernard Hopkins can be chalked up in the win column.

He also wanted to talk about LeBron James. On a nearby TV, sports anchors were updating the breaking news that James would be returning to the Cleveland Cavaliers. Hopkins praised James for sticking with an old friend as his agent rather than going with one of the usual suspects, a sign of independent thinking that qualified James in Hopkins's view as "a slave who's learning to read." But no matter how much James got paid by a team that owned his labor, said Hopkins, "It's still who can buy the slave with the most money. It's like, 'I'm gonna trade my Negro for your Negroes. Hey, this Negro got a ACL; I don't want him.' Like a horse. You think they love you, try to date they daughter."

Hopkins and I were sitting face to face—a little too close, in the manner he prefers, so he could poke and prod and hunch in to look into my eyes from very close up indeed. When he did this he appeared to be endeavoring to read my mind through them, his own eyeballs flicking back and forth, taking in data and analyzing it. I had been happy to just listen and take notes during my visit to the gym in Philadelphia, but in Las Vegas I had begun interrupting his recursions to his stump speech. My time there was limited, and I wanted to make sure I got what I needed for my story. To smother my impatience to get back on topic, he deployed some of his trustiest moves: interviewing himself ("You might ask, 'Bernard, how come . . . ?'"), going off on a riff (the LeBron excursus) so seamless that it left no room for me to wedge in a redirective question, playing to bystanders to stall me. At one point, he looked up and caught the attention of a man and woman sitting and talking quietly nearby. Pulling these strangers, who were black, into the conversation allowed him to restate in detail his analysis of the LeBron Situation, which they politely seconded, putting me in a position in which I would not only be rude to interrupt but would also be a white guy trying to stop a black man from talking with other black people about slavery so I could force him to talk about what I wanted to talk about. So I had to let him finish, which gave me occasion to sympathize with opponents whose elbows he controls in the clinches so that they can't let their hands go.

Because the LeBron routine ate up a stretch of clock during which I couldn't do anything but listen, it perhaps also gave him time to straighten out in his head the narrative of learning the boxing business he was about to recount to me. When Hopkins was good and ready, he let the temporarily dragooned couple go back to their chat and leaned back in to me to tell his own story, which resembled Frederick Douglass's account of how he learned to read and write—that is, making moves toward taking ownership of himself without letting his oppressors know what he was up to.

While we were talking about the boxing business, I mentioned that I had spoken with a judge who had been impressed by Hopkins's performance in court. He said, "The judge remembers me? That matters." He has ended up in court quite a bit over the years, where his opponents have included Don King, Lou DiBella, and other major promoters. Hopkins hasn't won every time, but he has acquitted himself well. "I'm still not very educated on law," he said. "The words can seem — so many options, conflict of interest, giving things up in the future. But I know a lot more now than I did then."

The federal judge I talked to, John L. Kane of the US District Court in Colorado, who heard Hopkins's countersuit against the promotional company America Presents in 2004, said that Hopkins conducted himself on the stand "like a true gentleman; he was prepared and articulate, and he respected the court." Testifying about the austerity of his life in training and his promoters' failure to secure a promised payday, Hopkins succeeded in presenting himself as an earnest victim of dishonest and incompetent partners. "The people on the other side weren't as reprehensible as some in the fight business," said Kane, an enthusiastic boxing fan named for John L. Sullivan, "but they had some kind of Englishman on their side" (the South African–born promoter Cedric Kushner), "a big fat guy who was totally obnoxious on the witness stand. I was repulsed, he was so cynical. He was saying, 'The fight business, it's dirty, everybody in it is dirty, that's the way it is.' Bernard Hopkins looked up and said, 'I guess I don't have to tell you any more about it than he just did.'"

Kane told me that as a young lawyer he once represented Joe Louis, who spent the last years of his life in a pitiably broke and damaged state. The cold logic of the fight world, masked by a facade of sentimental regard for beloved warriors, ordains that eventual fate for even the greatest champions. "People see a money tree and start trying to pick off the fruit," said Kane, "and to hell with the guy."

Having taken steps to ensure that he will not end up like Louis, Hopkins does what he can to help other boxers. He testified at Senate hearings in favor of the Muhammad Ali Boxing Reform Act — "not a perfect law," he told me, "but it has some checks and balances" — and he offers advice to younger men willing to listen. Andre Ward is the best of them, a young Hopkins in many ways. When I was working on my Hopkins profile, Ward was embroiled in his own extended legal beef with his promoter, Dan Goossen, who had been part of America Presents when it first sued Hopkins in 1999, which led to Hopkins's countersuit in Judge Kane's court. Ward told me, "Bernard's saying, 'Be patient, stay in shape, this will pass. I beat Goossen in court. You can do it. Don't get depressed.' Those are nuggets, and they're so valuable when you're going through it all and getting upset and impatient." When I asked Hopkins about offering advice to other fighters, he said, "Be the bad seed. Teach the other slaves how to read. 'Cause you get tired of just reading to yourself."

When we were done talking in the media room, we met up with Malik Chambers. It was time for the trip to Whole Foods and the Showtime shoot. Hopkins walked with great purpose through the casino, accommodating fans' greetings and requests for autographs without wasting time or motion. He welcomes attention and loves the camera, but he does not dive into crowds. The MGM Grand was holding some kind of dance competition featuring preadolescent girls in tarted-up gear. They looked horrible, over-made-up and underdressed, prematurely old. Hopkins steered among knots of them. When the gambling floor came into view, he said, "These people in there haven't been to bed. These people haven't changed their drawers." Passing a packed restaurant, he said, "I don't like buffets. You pay to try to kill yourself."

The crowds disappeared when we went through a locked door separating the public space of the casino from its backstage areas—housekeeping facilities, service elevators, empty hallways that led to an employees-only exit, outside which the black SUV was parked in a VIP spot. "Human beings are fucked up," Hopkins said, returning to our discussion of battling promoters in court for his rightful share. "Something is wrong with us. We the only creatures on this earth that's unpredictable. A shark is predictable. A lion is predictable." He watches nature shows on TV as if studying for an exam. "But humans—we grow up together, we know each other all our life, but then I cheat you. Why?"

*

The former opponents of Hopkins I talked to in the summer of 2014 were unanimous in feeling that Kovalev presented a dangerous matchup for him. When it comes to absorbing the effects of blows to the head, forty-nine is beyond ancient, and Kovalev was a big man in his prime with explosive power in both hands, not only at long range but also in close, where Hopkins normally counted on being able to score without taking much punishment in return. Hopkins had so far proven impossible to knock out, but the opponent most likely to accomplish it was Kovalev. It would be shocking, almost unthinkable, to see Hopkins reeling on rubbery legs around the ring, out of control and on his way to being counted out or saved by the referee's sheltering embrace. If that happened, he might cease to be recognizable to anyone at all as Bernard Hopkins. It would seem . . . *wrong*, like seeing Bill Clinton struck dumb by a hostile question, or Barack Obama sloppy drunk and spoiling for a fight. Joe Louis was knocked through the ropes by Rocky Marciano; Muhammad Ali was humiliated by Larry Holmes's pity; but nobody had ever seen Hopkins, even when he lost, get his ass comparably kicked. I asked him if, at any point in his life, he had ever been beaten so badly that he couldn't continue or had to give up, and he said, "Never. When it got bad, I always found a way to make it at least respectable." Nobody, as he put it, had ever managed to "undignify" him.

It seemed unlike Hopkins to allow hubris or greed to affect his judgment in choosing a matchup. If he had agreed to meet Kovalev, it was because he had coldly determined that he could beat him. A look at the thirty-one-year-old Russian's record suggested a disparity in experience so great that it could potentially negate his manifest advantages. Gary Moser, a former accountant whom I count on to use statistics to deflate the reputations of undefeated heroes, wrote to me to say, "I'm guessing that Hopkins has seen, albeit in a less literal numbers-driven way than is my meat, what I saw this morning by devoting a mere half-hour or so to deconstructing Kovalev's glossy 25–0–1 (23 KOs) record. A full 20 of Kovalev's opponents came into their bout with him with no more than a 1-bout winning streak. As for the other 6 opponents, the one with the most imposing record— Cedric Agnew, 26–0–0—came in having beaten 2 guys in their pro debuts, 21 guys who had lost their most previous bout, and 3 guys who HADN'T lost their most previous bout . . . but had records of 1–0, 1–0 and 10–12–1, respectively. PLEASE!!!!!"

Kovalev would probably have to go the distance to beat Hopkins, and he had never gone more than seven rounds. Lesser opponents like Blake Caparello and Cedric Agnew had proven that he could be hit and hurt by even an average puncher, a significant liability for a pressing fighter, and that he had displayed signs of becoming confused and frustrated when things didn't go his way. And Hopkins, who had been at ringside for Kovalev-Agnew, had to have noted that Agnew had cut Kovalev and put him down for the first time in his career with a headbutt, a genre of fouling in which Hopkins displayed great virtuosity.

It was possible for Kovalev to be both a genuinely dangerous puncher and an unseasoned champion who hadn't faced anyone who could have given him even an inkling of what it would be like to face an opponent as skilled and experienced as Hopkins. As Kelly Pavlik, Antonio Tarver, and other fearsome hitters who were supposed to destroy Hopkins had discovered, power that you can't apply doesn't do you much good, and Hopkins was remarkably adept at figuring out what an opponent wanted to do and preventing him from doing it. Still, beating Kovalev was a tall order for him. The Philadelphia boxing writer Frank Lotierzo told me, "Hopkins is already the best old fighter of all time, but if he beats Kovalev and Stevenson he'll be *unspeakable*."

*

Boxing offers frequent reminders that two men of about the same height and weight can be of drastically different sizes, but each fresh instance of this bedrock truth comes as a small revelation. From ringside at the Boardwalk Hall in Atlantic City on November 8, 2014, it seemed to me that Kovalev, who is an inch shorter than Hopkins and has a shorter reach, was twice his size. Hopkins, in his usual perfect fighting trim, looked like a big middleweight; the shovel-faced Kovalev, like a cruiserweight who had somehow squeezed himself into a vulpine 175-pound frame.

I figured that, beyond the usual business of interdicting Kovalev's leverage and timing, Hopkins was going to have to do something especially tricky or nasty to denature Kovalev's advantage in size, power, and youth. Hopkins would have to take a risk by leaving an opening to lure him in for a sneaky counter, or headbutt the shit out of him to scramble his wits and perhaps open a cut that would throw him off his game.

The challenge, for Kovalev, was to do something he had not done before: take something off his punches, sacrificing power for precision, and keep up the pressure without trying to take Hopkins's head off. Nobody was ever going to beat a defender as refined as Hopkins by loading up leverage to hit him flush with big shots. A bigger man stood a better chance of hitting him by shortening up his swing and just trying to make contact, going for singles rather than home runs. It's difficult for a big hitter to do that, to exploit his advantage in power not by bringing it all to bear at once, which is his inclination by instinct and training, but by distributing it into controlled punches that are still hard enough to win the fight. The hulking Wladimir Klitschko had done it against the blown-up middleweight defensive wizard Chris Byrd, throwing a steady stream of three-quarters-force punches that prevented Byrd from doing much of anything. But a lot of big hitters couldn't rein themselves in like that. Wladimir's brother Vitali, for instance, lost his own bout with Byrd, quitting on his stool and claiming the usual shoulder injury, worn out after nine rounds of trying to obliterate the much smaller man with titanic blows and leaving himself open to Byrd's shrewd harrying counterattack.

I knew Hopkins was in trouble when Kovalev knocked him down in the first round with a chopping counter right that clipped him on the temple as he came off the ropes—not because of the knockdown itself, which no more than disturbed Hopkins's balance for a moment, but because Kovalev didn't freak out afterward. Knocking Hopkins down could have sent him into a finisher's frenzy, going all-out to put him away and leaving himself open to counters. In that sense, the knockdown could have put the younger man off his game as surely as being hurt himself. But Kovalev stuck to the plan he had worked out with John David Jackson, his trainer, who knew Hopkins well, having been TKO'd by him in 1997 and then having trained him for the Tarver fight in 2006.

After the knockdown, just as before it, Kovalev kept his distance, cutting off the ring with unhurried persistence and stepping back whenever it appeared that Hopkins was going to find a way to close with him. He patiently held back his right so that he had it ready to throw over Hopkins's left. He didn't rush and he didn't get flustered, even when Hopkins did manage to reach him with a right or a lunging hook. Kovalev would step back, resisting the booming puncher's natural urge to respond with a broadside, and Hopkins would have to reset himself, faced all over again with the daunting task of working through Kovalev's field of fire to close with him.

Kovalev piled up rounds, winning every one on every judge's card. He wasn't giving Hopkins a life-changing pummeling, but he was decisively defeating him. Only in the final round, after Hopkins buckled Kovalev's knees with a counter left, did Kovalev open up and come after him with less caution, but by then it was much too late for Hopkins, who was no one-shot comeback puncher. Kovalev jolted him with several shots to the head in the final round, a sight startling to behold, but Hopkins weathered the surge, answering with punches of his own. It was that rarest of spectacles in a late-career Hopkins fight, an exciting action round, and he survived it by a slimmer margin than he let on.

The outcome wasn't close; a shutout: 120–107, 120–107, 120–106. Kovalev had fought a surprisingly astute and disciplined fight, and Hopkins had not come close to solving him. He had figured out what Kovalev and his corner wanted to do, but lacked the wherewithal to work his usual negating sorcery on a potent opponent whose desire was to *not* take his head off—a diabolically restrained objective for a seek-and-destroy hitter in his prime. It was by far the worst defeat of Hopkins's career, but in the end it was just a bad day at the office. About the only thing Kovalev had failed to accomplish on his night of triumph was to undignify Hopkins.

*

Hopkins dominated the postfight press conference, and Kovalev, whose English was a work in progress, seemed happy to concede it to him. Hopkins bragged only enough to demonstrate that his spirit had not been broken, and he was graciously but not self-servingly effusive in his praise of Kovalev and his corner. "He was smart and he was patient and he didn't get caught up in emotions when I tried to suck him in," said Hopkins, his right cheekbone purple with damage. He acknowledged the success of Jackson's game plan in dictating on what terms the fighters would engage, and he gave Kovalev credit for technical skill, not just for being too big and strong for him.

"Tonight he was the better man, and that's cut and dry," said Hopkins. "You can't water that down." When asked if he would seek a rematch, he said, "A rematch with *who*? . . . *What*?" When asked if he would fight again, he said, "Askin' me to fight right now is like asking a woman who was in labor to have another baby." The defeated fighter's tenderness, the vulnerability and introspection you will see in even the hardest tough guy who has taken a beating, showed up in him as rueful noblesse. When asked how he felt about passing the torch in the light heavyweight division, he said, "He already *got* the torch. I don't have to pass it."

Watching him at the podium, his sharp edges blunted by fatigue and his roughness smoothed by disappointment, I was reminded of a conversation I'd had with George Foreman before the fight

I had called Foreman, who staged a successful comeback and reclaimed the lineal heavyweight title in middle age, to ask what he thought of Hopkins fighting on at forty-nine. Like almost every other retired fighter I talked to, Foreman didn't like the matchup and wanted Hopkins to retire before he got hurt too badly to enjoy his dotage. "I'm sixty-five years old," Foreman said. "I roll on the floor with my grandkids, I have a good time. You want your brain to be in order in your older age, and one punch can change that. One punch can wreck every little dime you set up, the fortune, the scholarships for your kids, all that. He got nothing else to prove. Boxing is not a sport for the wealthy. It's not polo. Get your money and get out."

But, he added, old fighters do get better in some ways, if they're serious about their craft. They get wiser, shrewder, and they don't waste energy in the gym, in the ring, or out on the street. "I got to be a better boxer," he said of himself in his thirties and forties. "You practice more, work harder in the gym, instead of chasing after fast women and slow horses. You figure a man out. You always got an angle."

No fighter of our era—and few of any era—exemplifies Foreman's point as well as Hopkins. Watching him on the podium, defeated and fallen short of unspeakable, but not undignified, I thought that even this punishing day, and the next, would go in the win column for him. He would wake up in the morning and still be recognizable to himself as Bernard Hopkins, bruises and all. And I thought of something Foreman had said to me about what it's like to be an old fighter: "Your ego die a bit, but your intelligence come up."

TOXIC NON-AVENGERS

Boxing's Quarter Century of Acceptable Losses

Gary Lee Moser

Both as sport and spectacle, boxing is in a state of deterioration. There have been other recessionary periods in the last century, but they tended to be short-lived: the decade between heavyweight champion Jack Dempsey's second loss to Gene Tunney in 1927 and the young Joe Louis winning the crown in 1937, for example. The sport's preeminent writer A. J. Liebling lamented the state of the game at midcentury when he wrote, "Nineteen-fifty was no Golden Age of boxing, but, compared to 1960, it was at least gold-plated." Despite such down periods, however, boxing has a track record of rallying back from them to the forefront of the American sports scene. There may be another boom for the sport in the years to come; never say never. It has proven to be remarkably resilient in era after era, despite all of the long-anticipated showdowns that aren't worth the wait or never happen at all, not to mention the mismatches that border on criminal.

The current extended drought doesn't bode well, however, both in terms of the quality and quantity of ring performances. Although boxing's perceived corruptibility and unstructured nature have always been barriers to its gaining the acceptance and respectability of other major athletic endeavors, what now puts boxing most in peril of becoming irredeemable is the culture of risk aversion that has emerged in the last quarter century among almost all of the sport's top names. George Foreman was right when he declared boxing to be the sport that all others aspire to; its lifeblood is the primal passion of fans who value the directness of the contact and the possibility that a bout could end by knockout at any moment. But as those elements leach away from the sport's core values, its permanent impotence becomes a more realistic probability.

The most important aspect of boxing that has been lost in the recent period is the cultivation of rivalries; today's so-called greats hardly ever avenge a defeat. Three of the most-celebrated champions of the last thirty years, Oscar De La Hoya, Roy Jones Jr., and Mike Tyson, have incurred twenty-one aggregate career losses. Only one was ever avenged, when Jones knocked out Montell Griffin in their rematch after having snatched defeat from the jaws of victory via a senseless foul at the end of their first bout. In the last couple of decades, there have been fewer trilogies than ever before. Recent classics like Arturo Gatti–Micky Ward and Rafael Marquez–Israel Vazquez featured second-tier champions but nonetheless sparked oversized interest among boxing fans. Without such rivalries at the top, notwithstanding the laudable stubbornness of Juan Manuel Marquez against Manny Pacquiao, the sport will remain doomed to the shadows. Great fighters making great fights is what drives boxing, and both have been in short supply since the late 1980s. Julio Cesar Chavez beat Frankie Randall twice after "The Surgeon" ended his ninety-bout unbeaten streak, but it's the rare recent case of a great fighter avenging a loss.

What does it mean to call a fighter great? *How does one score a career?* My own four-point system addresses superior technical and/ or physical *ability* that translates into successful *results* achieved over *high-quality opposition* for a *long period of time.* These four elements are what make boxing special and ensure its preservation despite all the factors it has working against it. The current unwillingness by most fighters to avenge losses, the refusal by winners of close and controversial bouts to grant rematches, and the fact that most fighters produce next to nothing after age thirty, all fly in the face of what produces great boxing. Thus the new culture of risk aversion among boxing's top fighters threatens the sport in ways that even the worst scandals have not. The fractured economics and politics of the sport, which have taken hold over boxing in the last fifty years and produce far too many titleholders, also contribute to this decline. Undisputed world champions have gotten much harder to come by with each passing year, and the importance of the so-called lineal succession has largely disappeared.

Many people regard Sugar Ray Robinson as the greatest fighter of all time because of his comprehensive abilities, dazzling style, quality of opposition, and sheer number of wins. But what truly sets him apart from the other influential achievers in the sport is his knack for emphatically avenging defeat while courting outsized risk. Robinson's ability to beat those who initially beat him makes him boxing's all-time pound-for-pound king over the other masters who had in excess of 150 lifetime bouts, like Archie Moore, Henry Armstrong, Willie Pep, Sandy Saddler, Harry Greb, and Benny Leonard. Some of Robinson's most dramatic moments were in late-career return matches, like the feverish barrage that stopped Randy Turpin and the perfect left hook that paralyzed the iron-chinned Gene Fullmer. Perhaps topping the list would be Robinson's winning his first middleweight championship by stopping Jake LaMotta in their brutal 1951 bout, the sixth and final time they would meet.

The first five bouts he had with LaMotta, when Ray was not yet in his welterweight prime and Jake was a middleweight on the rise, represent an unfathomable degree of risk-taking by a fighter with such a bright future, especially given the details. Sugar Ray thumbed his nose at a great aphorism that has been attributed to old-time fight manager Leo P. Flynn: "A guy who goes into the lion's den and comes out . . . doesn't deserve to come out if he goes in again." But within his first fifty-nine fights, all contested before he was more than half a year past his twenty-fifth birthday, Sugar Ray Robinson went in again and came out again four more times. Their first bout was in October 1942 when Robinson was only twenty-one, with a record of 35–0, including wins over Hall of Famers Sammy Angott and Fritzie Zivic. It was on LaMotta's home turf at Madison Square Garden with the "Bronx Bull" sporting a thirteen-pound weight advantage, but after ten rugged rounds Robinson emerged with the decision. Four months later they met again, with Robinson 40–0 and giving away sixteen pounds. Sugar Ray was winning the bout until he was knocked through the ropes at the end of the eighth round, which resulted in his losing the narrowest of decisions: five rounds to four, with one even, per all three judges. So long, perfect record.

After such a loss you would think a fighter in Robinson's position might want a bit of a break before thinking about reengaging LaMotta in a rubber match, but their third bout took place only three weeks after Ray had lost their second. And in between those fights, Sugar Ray took on "California" Jackie Wilson, a veteran of fifty-four bouts who had won twenty of his last twenty-one, with the only loss being to LaMotta. After scraping out a majority decision over Wilson in ten rounds, Sugar Ray then met Jake and was again floored, but this time took the decision. Almost one year later, after chalking up eleven more wins in as many bouts against opponents that must have seemed downright tame in comparison, Robinson returned to the Garden for a fourth meeting with the Bull, who by this time outweighed him by about ten pounds. No knockdowns or other scares this time; Robinson won by unanimous decision, although one of the judges had LaMotta winning four of the ten rounds. Seven months later, still marking time for a welterweight title opportunity that seemingly would never come, they met for the fifth time, with Robinson taking a split decision after twelve torrid rounds—"the toughest fight I've ever had with LaMotta," averred Ray, which is certainly saying something.

Going through this gauntlet at such an early stage of his career enabled Robinson to achieve so much for so long thereafter. When he finally was granted his way-overdue welterweight title shot, against Tommy Bell on December 20, 1946, it was a scant forty-four days after he had survived another close call in yet another bout he didn't really need to take: giving away nine pounds to a hard-punching fifty-nine-bout veteran named Artie Levine who had never been stopped, Ray KO'd him in the tenth and final round after being down and almost out himself in round four. In retrospect, maybe he had such a tough time with Levine because five days earlier he was busy taking out Cecil Hudson, who had only been stopped twice in seventy-five previous fights. When some years later Robinson lost the middleweight title to Turpin in his first defense, he reclaimed it a mere sixty-four days later. Even six years after that, it was only a four-month interval between his loss of the title to Fullmer and the night he landed that perfect thunderbolt of a left hook to get it back. And on, and on, and on. By his thirtieth birthday Robinson had already engaged in 126 fights—no fewer than fourteen of them against future Hall of Famers—and had only that sole loss to LaMotta. Yet he is most often celebrated for what he achieved in his remaining seventy-four bouts. Is there any doubt this man was the greatest fighter who ever lived?

Having an impressive roster of opponents, of course, does not in itself make you an all-time great, as evidenced by the example of Oscar De La Hoya. If one looks only at the names on the Golden Boy's record, it appears at first glance to be a veritable who's who of modern-day boxing. Without question, his conquerors—Felix Trinidad, Shane Mosley (twice), Bernard Hopkins, Floyd Mayweather, and Pacquiao—have all been top performers in the sport over an extended period of time, which cannot be said about many of the fighters who defeated Tyson and Jones. But Oscar might very well be the biggest disappointment of this troika, because in addition to only once attempting to avenge a loss, and not granting rematches after narrow wins over fighters such as Ike Quartey and Felix Sturm, he appeared to fight "scared" in his biggest bout, against Felix Trinidad, even when victory seemed at hand. Risk aversion was for the most part the guiding philosophy of his championship years.

Unlike most highly touted prodigies, Oscar did not have his pro career launched against a succession of hopeless bums and stiffs; on the contrary, not one of his early opponents came in with a losing record. But everyone he faced was carefully selected, just the same, and after notching eleven straight wins De La Hoya was deemed ready to annex his first world title. Despite having never fought at a weight lower than 131 pounds, he received a title shot against WBO 130-pound champion Jimmi Bredahl, who had barely more experience than De La Hoya himself and didn't win a single round before Oscar stopped him. The bout established the model that almost all De La Hoya title fights would follow: the careful selection of opponents who were ripe for the taking. Oscar shortly thereafter won the lightweight title by stopping Jorge "El Maromero" Paez in two rounds. Paez was a clowning crowd-pleaser with some underrated boxing chops but had started to show serious wear and tear; having lost only six of sixty-three bouts before facing Oscar, thereafter he would lose three in a row. Over the ensuing five years, De La Hoya would stretch his professional unbeaten streak to thirty-one bouts as he moved up to the junior-welterweight class before eventually settling in as a welterweight. At first glance, it is a very impressive list of opponents he vanquished during this middle phase of his career. The majority of them sported glossy records featuring thirty or more wins against two or fewer defeats. But some were smaller fighters—John John Molina, Genaro Hernandez, Jesse James Leija—who had stepped up in weight for the lucrative payday, which is certainly understandable given the major attraction that Oscar had become. And a fair number of others were even bigger names—Chavez (twice), Pernell Whitaker, Hector Camacho—who were all in their mid-thirties with their best days behind them. Of the nineteen world title bouts that De La Hoya had engaged in up to that point, over a spectrum of four weight divisions, only his victory over Rafael Ruelas involved more than one organization's title belt. It was not a bad body of work for a twenty-six-year-old fighter in the modern era, but it was without a definitive victory over a top rival.

De La Hoya's 1999 unification bout versus 35–0 welterweight champion Trinidad, who was only twenty-five days older than Oscar, would be the most disappointing of his career. That night boxing fans bore witness to the increasingly rare spectacle of two young superstars squaring off against each other for the highest stakes in the sport, with all the essential elements in place: both unbeaten, each several months shy of his twenty-seventh birthday, both legitimate 147-pounders, and the classic stylistic pairing of a boxer who can punch a little versus a puncher who can box a little. On paper, it was the most perfect match imaginable. One would've had to look back to 1981's classic Sugar Ray Leonard–Thomas Hearns showdown for such a mouthwatering collision of young welterweight titans. Except these two didn't collide. Because both were wary of the other's power and perhaps overawed by his reputation, the bout was from the start a metaphorical chess match, with Trinidad winning a boring majority decision after De La Hoya largely disengaged over the final three rounds.

So the monster showdown, poised to be a true classic, ended with a resounding thud. While it was bad enough that such a long-awaited and eagerly anticipated mega-fight turned out to be such a tepid, safety-first affair, it got worse. Despite their young ages, the closeness of the decision, and the lack of physical damage to either fighter, there was no rematch. Moreover, Oscar would engage in only thirteen bouts over the next eleven years, losing five of them, before deciding to work on the other side of the ropes, making even easier money by promoting the superior risk-taking of others. The victorious Felix ended up campaigning even less, notching only six more wins in nine bouts before hanging up his gloves. For this very odd couple, that's a combined record of fourteen wins and eight losses from age twenty-seven to career end—and not a single one of those losses avenged. Thud, indeed.

The paucity of those remaining wins is compounded by the lack of a single victory that could be rightfully regarded as historic. It's easy to overlook or even dismiss Leonard having only eight more bouts after that 1981 epic with Hearns at age twenty-five because one of them was a landmark upset of the truly all-time-great middleweight champion Marvelous Marvin Hagler—even if it was by a razor-thin margin in what proved to be the loser's swan song. And Hearns went on to more than double his total number of bouts, including a savage punch-out of Roberto Duran and a sensational loss to Hagler, as well as decision wins over fellow Hall of Famers Wilfred Benitez and Virgil Hill. In contrast, Oscar and Felix both had only moderate success once they moved beyond welterweight. How in the hell could any fan awaiting the first bell on that evening in 1999 have had even the slightest inkling that these two careers would ultimately yield so little in the way of true all-time greatness?

Disappointing in a different way is Roy Jones Jr., for his lack of durability and a sudden collapse that is atypical in the extreme for an all-time-great fighter. Practically untouchable for his first fifty fights and fifteen years, Jones double-shocked the boxing world in an unprecedented manner in consecutive 2004 outings, being stopped in the second round by a single left-cross counterpunch by southpaw Antonio Tarver and then being dominated for eight rounds by the veteran Glengoffe Johnson before a right cross knocked him out cold. What makes it all the more stunning is that both opponents were slightly older than Jones himself, and that Jones had just gone twelve close-but-victorious rounds with Tarver while Johnson, as good a professional as he was, had never scored a knockout past the sixth round in any of his fifty-one previous fights.

Jones was tabbed as an almost surefire all-time great from the moment he turned pro after an extensive amateur career. His first five years were at middleweight, a 26–0 run that included winning the vacant International Boxing Federation (IBF) belt via decision over the less-experienced Bernard Hopkins in May 1993 and then defending it once. Jones then beat the 168-pound IBF champion, twenty-six-year-old James "Lights Out" Toney, a very strong and multitalented fighter who sported a record of 44–0–2 that included a good eighteen-month run as IBF middleweight champion before vacating that title to campaign in the higher division. But after winning the IBF 168-pound belt from Iran Barkley, Toney had engaged in seven over-the-weight outings as compared to only three defenses; he came in as heavy as 181 pounds for one of them. This perhaps presaged the outcome of his showdown with Jones: Toney was sluggish from the start, and Jones, despite scoring a flash knockdown in round three with a quick left hook, was content to outbox his dangerous opponent the rest of the way, winning at least nine rounds on each scorecard. Six defenses against nondescript challengers followed before Jones moved up to the light heavyweight division. Against the great Mike McCallum, who was fifteen days shy of his fortieth birthday—and, as it turned out, two bouts shy of retirement—Jones won all twelve rounds to cop the "interim" WBC 175-pound title.

In 1997, Jones suffered his first setback and won a rematch, but it was a somewhat dubious feat given that he never should have lost to begin with. The opponent, the five-feet-seven Griffin, had won twenty-six consecutive bouts, including eighteen by knockout. Twelve of those eighteen victims did not come in with a winning record, though, and the six who did each had a minimum of six losses with at least two of those by stoppage. The strength of Griffin's challenge lay in the modified bob-and-weave pressuring style he employed, which had been effective enough to carve out a pair of twelve-round decisions over the inconsistent Toney after his Jones disappointment. The unorthodoxy of the challenger did indeed prove to be a puzzle for the favored Jones, but, perhaps emboldened by the flash knockdown he scored in the final minute of round seven, he became more aggressive thereafter. Two minutes into round nine, Roy caught Griffin with a quick straight right that sent him skittering backward; an extended sequence of individual lefts and rights soon had Montell wobbling even worse. When Griffin went down voluntarily on his right knee to buy some time, Jones stepped forward and stood over him, hesitating momentarily before throwing a tentative right hook that barely clipped him, then pausing before launching an only moderately harder left hook. This resulted in Griffin toppling headfirst onto the canvas—genuinely finished or opportunistically faking it—and left referee Tony Perez with no alternative but to disqualify Jones for flagrant fouling. It was an abrupt and stunning end to what had been a competitive and entertaining championship bout. Five months later, Jones avenged his "defeat" with a first-round knockout that was equally startling.

Over the next five years, Jones would win twelve more bouts in the 175-pound class, defending his WBC title along with whatever other ones he appropriated along the way from vanquished opponents. There were a couple of recycled former champions to be found—Hill, who was coming off a punishing twelve-round loss at the hands of the 33–0 WBO champ Dariusz Michalczewski, who Jones would never fight, and Reggie Johnson, whose best days had been in the middleweight division. Eight opponents had fought fewer than thirty bouts, with no signature wins to recommend them. In 2003, Jones took on WBA heavyweight champion John Ruiz, whose moniker "The Quiet Man" some found highly ironic given the nineteen-second coldcocking he had suffered seven years earlier at the hands of the Samoan New Zealander David Tua, not to mention that Ruiz had emerged with only one disputed points victory in a desultory trilogy with the aging-by-the-minute Evander Holyfield. Jones came in at 193 pounds to Ruiz's 226, but was still much too quick-handed for the Puerto Rican and won an easy decision. Eight months later, it was back down to light heavyweight, where Roy faced Antonio Tarver for the first time and won a majority decision over twelve rounds; by the reckoning of most observers that night, Tarver won his rounds more conclusively, just not enough of them. But for Jones, it was all good: 49–1, with world championships in four divisions.

And then at age thirty-five came the fateful rematch with Tarver and the loss to Johnson, and suddenly Jones was easy pickings. He lost an emphatic decision to Tarver in their rubber match, and then engaged in eighteen more bouts over the decade that followed, which included losing a long-delayed rematch to Hopkins by wide decision, an equally lopsided loss to Joe Calzaghe in what was the final bout for "The Pride of Wales," and ignominious stoppages by unheralded foes like Danny Green and Denis Lebedev. There was an illusory eight-fight winning streak at one point; not one of those opponents came in with more than eighteen career wins. Finally—at least one fervently hopes that it's finally—there was yet another brutal knockout loss, this time at the hands of Enzo Maccarinelli in December 2015 as Jones neared his forty-seventh birthday.

Before his fall, it was conventional wisdom in many sports media circles to regard Roy Jones Jr. as a short-list candidate for pound-for-pound GOAT (Greatest of All Time) along with the likes of Robinson and Muhammad Ali. On ESPN, it was common to hear announcer Brian Kenny say that Jones was the greatest fighter he had ever personally seen. His colleague Max Kellerman did him one better: he stated flatly that if it were possible for Jones and Ali to meet when both were at their respective physical peaks, the only reason Ali would win was because of his greater size. What may not have been apparent then, but is perfectly clear now, is that Robinson and Ali were both undeniably the best of the best because they had, in addition to an insatiable appetite for risk, three assets in abundance: great athleticism, great boxing talent, and the ability to take big punches. To have a realistic chance of winding up a true all-time great, you need at least two of the three, but Jones had only one. Because no matter how much a fighter might have been blessed by the gods with lightning-fast hand speed and cat-like reflexes and legs that never seem to tire, those physical attributes don't last forever, and need to be backed up by either a superior chin or the mastery of techniques for protecting an ordinary or inferior one (i.e., blocking punches, slipping punches, rolling with punches). Ali fought numerous big punchers in his thirties despite no longer having the blazing speed and boundless energy of his youth: his famous battles with Frazier and Foreman and Norton instantly come to mind, but there were also rigorous bouts against hard-hitting contenders like Ron Lyle and Mac Foster that most of the top names in the division studiously avoided. A thirty-five-year-old Ali held off a life-taker like Earnie Shavers for fifteen rounds to secure victory in a thrilling bout; Robinson was thirty-six when he fought a pair of back-to-back fifteen-round wars with Carmen Basilio that *The Ring* magazine voted fights of the year for 1957 and 1958.

Roy Jones was unable to produce anything like that after he turned thirty. An essential part of being a great older fighter is learning to cope with the loss of your speed, as Robinson and Ali did. Dominant in two weight divisions over a full decade, Roy Jones was a very compelling spectacle in the ring. But the best boxers ever have a considerably longer shelf life than he did, and against stronger opposition. As the tandem of Tarver and Johnson demonstrated to us in no uncertain terms, having "the look" of this generation's Robinson or Ali is not synonymous with truly being it.

The same holds true for Mike Tyson. Although he has been the most compelling figure of the current down era in boxing, Tyson is not an all-time heavyweight great. He suffered defeat at the hands of five different opponents and never got payback for any of them, which is somewhat of an anomaly in modern boxing history, as heavyweight champions have been surprisingly good at avenging the losses they incurred in the early and/or middle periods of their careers. Years before winning the title against the giant Jess Willard, Jack Dempsey was KO'd in the first round by a very tough former two-time title challenger named "Fireman" Jim Flynn; he returned the favor a year later. An undefeated but prechampionship Joe Louis was taken apart over twelve punishing rounds by former champion Max Schmeling. After winning the title a year later over so-called Cinderella Man James J. Braddock, Louis largely rebuffed the accolades that came his way by proclaiming, in effect, "I won't feel like the champ 'til I whup that Schmeling," a vow he made good on a year later with a first-round blitz of the German in what was the third of Joe's record twenty-five consecutive successful title defenses. When a broken jaw caused Sonny Liston to lose his eighth career bout by decision to tough journeyman Marty Marshall, he responded in two subsequent meetings with decisive wins—the same way Ali would later against the man who broke his jaw, Ken Norton. Well, except for the decisive part. But the second Ali-Norton bout was less than six months after the first, which should earn just about anybody's respect. Tyson never joined this very select group of avengers, however, despite having a career that was quite impressive in other ways.

Having won a share of the heavyweight title less than five full months past his twentieth birthday, Tyson seemed poised to join the pantheon of all-time great heavyweight destroyers that fans and experts alike rattle off: Dempsey, Louis, Marciano, Liston, and Foreman. He started well enough; in 1987, he had four successful title defenses in the form of two brutal middle-round TKOs and two dominant twelve-round decisions. He was even more impressive the following year, when none of his three opponents made it out of the fourth round; for one of them, the comebacking Larry Holmes, it was to be his only stoppage loss in a seventy-five-bout career. Another, the undefeated Michael Spinks, was blasted out in ninety-one seconds despite having never before been dropped.

So, as Tyson celebrated his twenty-second birthday three days after the Spinks victory, his career prospects could hardly have looked any brighter. His record was 35–0 at that point, with no major threats on the immediate horizon, although the 18–0 cruiserweight champion Evander Holyfield loomed down the line. Perhaps for that reason he fought only twice in the ensuing nineteen months, battering British visitor Frank Bruno for a fifth-round TKO after a slow start and then crushing American Carl "The Truth" Williams in half a round. But in his next bout, on February 11, 1990, in Tokyo, he lost to the big and talented but theretofore underachieving James "Buster" Douglas, despite being a reported 42-to-1 betting favorite.

Sadly, the rest of Iron Mike's career reads like a mere pugilistic postscript: four comeback wins over fringe contenders or worse, followed by a four-year boxing hiatus after a rape conviction, followed by four more comeback wins over fringe contenders or worse, followed by a one-sided TKO loss to Holyfield, followed by a disgraceful ear-bite disqualification in the rematch two days before Tyson's thirty-first birthday. After that, he had only ten more bouts, which yielded five inconsequential wins, an eight-round pounding at the hands of a slightly older Lennox Lewis, two other middle-round stoppages by the relatively unknown Danny Williams and Kevin McBride, and two no contests against Andrew Golota and Orlin Norris.

The incurring of six losses in a fifty-eight-bout career, in and of itself, is not problematic. It's the fact that all six losses were inside the distance, and none were avenged. No other heavyweight champion regarded as one of the true all-time greats comes anywhere close to this: Dempsey had just one in seventy-five bouts, Louis two in sixty-nine, Liston three in fifty-four, Ali one in sixty-one, Foreman one in eighty-one, and Holmes one in seventy-five. Even the contemporaries Tyson faced, Lewis and Holyfield, as well as the ones he didn't for one reason or another—Ray Mercer, Tim Witherspoon, Riddick Bowe, and Michael Moorer—each had no more than four.

During his regrettably foreshortened prime, Mike Tyson was undeniably one of the most dangerous fighters that the heavyweight division has ever seen, and was correlatively one of the most exciting. But when someone who revels in the nickname "The Baddest Man on the Planet" is deposited on the canvas in five different bouts by five fellow planeteers and is unable to finish a single one of those bouts— let alone win one of them—and all of those losses go unavenged, then, no, he's not a short-list candidate for greatest heavyweight ever.

Assessing greatness in boxing is inordinately tricky; oftentimes people make top-ten-all-time lists in various categories without having any particular methodology. On the surface, it may appear that fighters like De La Hoya, Jones, and Tyson deserve consideration for inclusion in such rankings, but in the crucial areas that separate fighters like Robinson and Ali from other celebrated champions, they go lacking. De La Hoya took few risks, both in his selection of opponents and his big-fight game plans. Jones and Tyson both lacked meaningful longevity once the bloom was off the rose: the former could not take a punch, and the latter could not fight his way out of trouble. The rarity of risk-taking by big-name fighters in the current era is of great concern. The perpetuation of it, more than anything else, will prevent the fight game from making any kind of real comeback impression on American popular culture. As noted before, the lineal-champion concept has become largely passé. But the sport can no longer afford to have its young aspirants embrace a mindset of "Not only don't I have to beat 'the man who beat the man' . . . I won't even have to beat any man who beats *me*."

WHAT BOXING IS FOR

Sam Sheridan

Picture the ungentrified boxing gym, with a half-dozen professional fighters working on any given day. Pieces of plywood flooring over concrete, with terraced holes worn through where fighters skip rope, the metronome *tick-tick-tick*. Bags wound tight with duct tape. Fight posters on every inch of wall space, banners hanging from the high rafters. Older men, of varying hues, watching all day long, ancient eyes. Trainers judge men like horse traders judge horseflesh: slap the withers, check the teeth. The incessant ding of the timer, the call to prayer, the *hut hut hut* of young black men on the bags, in the ring, in the mirror.

Some afternoons during my workouts, I'd watch an older black heavyweight "work" with two young white men who were paying for training. They were kids, really, maybe seventeen or eighteen, good-sized but soft, beefy, unfinished. Formless faces. The pear-shaped heavyweight, in his forties, had fought pro, some twenty fights, with about an even record. He now taught boxing.

When I saw him teach mitt work, the first thing that popped into my head was *That dude should be arrested*. In the weeks I saw them work, the kids never learned how to throw a single punch. He never taught them any footwork; he just conditioned them. He worked them relentlessly on the mitts, sometimes without the timer, letting them throw bullshit "combinations" of pitty-pat punches from the hips, from anywhere, flailing away. Uppercuts that started at their knees, and ended in a *Seig Heil*. As long as their gloves made contact with mitts, from any angle, arms curled or straight, that was fine with him. Then he'd put them on a heavy bag and walk away for a half hour.

The real tragedy was yet to come. The heavyweight would put on his face-saver headgear (like a catcher's mask) and spar these kids for three or four rounds apiece. And he would absolutely *crack* on them, just light them up. If they started to press or he got tired, he'd fall back on pro tricks: he'd hold their head and jack them with upper-cuts. He'd feint them into immobility, and rip them with body shots and hooks.

It was unreal. These kids would leave the ring, strip off their cruddy borrowed headgear, and smile; the fronts of their T-shirts soaked with so much blood they clung to rolls of fat, belly-button indentations, shiny like a second skin. Like someone had carefully poured blood from a pitcher all over their shirts, too consistent to be convincing if you saw it on film. Probably had their noses broken on at least one occasion. I've had my nose broken a few times sparring; you bleed like a stuck pig.

Those poor bastards thought they were learning how to fucking *fight*. But they weren't; they were just getting the snot kicked out of them and paying for the privilege. They thought they were learning to be tough, and maybe they were, a little. But mostly they were role-players in this heavyweight's strange revenge fantasy, while a roomful of trainers averted their eyes. There absolutely was something messed up about it, if anyone cared. It was a corruption of sparring, because sparring is fighting between near equals, for a specific training reason, and this had the master/student relationship involved. The kids knew they couldn't and shouldn't win.

But nobody really cared; as they say, boxing is not a game, you don't ever play boxing. The whole scene happened kind of fast, before you were really paying attention; there was a car-accident quality to the experience. By the time you realized what you were seeing, it was over. The beatings landed just on egregious, the kids seemed to revel in the punishment; and besides, one of the gym rules on the walls was that trainers don't talk to other trainers' fighters. Everyone is judged, but only the longtime insiders share any information, and then only with each other, like an Irish terrorist cell. The only way to infiltrate is to hang around for eight years.

There was something dark in the beatings administered, something about *race* and *vengeance*, something cruel. Boxing is still a color game, segregated and tribal, although talent transcends color. Not all men are created equal in boxing, and we know it. When I complained about being easy to cut, about being a bleeder, an older veteran trainer looked at me with a frank look, "You're a white kid, right?" *You should know better.*

I was learning to know better. I had come to this particular gym ostensibly to research and write a book, but really, I was in the gym for the reason that most young men learn how to fight. I wanted to be a hero, I wanted to be a badass, I wanted the great instructors of the world to teach me their magic and make me invulnerable . . . reasons not too different from the reasons those kids had for getting the snot kicked out them. I could cloak it in the aura of respectability, with a book deal in my hot little hand (and a college degree in my back pocket as an unspoken excuse as to why I wasn't a good fighter). I'd traveled and fought in Thailand and the Midwest, I'd put my time in at the gym, but I recognized those two kids.

Wasn't I essentially doing the same thing as they were, albeit a fraction more seriously? Was I in this for masochistic reasons?

What is boxing for?

I think I know what boxing is. It's entertainment. Like pornography, flashing a female baboon's inflamed estrus rear at male baboons elicits a certain response. Similarly, watching men fight elicits a certain automatic interest in males (and some females) of the species. They'll pay to see it done well. But that's what boxing *is*; what is boxing *for*?

Maybe the first thing that pops into your head is the narrative established in countless promotions: boxing "is for" poor kids to find "a way out," a venue (like other professional sports) for the talent-rich and option-poor to make money. The dirty street kid becomes champ and buys a mansion for his mom. The Ruelas brothers were from a region of Mexico so poor that they had no electricity; they used to sell candy in the dusty streets until they stumbled into boxing and went on to win world championships . . . That's the story we all want to hear: the rags-to-riches path. Sure, boxing is for that.

Maybe more important but less obvious, boxing is a way for damaged men and women to find wisdom. For those for whom *hurting* and *hurt* are inextricably tied together in such a way that they become their own worst enemy, boxing can offer a path to manhood, a path to competence, a way to be respected. The violent kid can pour his violence into the ring, and the ring will absorb everything and still eagerly take more. The expected motivations are usually back there somewhere — the abusive or the vanished father.

Professional fighters usually have all the uncontrolled rage absorbed like a sponge by their trainers, by the heavy bags, by sparring partners; while they must cling tightly to their controlled rage, sharpen it like a spear, and hoard it for the opponent. If it runs out, so do their careers.

Professional boxing is about money. If it's about anything else, you probably shouldn't be doing it. When kids ask me if they should go pro, I respond with the old trainer's question: Could you be a world champion? Because if you don't realistically think you can be champ, you have *no period business period* in professional boxing. (There's an exception: if you're so damaged that if you don't box you'll end up in prison, then go ahead and box, even if you have no shot at ever coming near the big time or even being any good.)

So this is what boxing is for, for those talented and strong and young enough to do it professionally, to fight for titles someday. For money, for a way out; for the damaged to find wisdom, order, and an organizing principle.

What is boxing for, for the rest of us?

*

I discovered boxing at Harvard University, not the Harvard Janitorial School, as some have hypothesized.

The Malkin Athletic Center, or "the Mac," was the closest gym to the Freshman Yard, a gym for students who weren't playing school sports. I had spent a year in the merchant marine, gladly turning my back on football and lacrosse, discovering wine, women, and cigarettes; but I still needed to do something. If I don't exercise, insomnia sinks its fangs into me and tears me to pieces.

Entering the Mac was like stepping back in time; a trapdoor and wormhole that opened into a forgotten corner of 1950. Old white men checking IDs at the door, the hot air of the pool, echoing halls tiled in linoleum. There was an ancient, rattletrap weight room in the basement. I've seen prisons with more up-to-date equipment. You worked out in there and felt like you were in a black-and-white exercise documentary about the 1952 Polish gymnastics team.

Upstairs at the Mac, I attended some tae kwon do classes taught by well-meaning grad students. They were nice enough, but the scene was what we call in the martial arts world a "pajama party." Playing dress up in a white gi. I have no problem with traditional martial arts, as long as I feel confident that your black belts could kick my ass. I could have taken these black belts' lunch money on the first day.

Up another flight of the stairs, the timer's *ding* lured me in. Two small rooms with high ceilings, a dozen heavy bags, the walls lined with various speed bags. Working out, mostly typical Harvard kids: nerds and a couple of slightly more athletic kids who had dropped out of football or turned up their cool noses at collegiate sports (like me). Boxing, not that interesting . . .

But along comes Tommy, the boxing coach, and everything changed for me. I had no idea who he was, or what he was, but I could sense authenticity. His battered face, his carriage, the wiry-old-man strength inherent in his limbs conveyed a depth of knowledge; here was someone for whom boxing was breathing, was walking. His footwork was perfection; he couldn't throw a bad punch if he tried. He taught us to shuffle, and I could see the power and poise still inherent in his whole instrument. The integrity was physical.

Tommy was delightful and delighted. He was a goddamn treasure, and nobody knew it. A bunch of Harvard kids who might have picked

Mike Tyson out of a lineup but that was as far as it went, and here was a piece of living boxing history. Shake the hand that shook the hand of the great John L. . . .

Tommy Rawson had been a New England lightweight champ in 1935, and he'd known Jack Johnson; his father had been a bare-fisted fighter who'd apparently been friends with Jack Johnson. Tommy coached Rocky Marciano as an amateur; he'd refereed Sugar Ray Robinson. None of us really understood the prize we had in him, already in his eighties, uninterested in names. He'd still hit the bag, with a huge grin, strange half-gloves, "Hey sluggah . . . hey champ . . . don't start weaving until he gives you trouble . . ." His crumpled face wore the irrepressible beam of a man pleased with life. *Here we are, this is what we do, and ain't it grand.*

Tommy started with footwork. He had us line up in rows and for hours, weeks, shuffling up and down the hallways or across the dance studio floor. I shuffled up and down the hallways of the gym, just doing footwork, learning how to sync the jab with the shuffle, three or four days a week, *for weeks before* I ever gloved up and hit the bag. Just working on the jab, then the right hand, getting the feet right, not worrying about hitting something. I've never seen anyone teach boxing that way since. It felt like the way you might teach little kids, third graders.

Later, as I continued my fighting education, I would hear trainers say, "Those who get taught hands first, the feet never catch up." I see this a lot with men who learn to box as adults; they want to punch shit really hard and so they slam the mitts or the heavy bag, and they never learn to punch because they never get their feet right. You see guys in MMA who murder the mitts but can't land a punch inside the cage, because they're wrestlers or jujitsu guys who never learn boxing footwork. You want quick hands? You need quick feet. Power in punching, anyone will tell you, comes from the hips, the legs, the feet, the movement up from the toes—all of it working together. Guys who punch with their arms can't bust a grape. My footwork has always pleasantly surprised trainers. And I owe it all to Tommy, to his method. He understood the right way to teach boxing, even if it was hard because men are desperate to start hitting when they start boxing.

Tommy would also get us sparring, headgear and Vaseline. But he would strictly control it. For instance, if I was sparring with a new kid, I could only jab to the body, whereas he could throw everything to me. "Everything to the body, only jab to the head," he'd say to one guy, and then turn to the better fighter and say "Only jab to the body." I've never seen that anywhere else, either. It was a great way to keep kids safe while giving them a taste, and to make sure they were trying things in sparring, not just freaking out.

Fighting is a little like losing your virginity. Before you do it, there is a lot of speculation, a lot of anxiety, some wild flights of imagination. And then you start doing it, and you find *Oh, this is fighting, I'm still me.* You aren't transformed into something else, it's not some dark door you pass through, the world is still the world.

Little boys delight in the fantasy of the hero—Bruce Lee against a hundred, whirling through them like a dervish, lethal and untouchable; the potent man, free from fear, better than all those around him. Boxing punctures that fantasy. Even as a little boy, when I watched boxing I was surprised at how few clean shots landed, compared to the action movies I was used to. My four-year-old finds boxing boring, compared to cartoons and their perfect kung fu violence, and I remember feeling the same way. The myth of fighting is far more appealing than the reality, until you start doing it.

The truth is, not all men are created equal, and there is a limit to what you can do. In America, the land of eternal optimism and "anyone can be president" and the power of positive thinking, where "no excuses" rules the gym walls and *anything can be yours if you want it bad enough*, we are especially in need of a reality check. Nothing checks your reality like a good punch to the face; nothing reminds you as effectively that there is a real world out there, a hard-edged cold world of materials that have no interest in you, no sympathy for your desires. A world that doesn't particularly care how hard you work, if you don't produce results. You can philosophize all you want about how perception makes reality, about how nothing exists but that you perceive it, Schrödinger's cat and a tree falling in the woods, *but you get punched in the face and you better adjust.* The cat is dead, in that box. It's not in some limbo. You can train as hard as you want, run the stairs to the World Trade Center three times a week, but you get in the ring with a real puncher (God forbid) and you realize that life ain't fair. Some dudes can *hit.* When they land on you, the blows alter your world—and if you don't have that power, you can't reply. The comparison I fall back on is that of an adult sparring with an eight-year-old, or maybe a ten-year-old; there's nothing that kid can really do to you in the ring. The strength-and-speed ratios are too different. It may look fair, on the outside, if the two combatants are about the same size; but it ain't.

So yes, young man, young woman, go box. But use boxing to strip away illusions. By all means, take karate, go to kung fu classes, but you better, at some point, strap on a headgear and some fifteen-ounce gloves and get popped in the face. You'll understand on a whole different level what is possible, what range means, where you can operate. Getting punched in the face has a wonderfully trenchant effect of showing you what works in a fight. Martial artists may say that boxers will break their hands in a street fight, which may be true, but I've known and seen street fighters absolutely starch dudes on the streets of Boston or Tijuana without breaking the skin on their knuckles.

Part of this lesson is about identity. In boxing, you need to know who you are, and not lie to yourself. Tommy Rawson knew who he had; he knew what he was doing with a bunch of college kids who were never, ever going pro. He knew there was value in what he was doing, regardless. He set up sparring so that both the stronger and the weaker were forced to learn (by doing) to have any success. The kids at the ungentrified gym, getting the shit kicked out of them, were living in an illusion of toughness and manhood, of tests. I was getting their education because I knew enough to see it, but I doubt they understood or wanted the real lesson that heavyweight was teaching them. Those kids were learning how to lose a fight. Contrary to popular belief, that is worth something; but it's not worth the price they were paying.

Boxing, more than any other sport, forces *identity* down your throat. You need to understand who you are as a fighter to have success, or even survive. In the ring, the truth will out. If you're a boxer, don't brawl—make him box. If you're a brawler, don't get frozen—get in and let your hands go, get your shots in, make him fight your fight. I'm a tall white guy with limited athletic ability, good endurance, and a good work ethic. So, I remind myself, don't try to fight like Muhammad Ali or Floyd Mayweather. Fight like Winky Wright (in my wildest fantasies). If James Toney is in the gym and calling out for challengers to get in and spar him, *do not* get in there, no matter what he says about you. You're not gonna learn anything in there except the lesson you should already know: *Don't get in there with the wrong guy.*

By the time I got to that ungentrified gym, to watch that heavyweight whup up on those boys, I knew enough not to get in there with him. Sure, I could have done better than those kids—but that heavyweight was tricky enough and mean enough to do some damage if and when I got careless or tired. He could play in that area between sparring and fighting far better than I, lull me into a relaxed pace—*we're just sparring*—and then drop the hammer. He had legitimately bad intentions, and even when fighting I never really did. More to the point, I already knew the lesson that heavyweight was teaching, and he wasn't teaching anything else.

The true value in boxing for an amateur is to experience the nature of reality. You learn a very little bit about the fury of a fight for your life. Even at Harvard, the very first time I got popped hard in the face, I felt it: *He's trying to kill me. I better kill him first.* The ungentrified gym taught this lesson a little sooner, a little more harshly: boxing is ruthless. A real fight, what a sparring session can sometimes turn into, is kill or be killed, in its essence. Those kids sparring with the heavyweight weren't allowed into that equation—because they weren't sparring an equal, they were sparring a teacher, and the teacher was supposed to be teaching them. They already knew who was better, before they got in the ring; the outcome of the encounter couldn't be in doubt. Part of the learning process is testing yourself; and you can't test yourself against a guy you can't ever beat, who wears a face-saver so even if you do land you'll never bloody him up.

*

I sit here at my kitchen table, almost in my forties, I've been writing since three thirty this morning, thinking about my son, nearly five now (this essay has taken some time to write). I took him to a boxing gym nearby for the first time, a real boxing gym in Santa Monica (will wonders never cease), run by a bunch of Irish pros, and he got to hit mitts with a real boxing trainer, up in the ring, wearing my ratty bag gloves. His face was serious. So very, very serious. I can't stop thinking about it. His wide eyes. He hovered around me, staying quiet, staying close . . . what will this memory be when he is grown? I will let him box, if he wants. But I won't let him turn pro. The head trainer, a retired professional with an Olympic bronze medal, agreed that his own son would never fight professionally.

What else is boxing for? In the big picture? Is there something else, a value like the one Victorians sought in rough sports, promoting the gameness of the British fighting man? Of course, obviously, boxing by itself doesn't make you a good person. Learning to punch and getting punched in the face doesn't mean you achieve wisdom. But I think there is real value in learning to fight. There is something my son should know.

Contrary to popular opinion, violence in the world has greatly declined. Oh sure, the twentieth century was the bloodiest on record, and so forth—but not in the percentages. The likelihood of you dying a violent death before the dawn of civilization, in hunter-gatherer societies, was pretty high, anywhere from 15 to 60 percent. Since civilization started, violence has been in a slow decline in every single measurable category. The likelihood of you dying a violent death in the twentieth century was something like 3 or 4 percent. It's even less now.

You can feel the decline of violence in our culture: you can't get in a fistfight anymore; it's not allowed. Does anyone even know how to put on a chip on their shoulder anymore, to get it knocked off?

When I was growing up, kids could fight a very little bit in the school-yard—I got slapped around once or twice—but for the most part, any kid who throws a punch these days is headed into official trouble and therapy. If I got in a bar fight now, I'd be looking at thousands of dollars in legal fees, pretty much guaranteed. Sure, our movies are violent, our video games are violent, but the murder rate is remark-ably low, historically. Slavery is illegal, dueling is illegal and out of fashion, a samurai can't check the quality of his katana on me, the Spanish Inquisition can't torture me into confession, and crucifixion isn't an acceptable legal sentence in any country in the world.

Boxing is a holdover from a more violent era, from Regency En-gland, where watching a dog kill rats was considered very sporting for gentlemen. Boxing is incongruous in the modern first world. There is no longer any doubt about the brain damage, the CTE prion break-down caused by the thousands of blows to the head, the multiple concussions. Gabriel Ruelas, who had an opponent die—he essen-tially killed a man in the ring—once asked me, rhetorically, bitterly, "How safe can you make a sport that's about hurting people?" Boxing is a remnant from a rougher past, when violence was a part of life, when damage was normal.

Our understanding of violence here in the first world is laughable. Not only do we rarely experience it, we don't know death. We rarely slaughter our meat or handle our own dead. Violence and death are abstractions for most, abstractions based on abstractions, grow-ing more distorted down the kaleidoscope of movies, pop culture, first-person-shooter video games—designed and written by people whose experience with violence and death comes from earlier movies and video games.

Yet they fascinate: violence and death are still a part of us, a part of life, a part of our decision making. Violence can still come and find you. Anyone can be a murderer, the genetic disposition is there. If pushed, given the right circumstances, you would kill. We vote for officials who take us to war, and a big complaint among the drill ser-geants of today is that the new recruits have no connection to phys-ical violence, they've never thrown a punch in anger. We do most of our killing from afar with bombs, planes, and drones. American casualties are unacceptable. Our wars are fought over things worth killing for, but not worth dying for.

The first time I got cracked in the face, I felt a deep, twofold thrill. It was a combination of *that didn't hurt* and *he's trying to kill me, I better kill him.* The taste, the thrill, changed my life. The deeper I got into fighting, the more interesting I found it.

One of my most powerful revelations began at Harvard but was completed much later, sparring MMA at the best camp in the world, and boxing with professional boxers. A lesson that you first start to learn in kindergarten: *who's the fastest kid in class?* A lesson that runs antithetical to what every adult tries to teach you: *everyone is equal.*

Boxing, for me, has been about understanding, a chance to mitigate the supreme narcissism we're born with. I was a sheltered white kid growing up in rural New England; I needed a little damage to understand, for empathy, for comprehension. Damage is part of childbirth, of creation, of creativity, of growing up. I would argue that the end of the draft, the bombers, and the drones all extend our collective adolescence. Of course, getting punched in the face by an opponent of about your own size, wearing protective gear in a ring, *when you're ready for it,* is not a shortcut to enlightenment for everyone, or even a really truthful example of what real violence is and does ... but it's better than nothing. It's a crack in the door, a peek through the keyhole. It's a glimpse at the knowledge from an earlier era, as Ian McEwan wrote in *Black Dogs:* "out here the rules were exposed as mere convention, a flimsy social contract. Here, no institutions asserted human ascendancy. There was only the path which belonged to any creature that could walk it." The ring belongs to any man who can hold it. Boxing is a frontier to our savage past. A reminder of what you don't know.

There are more reasons to learn boxing. There is intense satisfaction even for those who will never be champ. Even if you'll never be very good, you can still make yourself better. You train and improve like the sun follows the moon. There is the satisfaction of learning how to move and punch, of becoming dangerous. To an untrained man, I'm a reasonably dangerous proposition. I know I can survive against low-level fighters, if only for a few rounds. There is a poetic joy in an action well done, a visceral thrill to solid punches, to digging hard shots into a bag. To floating like a butterfly, if only in a shadowboxing match. The intense satisfaction of landing a hard hook in sparring, and seeing your opponent change his style, knowing *that hurt him.*

Fight fans watch and watch, because in that one out of a thousand fights, you see something special. In two fighters of at least "good" caliber, the styles match up, and you get to see real courage, true heroism in the face of danger. It's electrifying. It has to be live—tape it and watch it days or months or years later and it's like reading about a fine wine versus drinking it. It has to be happening in the moment; we're all discovering it together, the tick of seconds, the real-time surge of real wonder in the crowd. We get to see qualities we aspire to: courage, confidence, competence, skill in an arena of savage risk. It's euphoric. There isn't much of that in the everyday modern world; it's beguiling and wonderful, addictive and emotional. Real human courage is the most compelling spectacle there is, the most riveting drama. It's what every movie aspires to, what every professional sport or spectacle ends up aspiring to.

There is value there, in risk and reward and damage—because the world deals in those terms, no matter how safe and secure you try to make it. As Mark Helprin wrote, "You must give everything you have." If you don't take risks—if you don't, on occasion, push yourself to the edge—you risk becoming one of those people who "continually expose their souls to mortal danger in imagining they are free of it, when, indeed, the only mortal danger for the spirit is to remain too long without it. The world is made of fire."

Boxing is a land of secrets and half-truths, where nobody knows anything and everyone is an expert, where survival is like finding water in the Australian outback; you have to know where it is or travel with someone who knows where it is.

But go; by all means, go.

THE MYTH OF DEMPSEY-WILLS

Carl Weingarten

None who saw last night's battle can doubt that Dempsey would have annihilated Wills four years ago, three years ago, or a year ago.

Milwaukee Journal, September 12, 1924

It was a terrible injustice that Wills never got a title shot, but those big, slower guys were made to order for Dempsey. [He] would have cut Wills down in a few rounds.

Ray Arcel quoted in Roger Kahn, *Jack Dempsey: A Flame of Pure Fire*

Between 1920 and 1925, contender Harry Wills, an African American, and his advocates pressed for a match with champion Jack Dempsey, which would have been the first integrated heavyweight title fight since 1915. In that year, the first black heavyweight champion, Jack Johnson, lost to Jess Willard, whom Dempsey would beat for the crown in 1919.

Upon Dempsey's title victory over Willard, the *New York Times* reported that the new champion would ignore all black challengers. The statement was a political gesture to the men who controlled boxing that this new and very young champion would uphold the status quo. Privately, Dempsey was not committed to this belief. Whatever his feelings about African Americans might have been, Dempsey was inclusive in his professional life. He had already fought black opponents and employed African Americans in his training camps, including contenders Big Bill Tate and George Godfrey. Within a year not only were his managers discussing the possibility of Harry Wills as an opponent, but also there was growing public support for the matchup as well. Jim Crow was still the rule of law, but some signs of racial tolerance, coinciding with the end of World War I, were beginning to emerge. The prospect of a Dempsey-Wills fight arose on the cusp of this new era. The possibility of a black man fighting for the heavyweight championship was still remote, but now no longer out of the question. Five years of efforts followed to make the bout, but when the climate was finally right, it was too late for both boxers.

Harry Wills's not getting a title shot, in a sport rife with tragedy, remains on some observers' short list of boxing's greatest injustices. While the five-year saga intertwining Dempsey and Wills represents one of boxing's most famous unfinished chapters, the clearly unjust circumstances of Wills's denial have led to unwarranted assumptions about who would have won. Whether Wills was an uncrowned champion or just a noteworthy contender has been debated for decades, but estimates of his prowess have become inflated over time, especially since he was inducted into the International Boxing Hall of Fame in 1992.

There's no question that the failure to match Dempsey and Wills was an injustice, but it actually may have worked out, ironically, for the best. First, outrage over the obvious injustice done to Wills has blinded observers to the strong probability that Dempsey would have crushed him at any time during the period they might have fought. Second, had the bout lost money it might have led to an even longer exclusion of African American heavyweight contenders. Third, regardless of the victor, the fight might have led to widespread rioting. Fourth, the public sympathy and support Wills generated in the press may have helped open the door for Joe Louis ten years later.

As a boxing and fight film historian, I wanted to learn how good

Harry Wills actually was, and the details of his quest to fight Jack Dempsey. Going back to the newspaper and biographical records, I researched firsthand accounts of these two men and studied films of both fighters in action, including footage only recently discovered. The story was of a challenger turned away not only because of race but also by a matrix of forces that left a baffling trail of claims, counterclaims, public debates, court battles, reluctant investors, lawyers, feuding business interests, and fearful politicians. It's not that Dempsey wouldn't fight Wills; it's that people didn't see it as a profitable enough venture to be worth the trouble that an interracial heavyweight title fight would carry. The failure to match Dempsey and Wills resulted not from a conspiracy, but instead from the gridlock and infighting between the parties that dragged out over six years. Boxing and American racial politics can both be cruel, but it's a mistake to regard the two as always governed by a single set of rules.

Harry "The Black Panther" Wills (born 1889) began boxing professionally in 1912 and was the youngest of a generation of African American heavyweights known as "The Black Lights," who had dominated the division even though they did not receive title shots from champions Jack Johnson and Jess Willard, who both drew the color line. This group included Sam Langford, Joe Jeannette, and Sam McVey. Wills's size and age distinguished him from most of the era's other great black heavyweights, who were usually smaller than Wills and who had aged considerably by the time Wills came into his own. Wills looks impressive in photographs—lean, imposing, chiseled—standing over six feet two and weighing 210 pounds. He seems like one of the few old-time fighters who could keep up in the gym with the behemoths of today. Wills's most celebrated victories were over Langford, one of history's greatest fighters, who, like Wills, never fought for the title. But Langford was near ancient when he fought Wills, and still their bouts were close. Wills also had at least a thirty-pound weight and seven-inch height advantage over Langford. This three-weight-class differential would have been considered a mismatch in most cases.

Jack Dempsey (born 1895) was one of the greatest superstars in boxing history as well as one of the most lethal punchers who ever fought. His kinetic style buried the previous generation of flat-footed heavyweights—Wills's stylistic equivalents—and paved the way for the modern big man. With each defense of his title, Dempsey became more of a sensation. When the Dempsey–Georges Carpentier fight of 1921, promoted by Tex Rickard, grossed more than a million dollars at the gate, boxing exploded from a subculture into what would become the nation's most popular sport.

Dempsey would have fought Wills, as evidenced by the many negotiations and multiple contracts the two signed over the years, the first in 1922, and the last in 1925. When interest for a Dempsey-Wills fight peaked in 1922, a national poll was taken over one week in March to determine the public's choice for Jack Dempsey's next opponent, according to the *Evening Independent*. Wills came in first with 131,073 votes, just edging out Tommy Gibbons, who received 125,000. Here was confirmation that the public appeared ready for an African American to fight for the heavyweight title. The color line was becoming blurred.

The 1922 Dempsey-Wills agreement was open-ended. No deadline for the bidding process, or fight date, was scheduled. When the bidding timeline ran beyond sixty days, Wills and his manager sued. From that point until 1926, the legal proceedings dragged on. A potential Dempsey-Wills fight hung in the air, often mentioned in the news as either under consideration, being planned, or "scheduled for next year," but never a done deal.

Boxing has produced its share of heroes in every community, but boxing at its core is a venture that enables a few people to make a great deal of money in a short amount of time, with most of the cash going to those who already have plenty of it. Dempsey was the central figure in the nation's leading sport, holding an esteemed title with huge earnings possibilities. At the same time, this made the potential for ruin also great. Dempsey, Wills, and their managers did not create the nation's racial problems. They were caught up in the times like everyone else, while investors, politicians, and other powers of the day played political football with the prospect of a mixed-race championship fight.

Boxing had only recently emerged from the aftermath of the championship reign of Jack Johnson, the first black heavyweight champion who held the title from 1908 to 1915. Johnson was a supremely talented fighter, and he defeated a short list of "white hope" challengers, including former champion Jim Jeffries in 1910. Law enforcement and politicians hounded Johnson, and he became mired in a scandal and court battle over his personal life. Johnson also fueled the fire. He dated and married white women when interracial relations were still taboo. He was openly unfaithful and self-aggrandizing. Johnson also drew the color line, refusing to defend against Langford, Jeannette, McVey, Wills, and other black heavyweights. Johnson argued that the issue was money, proclaiming the reason he fought only one African American challenger was that two black men fighting for the title wouldn't sell. But this was an excuse, and his claim was never substantiated. A Johnson-Langford title fight, proposed in 1915, might have been as successful as any other title defense that Johnson had. It would have matched a very unpopular champion with an established and respected challenger. A rally behind Langford could have galvanized both whites and blacks, easing race relations surrounding the event and making history by doing so.

But Johnson would have none of the above. Historians have yet to hold Johnson fully accountable for this choice, especially considering that he was an outsider, with more control in his choice of opponents than Dempsey had. When Johnson fled the United States to avoid prison, the heavyweight championship franchise, perhaps the richest in all of sports, lost much of its monetary value as Johnson and his nomadic entourage toured overseas. The promoter Tex Rickard spoke for the boxing establishment when he said that the heavyweight title in the hands of a black man "ain't worth a nickel."

Rickard was the leading boxing promoter during the 1920s, and it was he, not Dempsey, who ultimately decided who the champion would or would not fight. Rickard has been singled out as the culprit for blocking the Dempsey-Wills fight, and there's no question that he did not want it to take place. But Rickard was a businessman, who in fact had promoted several mixed-race contests, including the controversial Johnson-Jeffries match. But Dempsey-Wills, as a sporting event, just didn't merit the risk. Big fights were complicated and massive undertakings with no room for failure. A century ago, large-capacity stadiums had yet to be built in the United States, and the venues that did exist were made for field sports, not for watching two men in a twenty-foot ring at night from a quarter of a mile away. Stadiums were sometimes built for just one event, which meant acquiring acres of land, as well as property rights, in a location close enough to a big city to be accessible by thousands of people. Local officials had to sign off, including state governors. If any of those parties balked, the event was in danger of being canceled. All this took an enormous amount of credit, planning, labor, and months of promotion.

Big as boxing had become, Rickard and his associates were still at the mercy of the political winds. Even if a Dempsey-Wills fight ended fair and square, race relations were such that no one could predict what the public reaction might be. Would the bout trigger racial violence? Johnson-Jeffries led to the most widespread day of rioting in American history until Martin Luther King was killed nearly sixty years later. There was a lot at stake, a great deal of money to lose, a social and political cost, and possibly jail for those backing the fight. In short, there was too much risk and not enough reward to make Dempsey-Wills worthwhile. Rickard wanted no part of it.

Around the time Dempsey and Wills signed their first contract, Argentine heavyweight champion Luis Angel Firpo arrived in the United States and began to upstage Wills as Dempsey's most intriguing contender by knocking out a series of opponents, including Jess Willard. When Dempsey signed to fight Firpo, Wills sued yet again, insisting that he was the rightful challenger, but the bout was held anyway. Wills was not without means, money, or popularity, but suing into existence a championship fight that had no promoter is like suing a corporation for its stock price going down. That Wills was never given the chance to fight Jack Dempsey was grossly unfair in its day, but boxing history is filled with worthy fighters from all communities who never had their rightful title shot due to discrimination, circumstance, or bad luck. At least Wills got his case on the record.

Firpo and Dempsey met in September 1923 in one of boxing's most furious battles, famously captured in the artwork of George Bellows. Dempsey sent Firpo to the canvas seven times, but the champion was also dropped twice, including a trip into press row, nearly losing his title. During this period, Wills and his manager Paddy Mullins made a key tactical error. Many fighters other than Wills wanted Dempsey's title, and the contenders battled one another for position. But Wills and Mullins chose not to fight and perhaps eliminate the other leading rivals, a group that included Tommy Gibbons, Billy Miske, Georges Carpentier, Jim Maloney, Harry Greb, Young Stribling, and Jack Delaney—all of whom fought across racial barriers. As good a boxer as he was, perhaps Harry Wills's reputation has been advanced in part because of who he didn't fight rather than who he did.

In 1924, Wills could no longer stand on the sidelines and received the golden opportunity to fight Firpo. Jack Dempsey sat at ringside. Both Wills and Firpo were knockout artists of roughly the same height and weight. The *Times Daily* reported the odds as virtually even on the day of the fight. Staged in front of an audience of seventy-five thousand, it was the highest-profile bout of Wills's career. The contest went the full twelve rounds to end in a no-decision. Newspapers, including the *Quebec Daily Telegraph*, hailed Wills as the winner who "took almost every round and in the second round floored his opponent." Others were not as impressed. The *Milwaukee Journal* headlined, "Harry Wills No Match for Champion Dempsey."

How close Dempsey and Wills actually were to a bout is unclear. In March 1925, the New York State Athletic Commission reversed its earlier position and sanctioned a Dempsey-Wills match. The Associated Press reported on July 17 that Dempsey appeared before the New York Licensing Commission and formally accepted Wills's challenge. Two months later, acting without Rickard, Dempsey agreed to a second contract with Wills. Midwestern businessman and promoter Floyd Fitzsimmons, who had produced the Dempsey–Billy Miske title fight in 1920, proposed a Dempsey-Wills bout to be held in Michigan City, Indiana. Dempsey was guaranteed $1 million for the fight with $300,000 due upon signing. Dempsey accepted the offer. On

September 28, Wills, Dempsey, the promoter, and investors met for the contract ceremony. Wills received a check for $50,000. Dempsey's check was for only $25,000. Despite the $275,000 shortfall, Dempsey was still willing to proceed. The next morning, Dempsey accompanied Fitzsimmons to cash the check. The bank, wrote author Roger Kahn, reported that the Fitzsimmons account was in fact empty. The check bounced, and Dempsey walked away. Wills kept his $50,000.

In 1926, Wills received another opportunity. This time the offer was $250,000 to fight Gene Tunney in a title eliminator, with the winner to meet the champion. Wills turned it down, believing that he was already entitled to fight the champion. Others were also in contention now, including Jim Maloney, Jack Delaney, Jack Sharkey, Paulino Uzcudun, and Tom Heeney. Rickard may not have wanted to take chances with a Dempsey-Wills contest, but Mullins, too, didn't want to take chances with his fighter's career. By trying to tie up Dempsey in court instead of cleaning out the division, Wills may further have dimmed his own prospects.

Wills, already thirty years of age by the time Dempsey beat Willard for the title, had time working against him. But time ran out sooner for Dempsey. With the pathway for a Tunney-Dempsey match eventually cleared, Dempsey lost the fight and the crown to Tunney in what was the biggest-grossing bout of all time. One month later, Wills lost to future champion Jack Sharkey. *Time* reported, "Sharkey chopped and hacked at Wills, closed his eye, made his mouth bleed, all through the fight." Wills reportedly backhanded, butted, and hit Sharkey during the break in an effort to discourage his opponent. After numerous warnings by the referee, Wills was disqualified in the thirteenth round. Wills soldiered on for several more fights, but retired from boxing in 1932.

So the question remains: What would a Dempsey-Wills fight have looked like? Who would likely have won in 1922 or 1925? No single piece of evidence is conclusive. Boxing matches are fleeting events. Those that are close and competitive are complex, and judging them is subjective at best. The wealth of archival materials including biographical information, newspaper accounts, interviews, photographs, and motion pictures of Dempsey show him to have been a force of nature in his prime with supreme punching power, ferocity, fighting savvy, and determination. The question, then, is Wills. Aside from photographs, most of the testimony regarding Wills comes from newspaper accounts. At the height of boxing, newspapers often reported fights in great detail. Reporters composed their eyewitness accounts as the action took place. It made for exciting journalism prone to exaggeration. With newspapers hitting the streets just hours after events and no time to review fight films, the initial press reports of major fights were usually hasty impressions slanted toward popular sentiment. In any case, the accounts of Wills's fights were more than favorable. The condescending and blatantly racist narratives published in Jack Johnson's era were no longer en vogue by the time Wills contended. The press liked Wills and championed his cause. The accounts of his battles describe him as an exciting, skilled, and powerful fighter. But one valuable cache of evidence has remained missing—film footage.

For almost a century, the only accessible Wills fight footage, issued by Official Films as part of a series called *Monarchs of the Ring*, showed him in 1927 at age thirty-eight being clubbed to the canvas by Paulino Uzcudun in a fourth-round-knockout loss. Several newsreels from British and American archives also survive, showing Wills posing and sparring for the cameras prior to the Firpo bout. These provided a glimpse of his size and stance, but little else, leaving people to wonder about Wills's true abilities. The real breakthrough occurred in 2012, when boxing film archivist Steve Lott received a call from a woman living on Long Island who wanted him to identify some film she found stored in her attic labeled "Wills and others." She agreed to send him the footage for inspection. When Lott received the package it contained two reels of thirty-five-millimeter theatrical film on nitrate stock. The materials, in marginal condition, were carefully transferred to digital video. The footage showed excerpts of two fights: the Mickey Walker–Mike McTigue middleweight title match and the Wills-Firpo fight.

Though the reel contained only the first two rounds of Wills-Firpo, the footage has been a revelation. Remarkably well photographed, the film captures the match with amazing clarity for the period. From it, we finally get a good, if brief, look at Wills's skills and style, a true reading of what he could do inside the ring. Promoted as a clash of the titans, Firpo and Wills was anticipated to be an exciting display of punching power, but the match went the full distance. The fight has since been described as one of Wills's best performances and one of his best credentials for holding his own with or even defeating Dempsey.

The film, however, tells an unflattering story. In keeping with Jack Johnson's old-school stance, the one Dempsey would likely rip through, Wills holds his hands forward at waist level, with a pawing left jab and his feet spread wide for maximum balance and stability. But Wills was no Jack Johnson. Wills's footwork was limited, and he didn't have Johnson's speed or savvy to control the action. Firpo did little in this fight to enhance his own reputation, predictably launching one overhand right after another while Wills slipped them, though some just barely. Other than dodging punches, however, Wills had no tactical response to Firpo. He could make Firpo miss those broadly telegraphed overhand rights, but he couldn't make him pay for missing. The two spent most of the fight in clinches, dragging one another around the ring. The much-noted knockdown came in round two, when, the United Press reported, "Wills floored Firpo with a right to the jaw. When Firpo arose Wills swarmed him with a flock of rights." This sequence makes for better reading than viewing. The film shows Wills hitting Firpo illegally on a break. Firpo drops, but rises more surprised than hurt. The action resumes, with Firpo crowding Wills, and Wills struggling for punching room. The footage suggests that Wills was either a very slow starter, or as Firpo himself put it, "more of a wrestler than a boxer." Wills's greatest asset may simply have been the height and reach advantage he had over the majority of his opponents.

In addition to the Wills-Firpo excerpt, further film evidence of Wills has come to light. Footage from a European archive shows Wills's fight prior to Firpo, against Irish veteran Bartley Madden in

1924. Madden, who had also fought Harry Greb, Gene Tunney, Fred Fulton, and Tommy Gibbons, brought respectable ring experience to the fight. Wills-Madden went fifteen rounds, with Wills the easy winner. But even this victory exposed some of Wills's weaknesses. In the film, Wills, again the much bigger man, stalks Madden aggressively, but Madden has little difficulty evading Wills or quickly closing the distance to score on the inside. This vulnerability would have been fatal against a puncher like Dempsey.

Dempsey and Wills were also much closer in size than has been suggested. Wills had twenty pounds and three inches at best on Dempsey, still only half as much as Willard and little more than Firpo—two men Dempsey dispatched in less than four rounds each. In addition to his superior speed, mobility, and success against larger opponents, Dempsey sparred and trained with Big Bill Tate. A heavyweight contender who stood six feet six and weighed 220 pounds, Tate had been hired by Doc Kearns in 1918 and remained in the Dempsey camp until Jack's retirement in 1927. During those years, Tate continued fighting professionally. In fact, his resume lists five fights with Harry Wills, including a knockout loss, two close decision losses, a draw, and a win. Had a Dempsey-Wills fight actually gone forward, Tate's tactical experience with Wills would have helped Dempsey substantially. It's important to note that two of Tate's best showings against Wills, a disqualification win and a draw, came in 1922, the same year Wills first proposed to challenge Dempsey for the title. One has to wonder—what does it say that one man's difficult opponent is another man's sparring partner?

Hall of Fame trainer Ray Arcel witnessed both Wills and Dempsey in action as early as 1916. Arcel, who lived long enough to train both Benny Leonard and Roberto Duran, had apprenticed with Wills's trainer Dai Dollings. Arcel told author Phil Guarnieri that Harry Wills was surely deserving of a title shot but was also at best "a very good journeyman" who was too slow and did not hit hard enough to deal with Dempsey.

Although Harry Wills deserved a title shot in the 1920s, to include his experience in the pantheon of great boxing misfortunes is to ignore a number of key factors. First, Wills was no better than any of the other Black Lights, one of too many African American fighters to count who were denied a title shot because of the color line. Second, had he fought Dempsey, he would likely have lost badly. Third, the failure to hold a Dempsey-Wills match may have raised public consciousness and thus helped to open the doors to Joe Louis's emergence and historic reign as heavyweight champion a decade later, which forever made the division open to African American contenders and champions. Fourth, Wills had a good life after boxing. He and his wife were successful business partners, and, with the help of the $50,000 advance he received for a fight with Dempsey that never happened, he prospered more than the majority of African Americans. Finally, nobody "avoided" Wills. Dempsey wanted to fight him, but the bout was more a risk for promoters than for the champion. "I never blamed Jack," Wills was quoted as saying in a 1964 *Sports Illustrated* profile. "I'm sure if he had had his way, I'd have gotten the fight."

MY FIRST STRIPE

Robert Anasi

A slim black woman around forty stepped onto the subway car at the East Broadway station. My trainer scanned her anatomy from the floor on up and grinned.

"Hey," Daryl said. "How you doing?"

She didn't answer.

"You got a smile for me today?" he said.

Silence.

"C'mon, just a smile."

The woman looked away, at the handrail, the tunnel, empty space, anything but us. Louie was sweating her just as hard: up . . . down; up . . . down; up . . . down.

Adam, my second for the night, turned to Daryl.

"Maybe," Adam said, "she ain't smiling 'cause she don't got no teeth."

The three of them laughed and high-fived over my head.

Adam was a Puerto Rican of the New York City variety, which meant his occasional Spanish was all of the Caribbean and Lower East Side away from lisping Madrid. At eighteen, his handsome was near pretty, baby fat still nesting under his smooth cheeks. Adam was finicky in a way that bordered on neurotic: he kept his gear spotless and was always stroking his fade in the gym mirrors. Yet he was by far the best of Daryl's boxers, a lot better than me, even though we'd started at the same time. Adam could drop *Wall Street Journal* English when it suited him, but he was from Avenue D and had no problem flexing his street cred.

I didn't raise my hand in salute to the male gaze: suppressed panic didn't make for easy machismo. A black guy, a white guy, and two Nuyoricans (half-Italian Louie pledged allegiance to his father's people) were going to a show at Gleason's and it was the white guy who was fighting. That didn't make any kind of sense.

The F train accelerated toward Brooklyn, and Daryl turned serious.

"In the first I want you to be careful," he said. "Use your jab and work your defense. Remember, you can't think about what he's gonna do because you don't know what he's gonna do. You got to think about what you're gonna do."

I nodded. Jab? My jab was an ill-timed slap. Defense? I couldn't slip a punch launched from Westchester. In the ring, I'd paw at some equally deficient sparring partner and when one of us finally landed a hard shot, completely by accident, we'd rush at each other, swinging to kill. After my most recent sparring session, Adam had caught me as I left the ring. "You looked like a zoo full of monkeys in there," he said.

The only thing I could control was my weight. We'd signed up to fight at 132, and when I stepped on the medical scale at Julio's Gym an hour earlier, I'd weighed 132 exactly. I'd starved for a week in fear of that number and since it was still hours before the fight, I ran around the corner to Ninth Street Falafel. When I stepped on the scale again, I was four ounces of chickpea and pita heavier: 132¼. Daryl shrugged at the news. "You can always jump rope in the dressing room and work it off," he said. I didn't understand his equanimity—what if I was disqualified? What if I had to fight in a higher weight class? The next weight class up was light welterweight, and light welter held giants: Thomas Hearns had been national Golden Gloves champ at light welter and he was six feet one. Six feet one! Tommy Hearns! What if I had to face his latest incarnation?

The train rose from East River muck, upward slope gently pressing us into the plastic seats. There was no escape. I didn't want to fight, not right then, not that night. I'd changed my mind. Not today, thank you. It was one thing to get shoved in a bar and leap up in fury, another to count down the hours toward your execution. Time erodes courage like Chinese water torture—drip, drip, drip. I could have been talking to a pretty girl in my favorite café, working on an article, looking for a better job than part-time drywall framing. There was no obvious reason for me to be there. Boxing wasn't a family tradition like it was for Louie. I didn't plan on turning pro the way that Adam did. I was boxing because there was something wrong with me. And that night I was going to be punished for it.

Daryl tapped my arm, his eyes dark brown and oval, his lashes camel long. Bedroom eyes on a weathered face, a scar in a curving arc over his left brow, skin the color of milk chocolate and the first joint missing from the little finger of his right hand. His smile also lacked something—two front teeth catty-corner, top and bottom. Five feet three on a tall day, Daryl ran maintenance in a Midtown building and lived with a woman named Peaches who always answered his phone on the first ring. No matter the time of day, Peaches talked sweet and seemed gloriously inebriated. On my first day at Julio's, Daryl had told me he "saw something" in me and that he'd train me for free. It was the tender coupling of twin delusions, but nine months later that something remained nothing. I'd put myself in his hands, and we'd failed each other.

When I first walked into a boxing gym sometime after my twenty-fourth birthday, I was only a casual fan. After my second viewing of *Rocky* at age twelve, I ran home with my brother shouting the theme song and punching air. I'd seen a couple of the great middleweight and welterweight fights of the 1980s and, along with the rest of my generation, absorbed the legend of Muhammad Ali. My uncle, a neighborhood tough guy, had boxed in the army and had a heavy bag in his garage, three houses away from mine. Sometimes I'd cross the street, put on his stiff bag gloves and whale away until my fists went numb. That was as far as it ever went, especially as I came to hate jock culture. Instead of going to practice for some sport after classes,

I rode the bus downtown and hung out with the theater kids from the college-prep high school. In my college town, there was room for teenagers who had Mohawks, dropped acid, and hated Ronald Reagan. Theater geeks and punk rockers: those were my people; slam dancing: that was my contact sport. Boxing didn't even register as an option until a bad year in San Francisco when I was twenty-four.

The subway car deposited us at the dreary York Street station. I had time to think on the long walk from the platform, up the corridor with dingy tiles bordered in purple. Banks of black-and-white video monitors provided views of the tracks and corridor, the monitors a weak placebo for commuter fears of robbery, rape, and murder. We left the drab yellow-brick ventilation tower and stepped into the night under the vast shadows of the Manhattan Bridge. Daryl was still coaching—I had to move to my right, away from the power hand, make sure my lead foot was on the outside. He said something about throwing combinations and something else about staying focused but the words buzzed away into white noise. I'd heard it all before, many times, but that didn't mean I could do it. Adam interrupted with his usual encouragement.

"Just don't go through the canvas," he said.

That was the paralyzing fear—getting knocked out. Losing was bad but to have the referee count over you as you lay dazed or unconscious while the guy who'd dropped you pumped his gloves and preened before his friends, and people in the crowd laughed and nudged each other, yelling, "He fucked that kid *up*!" That fear lurked every time you stepped into the ring, even during sparring sessions. I'd seen it happen at Julio's—a shout turning you away from the punching bag as some muscular teenager was led from the ring. Minutes earlier he'd been all speed and braggadocio, but now he wobbled on shaky legs like a toddler with a full diaper. Getting KO'd was castration with a blunt scalpel.

Dumbo was a new frontier in the Brooklyn real estate stampede but at night it remained an eerie place. Friends of mine had art studios in the warehouses along Water Street but two blocks north loomed the dark towers of the Farragut projects. When I took the bus to Gleason's, I got off at the plaza in front of the highest tower as unfriendly eyes tracked the lone white boy with his gym bag moving south, past the only two legal neighborhood businesses—a C-Town supermarket gutted by arson and a liquor store with bottles behind bulletproof Plexiglas.

"You got to be the boss out there," Daryl said, his voice loud in the vacant street. "Remember, this is only a kid you're fighting. Seventeen, eighteen, probably. What are you, twenty-nine?"

I nodded.

"Well, there you go," Daryl said, slapping me on the arm. "You got to run out there and . . ."

He pumped his fist into an imaginary midsection. ". . . Mess that child up!"

Adam and Louie snickered, and Daryl laughed.

"Am I right or am I right?" Daryl asked. "Kid's probably a virgin. You ain't a virgin. You're a full-grown man!"

At our feet, asphalt ebbed away from nineteenth-century cobblestones, the warehouses shuttered for the night, the Manhattan Bridge on titanic columns roaring like an active volcano. Mist from the East River crept over the seawall, turning Dumbo into the Brooklyn waterfront of legend and the perfect site for a boxing gym.

We reached the unmarked entrance just as a van with the logo of a South Bronx boxing club pulled up and disgorged a cadre of Latin and black teenagers. The fighters wore green windbreakers blazoned with the same club logo; they had all the energy of a team before a match, talking loud and cracking wise in tough-guy poses as they pushed toward the door, a wizened trainer shouting in their wake.

Louie, Adam, Daryl, and I trailed them, no matching windbreakers, no team spirit. At the top of the wide warehouse staircase, I noticed a quote painted across the wall: "Now, whoever has courage and a strong and collected spirit in his breast let him come forward, lace on the gloves and put up his hands.—Virgil."

Louie followed my gaze.

"Wow," he said. "Virgil Hill talks as smart as he fights."

This wasn't some neighborhood club or church basement: my

audition was at Gleason's, New York City's fistic omphalos since the city fathers shuttered the Times Square Gym in 1995. So many of the great old gyms had closed—Times Square, Stillman's up on Eighth Avenue and Fifty-Fourth, Cus D'Amato's Gramercy Gym, the Fifth Street Gym in Miami. By 1997, boxing had been expiring for a long time, a drawn-out death rattle as Americans gave up the blue-collar pastimes of cities for suburbs and the big-three team sports on television. Still, Gleason's endured (although it had moved from the Bronx to Brooklyn). Every champion and contender who came to town climbed that staircase: Mike Tyson, Riddick Bowe, Julio Cesar Chavez, Hector Camacho; every New York pro headed for Madison Square Garden jumped rope, shadowboxed, and sparred there.

Gleason's might have been the most famous boxing gym in the world, but it was makeshift and squalid: plumbing exposed, windows crusted with grime. Fluorescent strips hung over gouged pine floors and the heavily taped bags looked like they'd been stuffed with pro-sected torsos. After registering, I stripped to my briefs, weighed in at 132—the quarter pound fretted away—and put my clothes back on. The doctor checked my blood pressure and asked me if I'd been KO'd in the last six months: I hadn't.

Back in the hall, the trainers greeted each other while the fighters hung quietly behind them. At the check-in table, officials and trainers juggled our "books." In order to compete, amateur fighters have to buy a license from US Amateur Boxing, Inc., which provides a passport-size white "book" with a photo and a record in place of customs stamps. Each decision inked on the pages was another border you'd crossed. The trainers played three-dimensional chess with the books, trying to find easy marks.

Daryl sidled over to the table and eyeballed the fanned documents exactly like a flea-market rube afraid of being taken for a sucker. He'd promised not to match me against someone with more experience—a difficult promise to keep since that ruled out pretty much everyone. In our nine months together, Daryl hadn't asked for a cent, motivated entirely by the fantasy that I'd become a champion. He paced the table, picking up books then slowly relinquishing them.

One book lingered in his hand, and after a brief conversation with the officials he called me over.

"This OK?" he said, presenting the book.

I looked at a photo-booth glossy of a scowling Latino with a thick neck and zero fights. Brian Garcia had weighed in at 134, and I suddenly understood why Daryl didn't care if I was over 132. This wasn't a tournament but a show, and in shows fighters were matched by relative weights, not by weight class. Daryl had only told me to make '32 to keep me away from McDonald's and Krispy Kreme.

"Sure," I said. It was the only answer I could give. Yet I was already worrying about the two-pound difference.

The other fighter's trainer was still negotiating the table. The man had aged in the way the thin and fit do—by desiccating, his face and neck all ridged veins and parchment skin. A flattened nose said "former fighter."

"So," Daryl said, presenting my book. "Your guy hasn't had a lot of junior fights, you know, like in the PAL [Police Athletic League]?"

The Mummy smiled beatifically.

"The kid," he said, "is green as grass."

I couldn't guess the Mummy's ethnicity—not with his version of English being more General American than mine. He could have been a light-skinned Nuyorican or a holdover from some ethnicity that preceded the Latinos and had all but faded away. (I never did find out why the trainer of a Bronx boxing team sounded like a newscaster from Tacoma.)

The two men exchanged polite words, nodded at each other, and we walked away.

"I know this guy from before," Daryl muttered as we headed toward the dressing room. "And I don't trust him."

Daryl was not making me feel better.

His suspicion didn't surprise me. Every trainer is always looking for an edge and would be more than happy to put a junior champion with two hundred fights into the ring with, say, me. An amateur boxer's record resets to a clean 0–0 when he turns seventeen, no matter how many fights he's had as a junior. And that's just US fighters. Latin

American boxers often turn pro by fifteen, and if you have thirty pro rounds under your belt in Oaxaca when you walk into a Harlem gym and claim to be a novice, well, your book will still read 0–0. I'd seen brutal mismatches at this level and did not want to be on the wrong end of one of them.

"He pulled some shit with me before," Daryl said. "Got one of my guys messed up. Thing is, he's a crap trainer. If I had all the guys he does . . ."

I'd never heard one New York trainer bestow a good word on another, at least not after the backslaps and smiles. As a relatively honest trainer put it to me, "I blow sunshine up their asses, just like they do up mine." First came that puff of rectal effulgence, inevitably followed by the knife in the back—all of it as petty, hypocritical, and vicious as a small-town beauty pageant. The hostility made plenty of sense. In boxing, a conviction of invulnerability was essential: no amateur stepped through the ropes unless he thought he had a chance. The trainer did everything he could to convince you that he made the best fighters. If, god forbid, one of his guys lost, it was by ludicrous accident or base treachery at the hands of corrupt or incompetent officials. Yet this attitude made it nearly impossible to learn from mistakes and was the main reason why so many fighters were demolished in lopsided fights. The same conviction of superiority extended to the teammates, to the girlfriends and to all the hangers-on. Your guy was the greatest, until he wasn't. Then a switch flipped and the team decided that their guy lacked heart, or didn't listen, or was lazy, or didn't have the killer instinct. He'd failed his crew and bruised the egos that had attached to his body. So they all walked away in disgust, forgetting who suffered the real injuries.

"Get changed and we'll do a warm-up," Daryl said. "Hurry. They could call us any time."

I was lonely as I'd ever been as I walked back to the dressing room. Sitting on a wobbly two-plank bench, I donned my dime-store wifebeater and the tacky pair of blue-and-gold shorts I'd ordered from the *Ringside* catalog. The shorts were a decade out of style and exposed my cadaverous legs to mid-thigh. I might as well have been naked.

"You ready?" Daryl said.

"I'm good," I said.

Daryl eyed the shorts but didn't say anything. It would be a few more fights until someone was kind enough to tell me how preposterous they were: "Rob," I was succinctly informed, "if they ain't long, they wrong."

I didn't start boxing because my old man made me or because I was from Mexico or Cuba where fighters were national icons; I started boxing because I was angry, and I was angry because I'd been castrated (figuratively, let me make clear). The castration, what Aristotle might have called the "material cause," came from getting dumped by my beautiful, charming, spoiled college girlfriend. Her father, a Depression-forged Hollywood tough guy, decided after our first meeting that I was area codes away from being man enough for her. "I'll take that boy seriously when he puts a fur coat on your back," he said. She eventually agreed with daddy but then so did I—her father was only broadcasting what I whispered to myself, whispers that said I would always be a failure. When she ran off to LA to be an actress, I was devastated but not surprised: the whispers said that it was exactly what I deserved. All my boozing and yelling came down to a terror of having my inadequacy exposed, a reason Aristotle would consider the "formal cause."

My fear went deep. As a toddler, I attacked my younger brothers because I thought my mother loved them more than she loved me. In nursery school, I bludgeoned other kids with the blocks and toys they wanted to share. By the third grade, I was spending as much time in the principal's office as I was on the playground. My father was as threatened by his sons as I was by my brothers and ran our house like a North Korean labor camp: imprisoning us in our bedrooms, rationing our food, driving us to escape. Intimidating us was his avocation—shouting, staring, and shuffling his feet in irritation, along with the occasional smack-down while my mother temporized. I suffered the abuse because I couldn't conceive of another option: his shadow circumscribed my universe.

Not growing to a size that befit my anger spared me a career as a first-class bully. By the sixth grade, most boys were bigger than me, often a lot bigger, and the bullies found their way to a natural target: Anasi, the bully manqué. Small and extremely nearsighted, I hid in books but even intellectual aggression provided a Day-Glo trail for the bullies to follow. In the sixth grade, I laughed when Sister Mary Catherine insisted that the moon was bigger than Mars. "But it is bigger," she snapped. "You can tell that by looking at them in the sky." When I proceeded to quote the approximate radii of both objects, the class fell silent. Every afternoon for the next three days, the largest boys in my class took turns jumping me. Not because of my disrespect to Sister MC per se, but because I didn't know when to shut up; I didn't know my place

By my sophomore year of high school, I was running every night after sit-ups and pull-ups, five to six miles on pavement in flat Chuck Taylors (yes, I got shin splints). Doing the most pull-ups in gym didn't help with the bullies: a varsity hockey player marked me as the perfect victim and tracked me down to bounce me off lockers, break my fingers, choke me to the edge of blackout. Punishing kids like me was considered his perk by the school administration, never mind the two years, four inches, and thirty pounds between us. As I walked home one night in my neighborhood, I saw him standing in front of a local bar. "This is the time," I decided. I'd heard the mantra that bullies are actually cowards, cowards who will wilt in the face of manly opposition. So I went up to him, shook his hand, and then asked him why he harassed me so much. My next memory was of rising from the pavement. The hockey player had disappeared. "I warned you not to do that," a classmate said. As the previous five minutes had been erased, I had no idea of what he'd warned me not to do. I just laughed and said, "What an asshole." I never found out what happened, but my jaw ached for a week.

When I walked into my first gym in San Francisco's Tenderloin at twenty-four, the owner, old Bernie, planted me in front of a heavy bag. Bernie was as frail as a potato chip, but he'd been a solid club fighter in some remote past before the hippie days. That afternoon I hit the heavy bag until I couldn't lift my arms and sweat inscribed a greasy circle around me on the floor. It was utterly satisfying, even though Bernie cackled at my ridiculous form. For me, it was a revelation: I didn't just like hitting things; I loved hitting things. Over the following months, I went to the gym four days a week to follow Bernie's parsimonious instruction—two steps forward, jab, two steps back—and looked up to see him still laughing from his glass-walled office. All the satisfaction of the heavy bag didn't keep the stakes from rising. Once you start on the bags you want to spar, and once you start sparring you want to fight. My skills didn't advance with my enthusiasm but I couldn't resist doubling down after every half step forward. It was the only way that I wouldn't despise myself when I said, "Oh yeah, I box a little."

Over the next four years, I never complained. Not when I got knocked down for the first time by an Irish kickboxer with a ginger beard. Not when a Junior Olympian broke my ribs. I was determined to pay until I could pass the bill to someone else, but it was taking long enough to seem like forever.

"Keep moving around him," Daryl said. "Don't let him get inside of you. Bring your left back quick after you throw a punch. Move."

It didn't seem like he had ever stopped talking.

At shows, the fighters arrive early and languish in the dirty locker rooms. After the weigh-in and the doctor and the matchmaking there's nothing left but the misery of waiting. Daryl told me to sit down, close my eyes, take a nap if I could. He chuckled.

"We've seen guys crumble before a fight," he said. "Ain't that right, Louie?"

Louie chuckled agreement. Slumped on the bench, I roller-coastered through frontiers of anticipation. A rush of adrenaline would come bringing thoughts of what I should do, visions of defeat, victory, random words coupled in nonsense rhymes. Then the wave would subside and I'd slump until the next hot surge set me shaking. It was like waiting for a firing squad, the only difference being that I'd volunteered to be executed.

On the bench beside me, Louie leafed through a back issue of *Fangoria*. A chunky twenty-three year-old with olive-gray skin and a perpetual grin, Louie was an interesting case. Although I'd never seen him train, he was in the gym almost every night. Two of his uncles had been local pros and he'd grown up around boxing. Like Adam, he was from the Avenue D projects and Julio's offered him a social club and daytime soap opera.

"Check this out!" Louie said, almost shouting as he pointed to the magazine. "They used real pig intestines in the scene!"

I tried to focus on a sequence of stills from *Dawn of the Dead* that involved the disembowelment of an unfortunate Hell's Angel in a shopping mall. As we marveled over George Romero's sanguinary verisimilitude, Louie revealed his master plan: he, Louie Villegas, was on the verge of directing his first horror film.

"I'm finally putting it all together," he said. "This summer I'm going to shoot a feature. It's called *Gangsta Zombies of the Lower East Side*. I got the script. I got the camera. I got the crew."

Louie's grin reached out and grabbed his ears.

"You can be in it! I've got a part that will be perfect for you."

"Sounds great," I said. "I've actually done some acting."

"It's on!" Louie said and shook my hand.

Word dribbled back to the dressing room: all the muttering and plotting of the trainers had produced a total of six fights for the night. Six fights, despite the fact that five teams and a dozen unaffiliated strays had appeared at Gleason's. With all their machinations, the trainers had outsmarted themselves. Anyone who paid the ten-dollar door fee would see fewer than twenty rounds of amateur fisticuffs. A few minutes later, a USA Boxing official dressed all in white limped over to Daryl.

"You guys are up first," he said. "Ten minutes."

Daryl bolted into motion. After massaging my fingers, he wrapped my hands tight, never stopping with the advice.

"Use the first round to figure him out," he said. "After that, be more aggressive. You don't have a lot of time so you want to throw. Don't try for a one-punch KO. You need to score: punches in bunches."

I nodded. I'd never figured anyone out. Telling me to "figure out" someone was like tossing a second grader Euclid's *Elements* in first period and instructing him to derive ax = bc by recess.

I blamed Daryl because it was easier than blaming myself. The truth was, Daryl really cared; training us was what he did with the biggest part of his life that didn't involve a paycheck. The first time I called his home number, Peaches already knew my name. "Robert!" she said. "This is Robert?!" Peaches was happy to hear from me. In the gym we never talked about our lives outside but Daryl, it seemed, went home and bragged on us. Somewhere in his late thirties, Daryl had accepted middle age, his muscular belly approaching second trimester in arc and size. He spent weeknights and all of Saturday at Julio's, gossiping, arguing, and putting his motley team through the paces. Because his fighters—with the exception of Adam—didn't win, the other trainers didn't show him respect. The civilized ones stayed quiet but the shit talkers, the angry barbarians, shot him down every chance they got. "That guy has crap for fighters." "He ruined that kid." "Oh, not this clown again." Always when he was out of earshot, but just. For any one of his fighters, he'd toddle off to the most distant corners of the five boroughs or even to the blue-collar suburbs of Long Island, all for a chance at a "W." In his best moods, he'd deliver gruff advice about romance and deportment: "I know you young guys don't like to wear T-shirts under your button-downs, but you can catch a chill that way. Plus the sweat stains will fuck up your Oxfords."

Daryl did have an edge though, usually concealed but razor-sharp when it flashed—the edge you needed to grow up small in Harlem. One day he took that edge to my face, a lesson he must have thought I needed. Although he never mentioned his own boxing career, on that night he had me stand opposite him and told me to avoid his jab. Or try to, anyway. He had surprisingly long arms on his squat frame and his up-jab was sneaky fast. I tried to slip or block, but almost every one of his jabs punctured my guard and snapped my head back. I laughed and swore on the way to a bloody nose and went home impressed by his speed. Yet the experience was more performance than seminar. Daryl had demonstrated that he could yo-yo my head but I hadn't learned a thing about slipping punches. Whatever lesson he was trying to impart, it was one that I couldn't absorb.

Back out in the main hall, Daryl led me to the shadows under a staircase and pulled on a pair of training mitts.

"Let's work some combinations," he said.

Not only was it the first time he'd worked me with mitts, it was the first time I'd ever used them.

"Jab, two three," he said. "Two three four. Double jab. Two three, two three! One two four!"

I tried to throw fast and hard, to catch a rhythm, but with every combination my punches went awry. After I hooked, Daryl swept a mitt toward my head expecting me to slip under it. Instead the mitt clanked against my head.

Behind me, I heard laughter. A few yards away, the Bronx-team soldiers were pointing out my struggles as they bumped shoulders and snickered. I didn't understand why Daryl had picked that moment to do mitts for the first time.

"That's enough for now," Daryl said. My hands dropped to my sides. We were minutes away from the ring.

"Don't worry about that," Daryl whispered. "I made you look bad so that the other guy would be overconfident."

You could have landed an Airbus in my open mouth. I didn't know what was worse—the possibility that he'd made me look bad on purpose, or the possibility that I was so terrible my own trainer couldn't make me look good and "I made you look bad" was the best lie he could come up with. Both options were equally devastating.

In a row of seats closest to the staircase, I saw the Mummy wrapping Brian Garcia's hands. Instead of the standard-issue cotton hand wraps used for sparring, the Mummy was swaddling Garcia with gauze: gauze, the stuff of pros. I wanted to shake Daryl and demand the same treatment. Maybe gauze was the final part of the boxing equation, the secret weapon that would make my punches harder, straighter, faster. Not only was Garcia two pounds heavier than me, he also had a secret weapon hidden in his gloves, tightly wound gauze that would turn his fists into dynamite.

Then it was time.

I was helpless, something else moving my limbs as I floated toward the ring on noise from a house suddenly full, a house waiting for blood, their sacrifice, me. As we reached the ring apron, Adam shouted in my ear.

"Just fuck him up," he said. "I hope you fucking kill him."

The words comforted me. An arrogant punk from the Bronx had made me suffer and now I was allowed to hit him in the face as hard as I could and I wouldn't get into trouble, not even if he died.

Garcia waited on the other side of the ring. He might have been an inch shorter than me, but his bulging pecs split the Puerto Rican flag on his wife-beater in two. As I stared across the ring, he boomed his gloves together.

"He's just trying to scare you," Daryl said with a snarl.

It worked: I was scared. Time had stopped, and all I could do was wait. I'd been carried to that point by a mechanism over which I had no control. Now the mechanism had halted and I would stumble into the spotlight on my own, chicken legs and all.

"Don't go out and touch gloves with that motherfucker," Daryl said. "That's pro shit. You run out there and hit him as hard as you fucking can."

As the referee spoke the ritual phrases at ring center—"clean fight," "obey my orders"—Garcia tried to lock eyes with me. I looked back at him, as surprised by the stare as if a stranger on Fifth Avenue had tapped me on the shoulder; in New York City, you never stared into the eyes of a stranger because bad things could happen. Daryl had told me to focus on the space between his eyes if I couldn't meet them. New York habit almost turned my gaze away but then I remembered, "I'm fighting this guy." Our gazes met and meshed and ground together. Less than a second later, his shifted to the floor. Staring at his exposed face, I saw the tough guy I'd seen in the photo and a boy too young to be taken seriously (his book said he was nineteen; his face said he didn't shave yet). I felt empathy—he was suffering as much as I was. But for the first time, I also felt strong.

The bell rang, and I trotted toward the center of the ring, straight into an overhand right. My nose detonated in a shower of blood and I reeled back in pain, shock, humiliation, the roar from the crowd an intense pressure vibrating in the air. Garcia followed up with wild punches but the big shot had erased my fears and I started to hit back. Thirty seconds into the round, I drove him into a corner. I wanted to kill the stranger who had been so rude. Trapped against the ropes, he covered his face with his gloves and crouched low.

"Break!" The referee shouted. "Break!"

Because Garcia wasn't fighting back the referee wanted to give him a standing-eight count, but rage had made me a lunatic. I kept hitting Garcia until the referee hooked my left arm and marched me to a neutral corner. While I stood there seething, he deducted a point from me for not following instructions. Seconds later, I was on the kid again. It was like being in a nightmare and being the nightmare. Through the adrenaline whirl, idle thoughts drifted through my mind like slow clouds on a summer day: the blood dappling the back of Garcia's shirt—was it his or mine? Would it be OK if I pretended to throw a hook and hit him with my elbow instead? Was Garcia just trying to make me overconfident? In this new articulation of time, a two-minute round seemed to go on for hours.

We did little boxing and much brawling. Garcia kept hitting me in the groin, and the referee deducted another point, this time from him. Great fights have dramatic tension that elevates the violence to something sacred. We spun like two roosters in a dusty yard until the round finally ended.

I went back to my corner, and Daryl swabbed blood from the mess of my face.

"This guy is nothing," I said between gasps. "He's mine."

The words were stupid but true. The first shot had set me free from all fear, from anything but the next punch. My will was crushing Garcia as his will shrunk away. The punches I'd taken and the public spectacle had lifted me up to the Himalayas. I could keep hitting

Brian Garcia and the more I hit him, the more people would cheer. I couldn't wait for the next bell so I could run out and hit him again.

Daryl agreed.

"He don't want to fight," he said.

It turned out that he didn't. The bell rang and I pummeled Garcia until the referee separated us and deducted another point for low blows, punches I never felt. We clinched and punched—throwing elbows, butting, shoving—until Garcia surrendered, crouching in his shell while I used him as a punching bag. The referee pulled me away but I didn't know that I had won my first fight on a TKO even when I saw Louie leap into the air while boos descended from the Bronx team.

As I left the ring, Bruce Silverglade, Gleason's Machiavelli, met me on the apron.

"Congratulations," he said, handing me a watch with "Gleason's Gym" inscribed on the face.

The trinket was a throwback to an era when amateur boxers received prizes of actual value after their matches—a good watch, cufflinks, silk ties. They didn't call it "prize fighting" for nothing. In the Great Depression, there were so many amateur cards at so many clubs across the boroughs that teenagers could fight four or five nights a week. Many fighters delayed turning pro because their purses wouldn't equal what they could get by selling or pawning the prizes.

I sent the watch to my father for his birthday. It never kept time and after a week it stopped.

In the steaming gray murk of the Gleason's showers, I rinsed away sweat and blood. Back in the dressing room, Garcia and the Mummy were waiting at my stall.

"Good fight! Good fight!" Garcia repeated as he pumped my hand, a smile parked on his round face.

"You don't want to come out slow like that," he said. "It made you easy to hit."

He wasn't wrong but it seemed strange for him to be the person saying it.

I found my crew watching the fourth fight. Adam and Louie sat me down between them and took turns smacking my shoulders and called me "Killer."

"Yeah," Louie said. "That's how you do."

"It gets easier," Adam said. "First is the worst."

He presented his fist. We dapped and I was a monkey no more, one rung up the Ladder of Evolution. As always, winning was much better than losing.

When the fight ended, Daryl stood up.

"I have to take off," he said. "Got to be in the office at seven."

He grabbed my arm with the thirteen joints of his right hand.

"You did a great job out there," he said.

Louie and Adam rose with him. They'd come out for the team, and it was time to move on. I felt displaced. I'd never won a fight before and didn't know what happened next.

Daryl scanned the crowd and then leaned closed.

"Those guys on the other team are really fucking pissed," he whispered.

"They're talking about jumping you outside. You better take off before the last fight."

I didn't understand. I'd won. That was supposed to be the end. The Mummy and Garcia had shaken my hand. We were all friends now. Besides, if there was a real problem, then why didn't Daryl tell me I should leave with him? The joy that came with victory was already turning into something else.

Through the first round of the next match, I scanned the room for threats. I couldn't spot Garcia or the Mummy or any of the Bronx jackets. Maybe they were already outside waiting for me. When the bell rang for round three, I headed toward the street, looking over my shoulder until I reached the subway.

The F train took me to friends on Ludlow Street and I kept drinking margaritas even though the first sip tasted like piss. In the barroom mirrors, I noticed that someone had stuck a bright-red clown nose on my face. I looked like I'd been crying for hours. Five margaritas didn't get me drunk and I felt too ugly to flirt so I sat watching my friends have fun. Past the polite "How did it go?" and the puzzled head shakes, none of them asked about the fight. Their world shared no connections to the world of boxing. For them, boxing was an idiosyncrasy, about on a level with collecting Star Wars action figures.

When I finally arrived home at 169th Street and Broadway, the phone was ringing.

"Yo Robert," a voice said.

"Daryl?" I said. The missing teeth always skewed his speech, but his words were more slurred than usual.

"How you doing man?" he said.

"I'm OK."

"I was feeling fine," he said. "So I stopped for a nightcap. Now I'm feeling even better."

Despite his dawn alarm, he'd managed to get drunk at his local on the block between the 6 train and his East Harlem apartment.

"You know," he said. "You did a lot of good things out there. You showed me something. You showed everybody something tonight."

"Thanks Daryl," I said. "You're the guy who made it all happen."

The words were banal but we were close. I wondered if Peaches was sledding through Dreamland toward that dawn alarm, or if she was hovering in the background waiting for her man to come to bed. In the gym, Daryl and I shared a real intimacy but it ended there. When I invited him to my parties he didn't come, and he didn't invite me to his. A few months earlier, I'd given him a bottle of Johnny Walker Blue for New Year's but there was a line between us that only failure or success could break. That night, we'd touched the line.

Daryl stayed on the phone, in the right mood to offer advice. That cute French girl I'd brought into the gym, well, it was all right to have fun, but I shouldn't let women take up too much of my time. He said I needed to find a serious job, one with benefits, as long as it didn't affect my training. He said there was no limit to what I could do in the world of boxing.

"You know the Olympic Trials are coming up," he said. "A couple of more fights like that and you'll be ready."

I didn't know much about boxing but I did know that Daryl was drunk. Still, the fact that I'd made him happy let me bask in his delusion. For once, I hadn't been a disappointment. A couple of more fights, then the Olympic Trials, sure, why not? It had taken four years to make my way into the ring and I knew that at twenty-eight, I was an old man in boxing. But for the rest of the night, I wouldn't let that worry me. No matter what happened next, I'd done it. I'd finally earned a stripe.

JIMMY BIVINS AND THE DURATION CHAMPIONSHIP

Louis Moore

Jimmy Bivins, who fought at a time when Americans supposedly closed ranks and rallied around democracy, not to mention the black heavyweight hero Joe Louis, was one of the most hated fighters of his era. In his fifteen-year career he took on the very best competition from middleweight to heavyweight and defeated several top fighters, including Charley Burley, Ezzard Charles, Joey Maxim, Archie Moore, and Lloyd Marshall. Despite great charisma, an appealing ring style, and a four-year undefeated streak between 1942 and 1946, Bivins never had an opportunity to fight for a world championship. In the era of World War II, the Second Great Migration of blacks from the rural South to the urban North, and increasing competition between black and white workers, Bivins was the wrong man to be champion. America was not ready for a bold, un-humble, self-asserting black champion like Bivins, who would have been a bridge between the eras of Jack Johnson and Muhammad Ali. Although during the war he won the "Duration Championship" in the light heavyweight and heavyweight divisions, Bivins's public persona meant that he would never receive a shot at Louis.

For Bivins and other ghetto boys, boxing became their salvation.

The choice to don the gloves and avoid poverty had a whiff of desperation. Bivins first boxed at age fourteen, pestering trainer Wilson "Whiz Bang" Carter to allow him into the ring. Carter had trained top fighters like "California" Jackie Wilson and was not willing to take on an underfed, 112-pound kid. But Bivins was a talented high school student with the gift of gab, a good painter who claimed he could have been valedictorian if he didn't box. He kept begging Carter, who eventually gave him a shot. Bivins impressed the trainer with his courage and moxie, and they would become inseparable for the next decade, plying their trade in the musty gym, where most of the boys could best hope for winning a watch in the amateurs or a few dollars for getting their brains knocked around in the type of lowly ranked pro bouts that were made to entertain workingmen looking for cheap thrills.

As an amateur in the late 1930s, Bivins entered a Cleveland boxing scene that had been discriminatory for decades. White promoters had kept African American fighters off the local cards altogether until the 1920s, when Dave Hawkins, a black trainer and manager, turned racial exclusion in the ring into a civil rights issue. Hawkins attended weekly city council meetings to protest the prejudice in pugilism, usually getting kicked out, until finally the council forced promoters to add black fighters to the city's cards.

Carter was another one of the pioneers of black self-assertion in the Cleveland boxing scene. A great amateur in the 1920s, he had a less-than-stellar professional career fighting for nickel-and-dime purses. Race and the reality of the ring restricted his revenue. Carter was a crowd-pleaser, a man who mixed it up. Back then, white promoters didn't appreciate aggressive black fighters, and the only way to make good money was to take a dive. Carter instead became the top amateur trainer in the city, guiding the likes of Wilson, Jimmy Reeves, Cleveland Kilpatrick, Art Tate, and Bivins to Golden Gloves crowns. Between 1934 and 1941, he had at least one fighter win a Golden Gloves title in every year except 1938. Bivins won in 1937 and 1939. Despite Carter's success, city leaders never selected him to be the head trainer of the local Golden Gloves team. A black man could not lead white boys.

The Cleveland amateur ranks mirrored the toxic racism that black fighters faced in their daily lives. From the referee to the fans, the onslaught never ceased. In mixed bouts, for example, if a black fighter had his way with a white foe, the referee would stop the bout early, saving the white boy from further injury to his body and his ego. But if a white fighter were pummeling his black antagonist, the referee would let the beating continue to the delight of the fans. Because few black fans frequented these fights, where they, too, would be subject to the crowd's racial animus, the black fighter was virtually alone in the arena. When he would hit his white opponent, white fans remained in dead silence, waiting for the right time, the white time, when the white fighter would hit back. In the meantime, they showered black fighters with boos and racial epithets. Some African Americans rationalized that this racism made black fighters tough and prepared them to face stiff competition in the future, but that was not true. Racism in the ring didn't toughen people; it softened their souls for what was to come next. Bivins would feel the bitter sting many times.

Bivins's pro career began well, as his body filled out and he beat all competition put in front of him and garnered his first ranking in *The Ring* magazine as a light heavyweight. Finally, with an adequate professional diet no longer confined to beans, greens, and pork chops, he easily transitioned from a welterweight to a light heavyweight. Soon he would become a heavyweight. The local press, black and white, touted him as the next big thing, the man who would save Cleveland boxing. He was "Joltin' Jimmy Bivins," the boy with the wide smile, a smile that was more deferential than defiant, more Sambo than savage. Whites didn't hate him yet. Luckily, a knockout loss to third-ranked heavyweight Lem Franklin about a year-and-a-half and twenty-five fights into his career—chalk up the loss to bad match-making by his people—did not derail Bivins's ascent.

In addition to a twenty-six-pound disparity with his opponent, the timing of the Franklin fight had also weighed on Bivins's mind. For the previous month, Bivins had been involved in a criminal case for reportedly having sex with a fourteen-year-old girl. Bivins denied the allegations, but what was not in dispute was the fact that she stayed with him for a few days while his wife was with their baby in Detroit. The fighter claimed he felt sorry for a wayward teen and let her crash at his house. The judge bought the story; Bivins got off.

Bivins escaped the law, but not Franklin, who floored him four times in the first round. Bivins kept getting up and trading punches with the slugger, showing his heart, until the ninth round, when the referee wisely stopped the bout, saving Bivins for another day. Franklin would eventually lose in 1942 to Bob Pastor, a white fighter touted for being able to beat blacks. In the last of a number of bad losses, Franklin would die in the ring in 1944. He was once a man with a promising future, but the duration for promise is not long in prizefighting. Boxing is cruel like that.

The demise of Franklin's career coincided with the rise of Bivins as a national sensation. Once Bivins started to regain his old form, he showed signs of greatness, even in his controversial 1942 loss to Pastor, a fight that saw Bivins drop his highly regarded opponent twice in the first round. Pastor didn't beat Bivins; prejudice won that night. It showed in the fans, the judges, and the local writers. "What do they care about [the] sacrifice of Jimmy Bivins, the ex–Central High School boy, the young Negro upstart?" asked John E. Fuster, a sportswriter for the *Cleveland Call and Post*, an African American newspaper. Whites wanted to see him beat. "There are white sportswriters who are tired of the domination of the ring by Negroes," Fuster fumed. "There are fight judges who cringe every time a black boy lays a right cross among his white opponent's whiskers. There are white referees who . . . go so far as to give advice to white battlers appearing against Negroes even when the white boy is a two to one favorite." Bivins internalized all this hate and took it out on his opponents. He got stronger and he got meaner. The smile got wider. If whites were going to hate him, fine, let them hate. He kept pounding all the foes they put in front of him, black and white. He pummeled Pastor later that year and didn't lose another fight for the next four years. At one point, he was both the top-ranked light heavyweight and heavyweight contender.

What made Bivins one of the best pound-for-pound boxers? The two-fisted fighter had the speed of a middleweight and the pop of a heavyweight. The black writer Alvin Moses said Bivins was the best 175-pounder since the 1920s. "He knows 95% of the prize fight answers every second of the time he's under glove-fire. He's pebble-game; brainy, (in and out of the prizering); is the best sneak-puncher extant, and—CAN PUNCH." A tenacious "tweener" whose size pitted him against top light heavyweights and heavyweights (and big middleweights, like the pre-prime Archie Moore, who thought they could try him), in most cases he was too strong for the light heavyweights and too fast for heavyweights. In either case, he was dangerous. Old-timers said he reminded them of a young Kid Norfolk, a great black fighter of the World War I era. The comparison to Norfolk was fitting, because like Bivins, Norfolk never got his fair shot. He was too dangerous for most top white fighters to take a chance on him, and too black for a promoter to push past prejudice. Bivins, like Norfolk, would be stuck in pugilistic purgatory, the great what-if of racism, held back by a public that could not see past color. Bivins let the discrimination fuel him, but using his boxing talent to push past prejudice could only last for so long. The punches, the real ones from his opponents and the jabs from the fans, would keep coming. On the way he claimed the Duration Championship, a title he never wanted: "I don't like sports writers who call me the 'Duration Champion'—I want no part of any title I don't win in the ring." He knew the limits of a fake crown.

What was the Duration Championship? Looking back, it's hard to tell if the title was a gift, or a joke, or a bit of both. With world titleholders like Joe Louis off to war, in late 1942 sportswriters and promoters suspended all championships, but to save boxing, or better yet, to keep the turnstiles turning, they created these fake titles. The Duration Champion was the king of the ring of those men that hadn't been called into Uncle Sam's army. With his 3-A status—he had a wife and kid—Bivins had time before he got the call. In wartime, being the Duration Champion gave the man an honorific title, something he could market, and it also gave him hope. If he kept the fake title long enough, when the war was over he would be first in line for the real title. But boxing hardly ever worked like that, on merit, especially for a black man like Jimmy Bivins who didn't hide his emotions. Instead, he was matched with tough foes that many people hoped would beat him.

Bivins defeated Ezzard Charles, an outstanding accomplishment, in an elimination match for the Duration light heavyweight title in 1943. Although he would lose their remaining four matches, the victory over the not-yet-at-his-best "Cincinnati Cobra" (also known disparagingly to white sportswriters as "Dark Dynamite" or the "Dark Destroyer") proved Bivins could fight. Before the first Bivins-Charles bout, Jack Kearns, famous for managing Jack Dempsey, said of Charles, "That colored kid has surely got it. Give me one of those fast, hard-punching, smaller fellas like him every time against the average heavier guy." This was one of those matches that modern-day fight fans are supposedly denied, in which the best up-and-comers of their generation battle each other in elimination bouts to take that next logical step toward the championship, with the loser falling a step back. But this was also one of those fights that made black fans cringe. Why were two young black battlers boxing each other in a bout that was supposed to knock one of them out of contention? The color line in boxing, and more specifically, the economic need to keep a white hope in the ring, meant that top black boxers constantly beat each other up as they angled for a coveted shot at the white hope or the championship. Charles would go on to have one of the greatest careers of any boxer, reaching his prime a few years later as a slightly heavier light heavyweight. In their first match, Bivins outweighed him by ten pounds.

Bivins and Charles were carbon copies of each other. In the ring, both didn't mind giving weight to their opponents, preferring to come in quicker and using their blinding speed to snap quick jabs. Like Bivins, Charles was born in Georgia, and his family moved to

Ohio to escape Jim Crow. Charles landed in the West End, one of Cincinnati's black neighborhoods, surrounded by want, poor people grinding out a living. Like Bivins, Charles turned to boxing to fight his way out, though few black boxers ever fully left poverty. They got a break from poverty, but poverty always awaited their return. In January 1943, after his bout with Bivins, it appeared Charles was heading back to poverty quicker than most expected. Bivins knocked him down four times en route to a ten-round decision. Bivins had one more fight to go until he could claim the Duration Championship, a rubber match with local rival Anton Christoforidis.

Bivins's third battle with "Christo the Greek," who was born in Turkey, was a grudge match. The two met twice in 1940, with Bivins winning a decision in their first fight, and Christo getting a controversial nod in the second affair. Everyone knew there should have been a third battle, but the politics of race and the ring dictated that Christo, the white man, get a shot at the National Boxing Association world light heavyweight title, which he won. Logically, Bivins reasoned that he would be next, a rubber match for the belt. But the Greek got a chance at a big-money fight with Gus Lesnevich in New York. Christo took the money, but lost the title, and Bivins lost his legitimate claim to a championship bout. So here they were, three years later, back at it again, this time battling for the Duration Championship. The naysayers said that Bivins couldn't stay the fifteen-round limit, but he proved them wrong. "Well, what are you going to say about fifteen rounds now?" Bivins bragged. "I guess you'll be asking if I can go twenty rounds." The *Cleveland Call and Post* reported, "Colored boys in North Africa, Australia, England, and all of the other army outposts know and are justly proud of their Jimmy." Perhaps the poor kid from Central High School would make it after all.

Most black fighters went broke. Very few saved what they made. "Old Chocolate" George Godfrey, Big Bill Tate, Harry Wills, Joe Jeannette, and Joe Gans—he went bust during the middle of his career but recovered his earnings—kept their money. George Dixon, the first black champion, spent the last ten years of his short life living in poverty. Joe Walcott, who owned a mansion in an exclusive white neighborhood at the peak of his career, spent the last thirty years of his life in poverty. As Bivins prepared to fight Christoforidis, Jack Johnson was operating a flea circus, Sam Langford was blind and living as a charity case in New York, Big George Godfrey was living in poverty in Los Angeles, Henry Armstrong was making a comeback trying to fight his way out of poverty, and Panama Al Brown, once the talk of Harlem for all of his flashy suits—he was Sugar Ray Robinson before Sugar Ray Robinson—was strung out on heroin living in poverty. The great Joe Louis, the American hero, the man who had recently donated all of his proceeds to the US Navy, was in serious financial debt.

The game is rigged so that fighters rarely come out on top. Within two years of his professional debut, Bivins went from making twenty-five dollars in his first local fight to earning nearly $25,000 in his 1942 hometown fights. All told, in his first three years, his fight earnings totaled $41,535. These figures, however, don't account for the percentages his managers took. In fact, three men (Claude Shane, Whiz Bang Carter, and Ed Kleinman) had a total of 60 percent of Bivins. The man who fought, who risked his life, didn't even own half of himself. To make things worse, Bivins got the short end of the gate when facing white foes. In his battle against Tami Mauriello, a fighter with considerably less talent than Bivins, Mauriello received a guaranteed $12,000, while Bivins earned a percentage of the gate, which turned out to be $4,000 before being siphoned off by his managers. Why the disparity in purses? White managers understood two interrelated factors. One, white men controlled the business of boxing. Two, black fighters needed to fight white men to make more money—interracial fights always sold best—and white fighters were essential stepping-stones for black fighters to climb the ranks of the ring. In other words, if a black fighter wanted to survive in the business of boxing he had to give up control of himself. As Bivins's manager, Claude Shane, explained to the *Cleveland Call and Post*, "the only way we could get a shot at [Billy] Soose who had dodged Jimmy since his amateur days was to let him get the big end of the purse. It was the same with

Mauriello and Pastor. They just wouldn't come here to fight for less money than they got."

In a sport that seemed to eat its young, the press held out hope for Bivins. Like every black fighter, he professed to the press that he saved and invested his profits. This was the fighter's chance to sell himself to the public and convince them that he was worthy. He was more than a fighter; he had the sensibilities and the middle-class qualities to ensure upward mobility. Poverty was a thing of the past. Bivins didn't drink, smoke, or gamble. If he wasn't fighting, or saving wayward teen girls, he was at home with his family. He invested his money wisely, sportswriters were assured. He bought war bonds, two houses (one for his parents, of course), and never splurged on items he could build himself. Gordon Cobblesdick, famed local writer for the *Cleveland Plain Dealer*, noted, "Bivins is making money in considerable gobs. And taking care of it, too. A large chunk of every purse goes into War Bonds." His trainer, Whiz Bang Carter, careful to sell Bivins in a Joe Louis "good Negro" mold, assured the white press, "High living'll never get this boy. He don't drink and he don't smoke and he don't like night life. You know how he celebrates after winning a fight? He gets a bite to eat and goes to bed." *Look* magazine sold the same Joltin' Jimmy: "Unlike most newly rich fighters, Bivins is conservative and thrifty."

Despite this favorable press coverage, white fans hated Jimmy Bivins because he embodied a bold black manhood they didn't want to see. Whereas Louis kept a stoic and emotionless look on his face, Bivins stalked his prey around the ring with a smile. His grin was big, wide, and unmistakable, like Jack Johnson's. Also like Johnson, he didn't care about what whites thought. Beyond his refusal to wear the mask, Bivins was braggadocious. He didn't follow the unwritten rules about black humility. He said he would beat his opponent, and he did. And when his foe fell in the ring, Bivins stood over him, taunting, and smiling at the crowd. He fought his fair share of whites and was always looking for the knockout. Cobblesdick observed, "You talk to the moon-faced colored boy with the twinkling eyes and the broad, slow grin and you wonder if this can be the same Jimmy Bivins who has been portrayed as a surly, snarling villain." His defiance was unforgivable in the midst of mass migration of blacks moving to cities like Cleveland, where antiblack violence would become more intense as interracial competition for limited housing and jobs increased in the postwar period.

The majority of white fans in Cleveland wanted him beat, and they filled up arenas and stadiums to see him get whacked. Take, for example, his 1942 bout with the Italian American fighter Joe Muscato, of Buffalo. As America went to war with Italy, the local matchmakers pitted a "popular boy of Italian ancestry and this unpopular boy of native American stock," so the fans could cheer the Italian American fighter and watch the black man fall. "The Italian boy is popular with Cleveland fight crowds," Fuster observed. "He has a natural boyish enthusiasm, which captivates the mob and (this is merely incidental of course) he has been given the warm side of the spotlight by local sportswriters." Bivins, however, was "not popular with fight crowds. Apparently they don't like the way Jimmy walks, or talks, or cuts his hair. Or it may be that the cocky grin he wears sometimes as he stalks his man . . . remember Billy Soose, and Lesnevich, and the great Bob Pastor . . . gets under the mob's collective skin." During the bout, the mainly white audience booed Bivins. But that didn't bother him. With a wide grin on his face, he stalked Muscato and knocked him out in the fifth with a right uppercut. It was like this for the next four years.

Despite the hate, most could not deny his greatness. The talk of the championship started early in his rise to the top. It was clear to most who saw him fight that Bivins, not Billy Conn, was the best bet in the business to beat the Brown Bomber. Louis called him a "damn good fighter," and in 1943 the champ named Bivins the top heavyweight outside of the army and placed a crown on his head for photographers to capture the moment. There they were, the deadpan Louis and the grinning Bivins, polar opposites, and only one could represent America. It should have been inevitable that the two black men had to face each other for the championship, but that was not the case. True, the war was partly to blame for Bivins never getting his title shot, but the war hero, Louis, also did his part.

Joe Louis, the most important race figure in the 1930s and 1940s, drew the color line. "Joseph isn't fighting able-body colored boys," writer Bud Douglass complained. True, Louis fought John Henry Lewis, but he did that as a favor. Lewis was his friend and needed the money. So Louis whipped the light heavyweight for pity and a payday. The champ wasn't scared of any man. He loved green, and interracial fights made him the most money. Lord knows he needed the money. As long as there was a list of white men lined up to fight, Louis always chose them. Black men like Franklin, Turkey Thompson, and Bivins would never get a shot until there were no white men to battle. In truth, Franklin and Thompson were not worthy of a shot at Louis. They were big bruisers, but could not hang with the Brown Bomber. Bivins? He was a different case. He had the speed and skills to baffle Louis, the pop to keep him honest, an unrelenting mean streak in the ring to put pressure on the aging champ, and a four-year winning streak. In other words, Bivins had a legitimate shot at taking the crown.

Louis would fight any white hope they put in front of him. Pretenders and contenders were all members of the Bum of the Month Club, but not just any black man would do. Louis received his shot at James Braddock because he wore the mask. His expressionless face showed deference and humility after he hurt his opponent. He publicly professed Christianity, was supposedly a teetotaler after prohibition, and most importantly he never was photographed with a white woman. In other words, he was the antithesis of Johnson, the so-called bad nigger who had reigned over the division twenty years prior and wreaked havoc on white America. Louis, on the other hand, was considered great for America, perhaps the first black man ever to have the prefix black, colored, or Negro dropped from his name to just be an American hero. He earned the distinction when he beat Max Schmeling in 1938, and doubled down on his patriotism when he went into the army and donated his fight purses to Uncle Sam. He was one of the greatest Americans of the greatest generation of Americans.

What would a Bivins championship reign look like? To only look at the pictures captured outside the ring, everything would be fine. In every picture you see of Bivins, he wore his classic wide-brimmed smile, a grin most black men learned to adopt to soften any suspicion about them. He posed for numerous pictures for the local press, and even in *Look*, with his black wife and child, he demonstrated to any doubters that he was not Johnson. Like Louis, Bivins professed his patriotism and told the press that he was ready to go into the army whenever they called him. And in 1944 when the army called his name, he put on his uniform, smiled for the cameras, and joined army life in the segregated South. Outside of the ring, there was no doubt Bivins could be portrayed as docile. But wearing the mask that America asked black men to don was a full-time job for a fighter, and in the ring Bivins did not don it. His smile said that he was his own man, relentless in his pursuit of his prey and always out to get blood. White fans could not get over Bivins's smile, Sambo outside the ring but savage inside the ring.

Bivins was not the right black man for World War II America. With millions of blacks moving north and competing for jobs, racial tensions boiled over in the streets and at the factories, and Bivins, who happily beat his white opponents in the ring, represented some of whites' worst fears of integration. He was coming to compete and take what was rightfully his. Only a select few got a pass from white America. Nationally, those spots were reserved for Louis and Jackie Robinson, and locally in Cleveland for baseball stars Larry Doby and Satchel Paige and football icons Marion Motley and Bill Willis. These black men, quiet in their strength, symbolized what whites would accept. Bivins never got his crack at the crown. The powers that be made sure of that.

By 1946, there was something clearly wrong with the once-bouncing Bivins. He seemed to have lost all his steam. What did him in? Was it the years of booing and racial animosity? The prejudiced politics of prizefighting? Or was it the army? He went into the service in 1944 and came out that same year, but it took something vital out of him. As Louis once said, "Can't understand why he didn't go farther than he is, 'cept for the condition he was in when he got outta that army." Rumors floated around that Bivins took a severe beating in camp, a racial lesson from southern white enlisted men. Bivins admitted to getting into scraps, but boasted nobody could beat him. But the rumors were true. Something bad happened to him while he was in the service. His sister, according to boxing historian Jerry Fitch, admitted that there was a serious beating.

He was never the same. After his discharge, he resumed his career and won fights, including a knockout over an undersized Archie Moore, but Bivins didn't look the same. He lost his reflexes. He lost his desire. And then he started losing matches. Jersey Joe Walcott, "the black Cinderella Man," beat him in 1946 and got a shot at Louis, the shot Bivins had earned. That had to hurt. But Walcott was safe; he had a hard-luck story and humility perfect for post–World War II America. The Walcott bout started Bivins's decline. The men Bivins once handled, Archie Moore, Ezzard Charles, Joey Maxim, and Lee Q. Murray, now dominated him. Soon he fell out with the one constant in his life, Whiz Bang Carter, and once Carter was gone, Bivins didn't have a chance to get back on top. His duration was done. Everybody knew it but Bivins. The fighter is usually the last to know.

By 1949 he was broke, or at least that's what he told a judge during a divorce proceeding prompted by the many beatings he gave his wife. Despite his downfall, or because of it, Bivins kept fighting and dreaming that he would get his shot at the title, but he never did. By the 1950s, the hate was gone, but so were his skills. To the public, he wasn't a threat any more, just another tragic tale of black poverty and a boxer hanging on too long. He did the retired boxer scene for many years after his career—a busted ex-pug waving his hand to the fans, showing up at the occasional banquet, soaking in whatever little glory he still could get. He drove a truck for a living and frequented the fights. And then he disappeared. The public abused him during his career, drained his spirit, and then it would be his daughter who was taking his life, leaving one of the best fighters of his generation to die in an attic.

Born poor in a southern shack in 1919, Jimmy Bivins was dying in a northern attic when the Cleveland police found him on that sad April day in 1998. Abused in his daughter's house, he weighed 110 pounds, or two pounds less than when he started boxing at the age of fourteen. His broad-beautiful smile, the one whites had hated and blacks had loved, was gone. He had a badly damaged finger, looked emaciated, and was covered in urine-soaked bedsheets. His fall from fortune seemed all too familiar for fighters. Most boxers, especially black boxers, died broke. For most of these black men who had climbed from the bottom and reached the top, only to fall again, the public didn't discover their poverty until it was too late. If one was fortunate enough to be found, perhaps the community might rally around him, as Cleveland did Bivins. The outpouring from friends and fans helped cover the pain, but to peel back from that moment is to discover deep wounds from years of prejudice that the Duration Championship could neither cover nor heal. Jimmy Bivins, the one-time Duration Champion, a man robbed by the ring because of his color, died in 2012.

THE MASTERS OF STYLISHNESS

Gabe Oppenheim

Style is *always* in the eye of the beholder. You do the research to be a well-informed beholder, but still, the final judgment is personal and subjective. You go on how you feel, and you should: *lo que importa es la sensación*. It might make humans more animal than we care to admit, but in the end, our greatest truths lie in emotional responses. And whatever rationales we attach to them are secondary and after the fact. As the neuroscientist and English professor Iain McGilchrist explains, the brain responds with emotions in the right hemisphere *before* the left hemisphere even assembles its worded reason.

And so: boxing. It's technical, sure, but above all, emotional. You can't really watch it and not respond—and that response is unavoidably composed of highly charged feelings, even if boxing also inspires an intellectual response. Analysis, even simple description, comes much later.

If I had watched but a couple fights in my life, my response to boxing would likely be to the oddity of blood sport in the twenty-first century. That's the feeling that colors nearly all novice responses today. But I've seen more than a couple bouts and, likely, so have you. What remains once the novelty has worn off is what the fighters themselves bring to the ring. Each arrives with training under his belt, previous fights, and sparring sessions. Each is a product of these experiences and also whatever touch and spin he has—perhaps, unwittingly—put on them. They've placed personality on those punches—and in their defensive slips, too.

Call it style.

*

I once watched in person the most stylish fighter in the world. It was eight years ago, at a card copromoted by Peltz Boxing and Top Rank in South Philly. The main event was supposed to be the lightweight Almazbek "Kid Diamond" Raimukulov against a Mexican challenger, Antonio Pitalua, who had an impressive 43–3 record but one that had been compiled entirely in Mexico against unknowns. It could've been a blowout, or maybe that record, despite being a cipher to us, was a reflection of the man's ability, in which case it would've been an evenly matched and possibly brutal fight. But Pitalua wasn't able to secure a visa despite frantic appeals, so at the last moment, as had happened so many times before, the world's most stylish fighter was called in as a replacement.

Enter Emanuel Augustus. By this time in his career, Augustus—who originally fought under the name Emanuel Burton, out of Baton Rouge, Louisiana—was a bedraggled thirty-two years old. He had made a habit of taking any fight offered him, no matter how late the notice, or how biased the venue, and he had been screwed out of plenty of decisions as a result. His ugly record was thirty-four wins, twenty-seven losses, and six draws.

Here's what the record masked. All the fights the judges in Texas stole from him early in his career. The draw with hometown hero Soren Sondergaard (38–1) in Denmark that should've been a win. The loss to Pete Taliaferro (31–5) in Mobile, Alabama, that the crowd booed, because Augustus had surely won. He schooled an unbeaten Allen Vester in Denmark, but knowing he was down on the cards, he took a dive just to demonstrate the sliminess of the proceedings.

When Augustus lost a tight decision in Mississippi to Teddy Reid—two judges had him down a single round, the third down two—the crowd booed just as they had in Alabama.

In 2001, he fought Micky Ward, the man whose life story was later made into the film *The Fighter*, in what *The Ring* called the fight of the year. Teddy Atlas, the ESPN commentator and former trainer, scored the bout a draw on television. But the judges saw it the way they always did with Augustus. Ward was the name fighter. Augustus was the boxcar nomad. One scored it 98–90 against Augustus, as part of another unanimous decision not in his favor. There were undeserved draws, as when Augustus schooled a 16–0 fighter named Aguilar in Las Vegas and was handed even cards—essentially a concession that his efforts were so superior that there was no plausible way to give him a loss. In Hidalgo, Texas, Augustus was disqualified for not looking at the referee. The ESPN article on the match was headlined, "Augustus Can't Win."

"They say you don't have no manager, no promoter, you don't deserve this fight," Augustus said afterward. "I don't know how to act." The man was no fortunate son. And none of the other injustices compared to the devastation of his first fight against Courtney Burton, in Muskegon, Michigan. In the ring, Augustus was penalized a point for spinning, which was part of his sui generis style but not a violation of any rules. The ref called two hard body shots that Augustus threw low blows and gave Burton time to recuperate from them. And then came the decision: One judge, bless him, gave Augustus the deserved victory. The other two barely gave him a round. On ESPN, Teddy Atlas, after scoring the fight for Augustus, confronted the Michigan Boxing Commission officials. Fight writers urged fans to send letters to Michigan in protest. Eventually, the referee and two judges were investigated.

The decision stood, as it almost always does. It's boxing. Everyone may agree you were jobbed, but no one will offer redress. Two years after I saw him, in the waning moments of his career, he was screwed out of yet another decision, against prospect Francisco Figueroa. In his final match, four years after I saw him, he faced an undefeated prospect in Detroit, pressed the kid past his limit—and then had two points deducted by the referee for nonoffenses. They couldn't even let the man leave the sport in the peace.

Despite all that, Augustus had a hell of a career. He was at one point the number-two-ranked fighter at 140 pounds. He beat 23–1 Alex Trujillo, knocked out 47–10–2 Ray Oliveira, knocked out 37–1–2 Carlos Wilfredo Vilches, knocked out 25–1–1 David Toledo. He drew with Leavander Johnson, who'd go on to become a respected world champ.

And he had pioneered a fighting style all his own—one soon dubbed *Drunken Master*, after the 1978 Hong Kong martial arts picture and the subsequent variations on it that became a staple of the kung fu genre. Of course, Augustus was stone-cold sober when he let his limbs dangle and his legs bend as though he couldn't stand straight. These were moves that only *appeared* loopy, and even then, only for a few moments. It soon became clear to any observer that the jester possessed a kind of genius: *Stylishness*.

*

Style and *stylish* suggest slightly different things in the boxing world. Begin with *style*.

Boxing may look like brutal chaos to the uninitiated, but it's bound by strict rules. You have to stay within the ropes. I think it's helpful to think of the ring as the Spanish do—*cuadrilátero*—a four-sider, a quadrilateral—because boxing is bound in a mechanistic way, a compact way. It feels to me as if each of the four walls bears down a little harder on the participants with each passing round. And so that's your four-sider—your canvas, literally and figuratively.

Within that frame, you can be as inventive as you want, so long as you stay vertical and don't foul. And so there's combustion, but instead of pushing air and fuel into a cylinder, you're pressing two highly trained men into a constricted quadrilateral and asking them to put on a beat-down show. It may be a cruel rite, but no matter, the arrangement is what matters here. Everything before and after the fight is orchestrated. But during the fight, no matter how well-thought-out your game plan, you must improvise. The only boxing without improvisation is hitting the heavy bag—because even a shadowboxer sets a part of his brain aside to surprise himself.

That improvisation is *style.* And just as poets, in Harold Bloom's estimation, feel the anxiety of influence and so deviate from a previous generation's style (at least the originals do), so do boxers try to create a new look for themselves. The parallel isn't as fantastic as it may seem at first. The best boxers take seriously the training they get from their elders and incorporate the relevant boxing canon into their work. But, at the least, this means they have to engage with styles of the past. Start dipping real low as a light southpaw, and you'll inevitably draw comparisons to Pernell Whitaker. And bully for you if you do—he was one of the most elusive fighters of all time. But you have to figure out whether you want to press further in that direction, become a closer mold of the original, or whether a little of his defense is enough, and now you want to see whether a Sergio Martinez up-jab might be a nice companion piece to a low stance. And so on.

Take away the combat component of boxing—the fact that the end result of movement is to score and win by inflicting pain—and focus on the movements alone, and you arrive at style. George Bellows captures two combatants in his painting *Stag at Sharkey's* who together resemble a Francis Bacon–painted piece of meat. It looks like pure brutality. But look more closely, and you see energy flowing through one guy into the other and back. The fighter on the right leans over his opponent with an arched spine, pulling back his right fist, letting the weight of his musclebound shoulders fall onto the rival, as though he wants his challenger to absorb not only a punch but the quintessentially human burden of standing up beneath a load—of carrying baggage. The rival on the left's response is what lends the scene its looping style: he springs forward off his toes, pressing into the brute before him, nearly lifting him up with the linear force of his calf muscles. Bellows has frozen a single moment in a fight so that we'll never know who prevails. What we're left with instead is the constant cycle of thrust-parry, push-pull—of boxing style.

*

When boxing bears a very personal imprint, when it becomes perhaps unnecessarily personal, that's when *style* becomes *stylishness*. It is idiosyncrasy harnessed for a purpose—inimitability within the flow of the game.

When Joe Louis pulls his right elbow up high to drop his gravity-propelled right in the slot, that's style, not stylishness. Louis was a completely practical fighter in an era when a black champ who was more outré might lose his white audience. Who knows what other moves Louis could've employed had he lived in the swag era—or maybe he would've stuck to the book anyway, which has its own virtues.

Stylishness is different. I first began to notice it myself in the fight tapes of Sugar Ray Leonard, in his windups—you're never supposed to bring your elbow that far back before punching, and yet he did—and his occasional bolo punches. No, he wasn't the punch's progenitor, but I didn't yet know who Kid Gavilán or Ceferino Garcia was. There was something about the way Leonard moved that was apart from the standard procedures taught in gyms, something nonpareil. That quality of apartness explains why, in the late nineteenth century, so many fighters adopted the nickname "Nonpareil"—because the truly original fistic artist causes viewers to marvel and muse, *That dude is the only one who could get away with that.*

Being a millennial, I was introduced to the next level of *stylishness* by Roy Jones Jr. He is very likely one of the best athletes ever to fight—and one of the sportsmen signed to the Jordan brand on whose shoes the Jumpman logo never seemed incongruous. In his prime, RJJ seemed like Jordan in a ring, bending his knees, sticking out his chin, lowering his arms and then snapping up quicksilver hooks and haymakers. He was athlete enough to fly despite that unconventional and dangerous positioning. The man knocked guys down from inconceivable angles.

The ultimate example was Jones's takedown of James Toney in their fight for Toney's super middleweight title in 1994. Going into the bout, *The Ring* had Toney ranked second in the world pound for pound, and Jones third. Toney was the betting favorite, too. But Jones destroyed him from the opening bell, in part because of his unparalleled *stylishness*. Toney came out utilizing his usual shoulder-roll defense, which protects the chin, but Jones rendered it useless by lashing Toney's flanks with whip-like body blows. When Toney dropped his hands over his torso, Jones swooped in with hooks to the head, in the vein of Floyd Patterson, only with an unparalleled plyometric burst. When Jones missed a straight right, his burst was such that he could land a left hook before Toney could even capitalize on Jones's imbalance. Jones had the answers before Toney could even ask the questions. By only the third round, Toney had an air of des-peration about him. He needed to turn the tables somehow, because if he didn't, he'd lose undoubtedly. So Toney lowered his arms to his sides, stuck out his chin, and generally clowned about as though assuming Jones's style. Who knows precisely what Toney was think-ing, but it seemed to be something near this: Maybe Jones's *stylish-ness* is a trick. Maybe it's so psychologically depleting to see yourself beaten by a technically unsound fighter that Roy Jones wins via the head game. And so, if I can land from this posture, Jones's entire aura of invincibility will dissolve.

Of course, if *stylishness* were so easily copied, it would cease to be *stylishness*. It wouldn't bear emulating. No, Jones's moves were an organic extension of Roy Jones the athlete, Roy Jones the man. No one else could hear his internal radio, and no one else had the fast-twitch muscles to realize those sounds in movement. With his arms low to the floor and his head jutted out, same as Toney, as if in a Wild West stare down, Jones launched a left hook toward Toney's chin in a split second. Down went Toney. And the fight, for all intents and purposes, was over in the third round.

And yet, as much as I love Roy Jones and could watch him in his prime on loop endlessly, particularly those moments when he moved his hands behind his back and then whacked his opponent on the chin with both fists simultaneously, he falls just short of being the *most stylish ever.*

*

Don't take my opinion for it. Go to YouTube or Dailymotion or whichever website currently has the video that has been constantly posted, taken down, and reposted for a decade. It's a montage of Emanuel Augustus's *Drunken Master* highlights—high-stepping, swinging his arms like a pendulum, raising his chest toward the ceiling like a member of a southern drumline—set to the hip-hop song "I Think They Like Me," by Dem Franchize Boyz.

It doesn't matter whether you like hip-hop. Just pay attention to the beat—and watch as every single move Augustus makes is in sync with the song's rhythm, as though it were playing on a loop in his head. You see this in gyms sometimes, because a boom box will play while guys are shadowboxing or hitting the bags. But no one else I've ever seen has achieved anything near this singularity. Not even Roy Jones. It's more than uncanny. It's as if Augustus had the song in his head his entire career.

Like all good artists, he drew inspiration where he found it. Many moves were cribbed from his favorite combat video game—the Japanese *Tekken*—and from the Brazilian martial art–dance capoeira. That Augustus had the musical and athletic talent to then time these moves to a discernible beat, to a legitimate pattern, is all the more incredible. Lots of boxers shimmy and groove, but no other spins, swings, kicks, and flows to a metrical pattern while enacting video game blows that actually land. Augustus KO'd Burton when he finally got a rematch with him, and Floyd Mayweather Jr. called Augustus his most difficult opponent for years after their nine-round contest in October 2000. That was a little more than six years before I saw Augustus in person in Philadelphia when he was a worn-out thirty-two.

*

The Cubans may be the most stylish national cohort of boxers, for Cuba has long been a man-made incubator of unique flair in the arts. Much like the Japanese during the shogunate's ban on foreign entry,

Cubans have evolved culturally apart from the rest of the world, because of Castro's policies and the US embargo.

Obviously, impoverished Cubans didn't choose to have it thus, but ex post facto, they've done the best they can on their prison-island. Like their inventiveness in restoring cars without most tools and parts, their boxing—defensive minded, technically infallible, almost severe in its fast-reflex execution—is both economical and elegant. You see it whenever a Cuban boxer defects and turns professional or, in smaller dollops, during world amateur tournaments and the Olympics. That the Cubans often resemble each other in the ring—the same way stereotypical Mexican fighters do, wading in to throw body shots—underlines their collective stylishness but keeps them as individuals out of the running for *most stylish*.

Still, watching them is a first step toward understanding how mastery of boxing fundamentals, carried to extremes by brilliant talent (the Cuban system lets only the island's best into the national training center, known as The Farm), can become its own style. The moves may be basic—occasionally, even robotic—but their sum total is a marvel.

Enter "Gypsy" Joe Harris, the only other fighter besides Augustus I considered for *most stylish*. Gypsy Joe's moves and world, somewhat like the Cubans', were determined by circumstances beyond his control. As a teen, Harris robbed children of their candy on Halloween night. One of those kids threw a brick in retaliation that permanently blinded him in his right eye. Far from distancing Gypsy from boxing, his incapacity made him a star in the sport.

Gypsy Joe crafted a most unusual style that allowed him to account for his opponent's positioning at all times—or, at the very least, rob the rival of sight, too. This could mean turning his back on an opponent, who would be forced to rush him, allowing Gypsy Joe to catch him coming in. It could mean positioning himself perpendicularly to the ropes, one hand holding on to them for balance, so that only his left eye faced outward. It could mean fighting backward, his spine facing the opponent's face, his arms swinging like oars. He didn't slug so much as fling, his fists buzzing about like demonically possessed flies.

Because he had the athleticism, despite his boozing and womanizing, to win big with this style, Gypsy Joe became a sensation. At first, it was just in Philly, the home at that time of champs or contenders in every division (welterweight Gypsy Joe's best friend was the other Joe—heavyweight Joe Frazier), but he broke out nationally when a *Sports Illustrated* writer in his prime, Mark Kram, spent days with Gypsy Joe on the streets of North Philly, known as the Badlands. Kram was a stylist in his own right. His June 19, 1967, article on Gypsy Joe became that week's cover story, making Gypsy Joe the only boxer to have appeared on the cover without being either a heavyweight or a champion.

Sadly, though Gypsy Joe beat welterweight champ Curtis Cokes (in a nontitle fight that conferred no honors on the winner), almost no footage exists of him enacting his whirling dervish tactics. Russell Peltz, the Philly promoter, has an audiotape (from the early 1970s, seemingly) of Gypsy Joe begging manager Jim Williams to find him matches anywhere, after the commission banned the boxer for his blindness in 1968, reputedly because Gypsy Joe had threatened to leave his management team of Yank Durham and Eddie Reddish, who had for years coaxed the commission into letting him fight.

For years, collectors of old footage would mention online that there did exist a fragment of Gypsy Joe on film, though no one knew where. I searched for it for years while writing a book on the history and culture of Philly fighters. Then, one day a few years ago, a clip popped up on YouTube: Gypsy Joe against former welterweight and middleweight champ Emile Griffith in the Spectrum in South Philly. It's just three minutes long, and it has no sound—it looks like a tape taken from a TV station's archives. And this was the lone loss on Gypsy Joe's record before he was banned. There are various explanations offered for why he seemed so disengaged during the bout: Gypsy Joe was upset his managers were spending so much time with their prize heavyweight Joe Frazier and had already begun parting from the team; he hadn't trained right because he was too enamored of the nightlife, particularly his many women and his favorite drink—whiskey and milk; he had needed to spend time in the sauna *and* take diuretics to cut enough weight to make the 160-pound limit.

None of these reasons, though, stopped Griffith from crowing afterward, "They wrote that all Gypsy had to do was show up and boogaloo and he'd win."

But even in this fragment, you can see glimmers of the Gypsy Joe style. He buries his head on the opponent's shoulder to smother incoming blows and also to get a better look at what's heading his way. He slips punches; he turns Griffith in the corner so that the offensive fighter is on the defensive. He throws out a right hand as a distraction then pumps a hard left jab. He curls his back and covers up his body crosswise, utilizing the famous "Philly Shell" for defense.

No, the razzle-dazzle isn't there. But the blind man's polish in executing these more conventionally stylish moves makes the legend of the wilder ones he was known to favor in his prime all the more believable.

*

The best article to date about Emanuel Augustus was written in 2015 by Michael Dolan for *Athletes Quarterly*, the magazine he edits. Dolan had traveled from New York to Baton Rouge, Louisiana, to look into Augustus's condition; the previous fall, Augustus had been hit in the back of the head by an errant bullet fired by a stranger. The stray bullet fractured a vertebra, cut an artery, and left the boxer in a coma. Augustus already had fight-induced vision loss and memory problems.

But Augustus came out of the coma and underwent physical therapy—to regain the ability to feed himself, among other capacities. Dolan found Augustus living in a shabby home just feet from the Mississippi River, debilitated but not completely diminished. Surrounded by loved ones, Augustus could still recall fights of yore and the video game he tried to mimic in the ring, but he needed prompting. He was emotionally labile. The shadowy black-and-white shots taken by Dolan's photographer, Mark Peterson, revealed the permanent disfiguration of Augustus's face. It was pulled back to one side, as though he had suffered a stroke.

Here's how Dolan described Augustus's *Drunken Master* style: "It was so unorthodox and unique, it paralyzed fighters, hypnotized by its bizarre sequence." Augustus's longtime friend L. J. Morvant said, "You couldn't ask Ali to fight like Tyson or Tyson to fight like Ali. Emanuel had to be himself in the ring. The showboating—that's who he was!"

Only a small bit of that performance art was on display on January 11, 2007, in South Philly, when I saw him fight in person. Augustus had 532 rounds to his name when he entered the ring against the favored contender, "Kid Diamond." I kept waiting for Augustus to break out of a conventional stance and tap his inner syncopated beat. There were small moments, sure. In the first, he slipped and ducked punches without even seeing them, as if by instinct alone. He threw old-school jabs to the body (a larger and more stationary target than the head, as well-trained fighters know) and parried punches with his right glove before countering—the ol' catch and counter. None of these tricks was especially spectacular—but they were crafty enough to indicate the man could do far more were he so inclined. It was scheduled for only ten rounds, but if that was Augustus's first, one could easily picture him dancing around Kid Diamond by the fifth.

The second-round bell only reinforced the notion, as Augustus came out slightly more offensive minded. Kid Diamond jabbed, and Augustus threw a counter right over the receding jab. It wasn't a hard shot, but it wasn't supposed to be—it was the rare counter meant to set up a secondary counter. As Kid Diamond avoided Augustus's right hand, he bent his upper body straight into the path of an Augustus left hook. *That* was the thumper. When the round ended and Augustus returned to his corner, he declined to sit on the stool.

You know the old film trick—executed famously well in *Citizen Kane*—in which we see a character age greatly in just a few shots, underscoring how fast it all goes by? That's what the following rounds resembled. Already in the second, Augustus's defensive head movement began to slow. Kid Diamond popped him to the head a few times—just to see whether Augustus was laying a trap. But as the punches kept landing, Diamond grew more confident that there was no trap. In the third, Kid Diamond pounded the body until Augustus slumped, and then Diamond launched uppercuts. You could see Augustus trying to mount an ordinary combatant's defense—hands held high, chin tucked—but he did it without strength or conviction. Ordinariness, not his strong suit, wouldn't help him now. After the fifth round, Augustus sat on his stool for the first time all night.

As sad a sight as it was, it gave the man some pep. Ever so slightly renewed, Augustus opened the sixth round throwing Joe Frazier–style left hooks, only his body didn't fall forward but pirouetted in place. Those were some balletic shots, and they scored. He landed a few rights next. Now, he started to dance to avoid punches, sliding under each one before popping back up and grinning—at Kid Diamond, the crowd, the cameras. "He's gotta get back to being who he is," said Bob Papa, the TV announcer, as though Augustus could turn on this charming litheness at will. If only. A minute later, the sixth round still very much under way, with about half the fight to go, Augustus looked depleted. In the seventh, when the referee tried to break up a clinch, Augustus shimmied out of it himself. Cute, but he immediately ate three hard shots to the face.

In the ninth, Augustus came out slugging, landing rights and lefts. Seconds later, he was sapped. Kid Diamond doubled up the left hook—banging Augustus to the body and the head in one smooth sequence—and shot a clean straight right that knocked Augustus to one knee. Augustus wasn't dazed—his backside never even touched the canvas. He didn't look disheartened, just spent. He took a deep breath—you could see his cheeks expand—and shook his head, then stood up at the count of eight. That combo that floored him had been *his* kind of combo, one that in his earlier days he could have deconstructed and rebuilt better and more cleverly. Now, though, he was powerless to defend against it.

Before the round, Augustus had told his trainer, "I don't feel so hot."

*

Maybe "sad" isn't the right word, but it's at the very least dispiriting, maybe even disturbing, to see a man of nearly unimaginable talent diminished. Think of Roy Jones, his left held low as usual, finally being caught by a killer left and then a right after fifteen years as a pro, when Antonio Tarver and then Glen Johnson knocked him out and permanently vaporized his aura of stylish invincibility.

All fighters eventually lose (yes, Rocky Marciano retired undefeated and early, but that's exactly the choice still held against him by his detractors), but some losses are harder to take than others. At a proper bullfight, the crowd wants the clever bull, the one who has conned the matador into missing him brilliantly, to be pardoned. So, too, men of mercury should never be reduced to molasses.

I didn't see the best Emanuel Augustus that night, nor did the friend I persuaded to join me by talking up Augustus's past exploits. Even as I hyped the event, I knew I was perverting the game. It was precisely *because* of those 532 rounds already logged that Augustus couldn't be the fighter he once had been. A very capable veteran, sure, but not the stylist par excellence.

That may be the ultimate sign of stylishness: the unyielding faith of those who have beheld it. Hell, if someone gave me tickets to see Augustus right now—the disfigured, wounded Augustus—despite every rational qualm I'd have, a small voice inside me would nevertheless wonder whether he still might have it. One more fight, or one more round, or even just a minute, a single exchange more. My curiosity hasn't dissipated at all.

"Do you know how much boxing fans loved watching you fight?" Michael Dolan asked the broken-down Augustus last year. "For real?" Augustus said. "You're bullshitting me." No one has managed to impart to Augustus what he meant to us. Very likely no one ever will. But even if we could, what would we say beyond that his exploits were pleasurable to the eye, that his movements were at times breathtaking, that if we could fight a lick, we'd love to do it the way only he could?

Not that those aren't very fine compliments—and true. But they wouldn't do justice to the element of stylishness. We can't aspire exactly to emulate those who live in extremis, acting at the periphery of society and the possible, attempting the ordinary in spectacular fashion. We know we don't have the innate talent to match them, or perhaps even the inclination. But the stylists reveal such goals as attainable—if not by all of us, then by our very best; if not for a full career, then for a brief moment. And those who enact impossible-seeming moves with their bodies teach all of us a new understanding of the boundaries of our world, because we're all stuck in the same basic situation, all subject to corporeal bounds. The stylists sketch in neon just how expansive those boundaries can be.

*

After Augustus climbed back up from the canvas that night in Philly, exactly two minutes remained in the ninth. Augustus would never have quit, but at the very least, with so much time left on the clock, he could've held on to Kid Diamond, grappled with him if need be, in order to last the round. It's what I expected, what everyone in the arena likely did. So, of course, the master of style did essentially the opposite. He wrapped *himself* up, crossing his arms in front of his body in the "Philly Shell" defense Archie Moore had used fifty years earlier and George Foreman had adopted thirty years after that, a defense that relies upon technique, as opposed to brute clinching. Augustus was a stylist to the end, even when it was far too late for him to do anything but go the distance.

ROY JONES JR.'S LONG GOOD-BYE

Brin-Jonathan Butler

> What is vertigo? Fear of falling? No, vertigo is something other than fear of
> falling. It is the voice of the emptiness below us which tempts and lures us,
> it is the desire to fall, against which, terrified, we defend ourselves.
>
> Milan Kundera, *The Unbearable Lightness of Being*

ROUND ONE

Back in 1996, when Muhammad Ali went down to Pensacola, Florida, for an event with Roy Jones Jr. and spoke to thousands of school-children bused in from around the county, Ali asked to go where Jones trained so they could playfully spar a few rounds.

Even on good days, Ali's speech was pretty limited, but he was still strong enough to move around and exercise back then. After Ali and Jones had circled one another in the ring and only really feigned jabs, at one point Ali smiled and gestured at Jones that he'd spotted a weakness.

Ali imitated and exaggerated the flaw he'd discovered in Jones's jab and left them both in fits of laughter at his shrewdness. Jones nodded after he'd caught his breath and confessed, "Yeah, you found it. But I'm so fast I can get away with it."

And then, one day some years later, he wasn't, and he couldn't.

"Old fighters don't fade away," the late Budd Schulberg wrote. "They just slowly die in front of our eyes." Jones, whom Schulberg described as a "genius" and "Hamlet with a mouthpiece," is just shy of his forty-seventh birthday, yet he refuses to let go of his career as a prizefighter. On December 12, Jones will fight Enzo Maccarinelli in a cruiserweight bout in Moscow. It will be the seventy-first bout of his career and the fourth of this calendar year.[1]

How much longer can he safely hold on? How safe is it for a man to release a grasp he's clutched with a death grip all his life? How much longer will the choice remain his to make? Does anyone have the right to talk this man off the ledge he first climbed onto at the age of five and has remained on ever since?

Over a professional career that's spanned a quarter century, after fifteen years dominating a sport like few athletes before him, in these last ten years, Jones has taken his share of beatings. He's lost eight times in his career, with some of those losses delivered by chillingly iconic blows and aftermaths.

Jim Lampley, who was ringside in Tokyo calling Mike Tyson versus Buster Douglas, said witnessing Roy Jones Jr. getting knocked out for the first time—via an Antonio Tarver left hand in 2004—was the most shocking thing he ever saw calling fights. It was the first time Jones had been knocked out in his life.

Before the boxing world had recovered from the shock, four months later, on September 25, 2004, another punch drove Jones's head against the canvas like an auctioneer's mallet, where he shivered and remained nearly motionless save for eyelids that strained to raise. This time, even with medical assistance, it required almost fifteen minutes to safely remove him from the ring and load him into an ambulance.

---

1. An earlier version of this essay appeared on BleacherReport.com on December 10, 2015. Two days later, Jones was knocked out cold, face down on the canvas, in the fourth round.

Early on, back in 1995, Jones had seen his friend Gerald McClellan, who once beat him in the amateurs, bludgeoned by Nigel Benn until a blood clot in his brain nearly killed him. After this event, Jones promised we would never see him risk suffering anything like what befell his friend. At the time, he claimed he was even more terrified of inflicting such damage on an opponent. The scene would continue to haunt Jones, though it didn't dissuade him from remaining in the sport.

Twenty-five years since his professional career began, a wife and six children later, amid rumors of money troubles and numerous calls to retire, here we are anyway. If you're hoping for happy endings for your heroes, boxing remains one of the worst places in America to look.

He's hung on ten years longer than Joe Louis after being knocked senseless through the ropes by Rocky Marciano. Nine more than Ali, slumped over and swollen on his stool against Larry Holmes. Seven more than the spectacle of a bankrupt and battered Mike Tyson, finally abandoning the cruel charade of his late career, caving in and quitting on his stool against someone named Kevin McBride.

One way or another, if Roy Jones continues to fight another year, he will be the same age as George Foreman when he hung up the gloves. Only Jones, unlike Big George, never took a full decade's hiatus from the sport. The further along we get, the scarier the station Jones's train threatens to stop at—that is, if it doesn't derail terribly along the way first.

Many have asked, and indeed asked Jones personally, what he could possibly have left to prove after being the first middleweight champion to win a heavyweight title in 106 years and having once had his name frequently raised along with Sugar Ray Robinson's in conversations about the greatest pound-for-pound fighter who ever lived. It turns out, at least in his own mind, everything. The stakes have never been higher, and "kill or be killed" is a thread that's stitched Jones's lifelong relationship to boxing.

"If God truly wanted me to stop," Jones told me, "all He'd have to do is have one doctor at the Mayo Clinic find something wrong with my brain. Just one little CAT scan showing any sign of trauma or damage and I'd be done. Am I slurring right now? I'm right where God wants me to be. To stop now would be to spite God with everything he gave me and everything he has planned, yet. That's why I'm here . . . and nobody can tell me different."

ROUND TWO

On the flight over to the Gulf of Mexico, I was thinking that they say you can never go home again, but many people, regardless of how many years or miles they put between themselves and where they were born, are never truly able to leave home.

Burning up in mid-September Pensacola's muggy late-afternoon heat, I stepped inside the air-conditioned taxi's reprieve and jolted the slouched-over, nodding-off Butterbean-look-alike cab driver at the airport. After I offered Roy Jones Jr.'s address to punch into his GPS, he inauspiciously turned back with a furrowed brow and look of concern, "None of my business, but you seem kinda jumpy. This house expecting you?"

"Hopefully." I shrugged optimistically.

"First time in Pensacola?" the cab driver asked.

"Yep."

"I'm not much of a tour guide, but out your window is our very own methadone clinic. Big ol' line kicks up every morning like clockwork."

I looked out the window and lingered a while on the roadside attractions: nearby fast-food chains, drifters along the side of the highway, a distant water tower, car dealerships with shiny red-white-and-blue triangular streamers flapping in the breeze, truck stops, local cemeteries, feed stores, an empty theme park with a miniature Statue of Liberty at the gate greeting nobody in particular, small children laughing in the back of pickups.

When Roy Jones Jr.'s father, Big Roy, returned to this small Florida Panhandle town from Vietnam as a war hero, he put food on the table by working at the local naval base as an aircraft electrician. Pretty soon, in 1975, when Little Roy was six, Big Roy gave professional boxing a whirl for a few years. He won his first eight fights in a row before getting knocked out. He fought on and went undefeated for a year until he landed a bout against a rising contender named Marvin Hagler, who stopped him in three rounds. Big Roy hung around boxing another year and lost his last four fights in Las Vegas before moving over to training his son and other poor kids around the neighborhood back in Pensacola.

"Say," I said. "Just curious, who would you say is the most famous man out of Pensacola?"

"Some folks would say Emmitt Smith, but he's kinda disowned us. I guess a lotta folks would say Roy Jones Jr. Fastest fighter I ever saw. Fastest fighter my daddy ever saw, too. And he watched Ali back when he was Cassius Clay. I ain't seen Little Roy around town in a long time. Wonder what he's been up to since he finished with boxing."

And here was the rub with plenty of folks to whom I'd mentioned covering this story.

"Actually he hasn't finished with fighting," I said. "Still going."

"Shee-it, that right?"

"The address I gave you is his house."

"He's still fighting? He must need the money. All them boxers do. How long he been fightin' for anyhow? Seems like forever."

Close enough.

"Hey, pal," the cab driver announced. "We're gettin' close."

We passed a lonely stretch of train tracks followed by the Escambia River. As the car slowed, we spotted the opened set of black gates off to the side of the road with four fighting rooster figurines greeting visitors. It was another quarter-mile drive under broad oaks and pines until we saw the fenced-in cows and hundreds of looming rooster cages next to the main house.

As we neared the main driveway, three men were playing with a little boy and girl circling around them on scooters. A large pit bull trudged along in pursuit of the children until a peacock and a turkey raced over in front of the crowd to cry out a horribly off-key alarm about the taxi's intrusion on the property.

I stepped out of the cab, and the cows and roosters joined the ear-piercing duet the turkey and the peacock had begun.

"You lost?" the tallest man from the group hollered as he slowly started in my direction. He was wearing an old, greased-up Roy Jones Jr. T-shirt.

I waved a little nervously and asked if Roy was around, as the group sized me up cautiously.

"You have business with him?"

"I'm just here for an interview with him," I said. "He texted me just now to say he's on his way."

The stranger got closer and reached out a hand while flashing a smile composed of mostly gold teeth.

"I'm Coco," he said. "That's Roy's cousin back there and his kids Roycen and Nalaya on the scooters."

"Nice to meet everybody," I said. "Any idea when you're expecting him?"

"Not long," Coco grinned. "He's out at the naval base playin' ball. We'll keep you company till he gets back."

Before Coco had finished proudly showing me all his bullet wounds, Jones's six-year-old son discarded his scooter on the pavement and threw me a lifeline. Roycen had braids hanging down over his shoulders but otherwise was his daddy's mini-me.

"You wanna play some ball before daddy gets home? We got a hoop next to daddy's gym."

"Sure," I said.

He pointed the way about fifty yards off from the house, just beyond the endless rows of chicken cages.

"C'mon, I'll show you around."

Roycen took me by the elbow and dragged me along for the dime tour of the property while his ten-year-old sister Nalaya gave chase.

As I watched the little girl stomp the pavement to accelerate her scooter, I remembered a story Thomas Hauser had told me about her being in the dressing room at Madison Square Garden after her daddy had lost to Joe Calzaghe. She noticed another child in the room crying after seeing the blood on her father's bruised and swollen face. She pulled at her daddy's boxing trunks to get his attention until he gave her a kiss and looked at her. "I'm a big girl, daddy," she beamed. "See? I don't cry."

Together they showed me his gym housed in a gigantic garage next to a few guest houses.

Once inside the gym, a giant thirty-foot poster of Jones in his prime greeted visitors, along with many other cobwebbed posters hung on the walls from dozens of his old fights.

Roycen climbed into the ring and shadowboxed, staring at his reflection in a soot-smeared mirror, while his sister tinkered around with aging gym equipment littered everywhere.

"Where does your daddy do his roadwork around here?" I asked Roycen.

"Roadwork?" his face pinched up in disbelief.

"Where he runs in the morning."

"I know what roadwork means," he laughed. "Daddy hasn't done roadwork since way before Nalaya was born. His knees ain't no good no more."

Nalaya nodded matter-of-factly in agreement.

"He can't run?"

They both shook their heads in unison from different corners of the gym.

"I thought he was off playing basketball."

"Daddy tries," Nalaya shrugged.

Suddenly the kids' faces lit up when they heard the peacock sound the alarm about a car pulling up in front of the main house's driveway.

"Mommy!" they screamed, abandoning me in the gym to sprint off just as Coco returned with a CD he'd recorded during his most recent spell in a prison.

"Is that Natlyn?" I asked Coco.

"Nah, son," Coco corrected gravely. "That's Missus Jones who arrived."

ROUND THREE

The inside of Roy Jones Jr.'s home warehouses the spoils of one of the most decorated athletes in history: trophies, framed posters, medals, ribbons, an Imelda Marcos–worthy stash of sneakers lying around from his expired promotional deals with Michael Jordan and Nike. Pride of place in the family home, however, is devoted to family photos and elaborately illustrated portraits of fighting cocks.

Roosters stare down from nearly every wall, and Jones's mantel, located a few steps after you enter the front door, advertises his numerous accomplishments raising prize-winning chickens. Louisiana was the last state in America to legally ban cockfighting back in 2008. At one time Jones had owned in excess of 2,500.

Natlyn Jones, a Florida native herself, invited me into her kitchen while she made tea and heated up some food for her children. Her elegance refused to give anything away despite being dressed down in a large Mike Tyson hoodie and wearing her hair in a ponytail.

She met Roy Jones back when she was still a teenager attending Florida State, intent on becoming a lawyer. She fell in love, and he became her first boyfriend. They got married and started a family in the early 2000s, and she abandoned her law school ambitions. It was obvious how her beauty had caught Jones's eye, but her keen intelligence, warmth, and effortless way with children made a far deeper impression.

I noticed it was already dark outside the window.

"I'm sorry you had to wait here and hang around so long for Roy to make it back from basketball. I hope these monsters weren't too much to handle."

"They were great," I said. "They showed me around."

"Did Coco lay his usual spiel on you?"

"Mommy, that man's crazy," Roycen shook his head.

"Their daddy's got a big heart," Natlyn smiled to herself. "When he gets here, you listen how many times his phone jingles. Every two minutes from dawn to dusk, his Morse code ring tone is chiming away."

"What percentage of those texts or phone calls are people with their hands out?"

"These days?" she snickers.

"How do these days compare to when he was on top?"

"On the way up? After he won the heavyweight title? I'd guess 95 percent of people reaching out wanted something from him. Now things have slowed down a little, but I'd still say 70 percent. Everyone thinks how much easier life must get when your boat comes in, but there's a lot of other stuff you have to be ready for, too. Not all of it's that easy to deal with.

"But I guess going into marrying a professional athlete, you have to know what you're marrying into. Not that I did. I just couldn't believe how nice he was, and, you know, you fall in love."

"I didn't remember until right now that I've actually seen you once before," I said. "Do you go to a lot of Roy's fights?"

She nodded.

"I think I saw you after a fight of Roy's in Moscow."

"Oh boy," she moaned, running her hand over her face. "Lebedev fight. Yeah, that was me crying my eyes out after that one. You watch somebody you love, and all you're waiting for is that final bell knowing everyone is OK, and we were almost there and then that happened.

"While you're breaking down, everybody else, ten thousand people or whatever, are busy losing their minds cheering. He's lying there, and you're in a panic that when he wakes up, he's the same guy as before. That one was a real long night for us. But we made it through, and here we are."

"Are all those highs you've been through with him worth the lows?" I asked.

Natlyn leaned over her kitchen counter and glared up at the ceiling.

"Not even close."

Soon, Jones entered the house in slippers with a large gym bag slung over one shoulder. We watched as Dusty, his floppy-eared golden cocker spaniel, pleaded to come inside with no luck.

He was still in shape but was holding over two hundred pounds on his once-middleweight frame now. When he flicked the light and sighed relief at dropping his gym bag, I could see his hairline had crept up some from his early days. As I watched him walk with an agonized expression wrenching his face, I realized his knees were far worse than I'd imagined. It took me a while to adjust to seeing someone who expressed youth so vibrantly throughout a career under the lights confronting middle age.

ROUND FOUR

Roy Jones Jr. started boxing at five and was competing at the age of ten in 1979. Between then and being the youngest member on the American Olympic team, his grueling roadwork over Pensacola highways, train tracks, or back trails carried him to a distance somewhere close to the circumference of the earth.

Nearly every afternoon, he sparred until exhaustion against bigger, older kids under an angry sky in Big Roy's backyard. His father was ruthlessly abusive, beating him with "anything he could get his hands on." That included a PVC pipe, broom handle, switch, bungee cord, and old gym equipment. Big Roy never hit him with a closed fist, but, according to Little Roy, "That was only because he'd caused brain damage to a guy fightin' when he was young. Otherwise I'm sure he would have."

Coming of age, Little Roy fought 134 times as an amateur. He won all but thirteen, first capturing the Junior Olympic title in 1984 at 119 pounds, followed by the national Golden Gloves at 139 and then 156, just before flying to Seoul for the 1988 Olympics as one of the most promising prospects in the sport's history. Before he flew home, wiping tears from his eyes with a towel, Little Roy gave an interview in Seoul where he talked about retiring before he ever turned professional.

Back in Pensacola, Little Roy changed his mind. For the next twenty-seven years (and counting), he said, he never again considered hanging up the gloves. By now, he's fought 461 rounds across seventy fights, spending almost an entire twenty-four-hour day in the ring over the course of his boxing career.

"Glad you made it," he smiled. "When Jim Lampley called and vouched for you—that was good enough for me. I don't usually let people into my life here. Let's go sit down and talk."

As we shook hands and he sheepishly apologized for arriving late, for all his accomplishments and abilities, Jones wasn't an especially charismatic presence. Nothing about him lent itself to becoming a brand. As I'd been told by numerous folks in the industry, "He's still that same country boy."

We talked for an hour on his couch about the state of boxing, until his children approached him for a good-night kiss. His wife was doing the dishes. I changed the subject to the elephant in the room: his own story in boxing.

"Given all the stories about how afraid you were of your dad," I began. "It's quite something to see just how much your kids adore you."

"I never wanted my kids to feel about me the way I felt about him," he said.

"How do you separate the killer you were in the ring with the man you are with your family?"

"Battling the fighter in me and the other guy with this life here has been a struggle every day of my life."

"How long did it take from when you started for boxing to stop being fun?"

"A week," he said.

"Was there ever an opponent who scared you as much as your dad?"

"Never," he said under his breath.

"You never wanted to get away from him and Pensacola?"

"I'm gonna leave my home? For what? That gonna make me happy?"

"I was born in 1979, the same year you started."

"Uh huh." He nodded.

"That's an awful long time putting yourself through what you do to be a fighter. Is there any part of letting go of boxing that offers you some relief?"

"Nah," he laughed. "But if I stepped away, there'd be relief for my wife and family."

"Huh?" Natlyn hollered over.

"I was just tellin' him, if I stepped away, you'd get some relief from boxing."

"Why would you say a thing like that?" she asked him.

"She'd be happy," Jones smiled and lightly tapped me on the shoulder.

"I mean," Natlyn turned it over, "a part of me would be happy."

"She'd be happy."

"A part of me would be happy because of all the stress around him fightin.'"

"You never thought about giving it up?" I asked.

"After the Olympics I did," Roy shook his head. "If Tyson had taken the fight I wanted with him after I won the heavyweight title, that woulda been it. Can you imagine if I got that fight?"

"You really wanted that fight?"

"Hell yeah," he laughed. "I woulda made 50 million easy. And look what Toney did to Holyfield when they fought. Look what I did to Toney. I woulda come at Tyson just like Holyfield did."

"You woulda tried to knock him out?"

"I woulda knocked him out. That woulda been it. I did everything I could to make that fight happen. He wouldn't take it. That woulda been enough."

"What's enough now?" I asked.

"Cruiserweight title. Nobody in history has won all the titles I've won and the cruiserweight title. I'd be the only man in history. That's when you die and go to heaven, and God can look at you and know you did everything with the gifts he gave you. If I died today, could

I really say that? If I stopped fighting, could I live the rest of my life knowing I didn't do everything I was put here to do?"

"I think a lot of people would say you've done more than enough to justify a place in history."

"After I win that cruiserweight title, it'll be enough."

"You sure?" I laughed uncomfortably.

"Unless they threw crazy money at me for one more. Yeah, I figure it'd be enough. Maybe after I win the cruiserweight title, just one little fight in my own backyard."

ROUND FIVE

The next morning, Jones spent a few hours clearing brush with some heavy machinery between his house and the pond. When I arrived at the house, he was off proudly giving his wife a tour of his progress.

They returned hand in hand, and Jones offered to take me for a ride in a vehicle that looked like a cross between a golf cart and a four-wheeler. Dusty and Bullet, a pit bull, tagged along.

The vehicle nearly flipped over three times along the newly shorn bumpy trail over to the pond, and the man at the wheel howled the whole way. When we arrived at the edge of the pond and he cut the engine, I spotted a tennis-ball-green five-inch lizard, and we spent a minute cornering it until I had it by the tail, pinched between two fingers.

"Give it here," he told me.

A little puzzled by his grim tone, I gave him the lizard.

"Now you just watch this," he laughed, tossing the lizard into the shallows of the pond.

The lizard drifted motionlessly.

"What's wrong?" he asked me. "You wanted him for a pet?"

"No," I said. "I was just trying to have a closer look at him."

"Keep your eye on him now. See that ripple from where he landed stretching out over the surface of the pond? In no time, a bass is gonna be on that shit and come lookin' to tear your lizard's ass up. Give it a sec."

True to Jones's forecast, a few seconds later, a bass auditioned for the starring role in *Jaws* and reenacted that film's movie poster with the lizard standing in for the woman swimming on the surface of the ocean.

"I tol'ja! Goddamn. Tore his ass up."

Welcome to Roy Jones Jr.'s world.

After we got back to the house, Jones offered to take me over to his old house on Barth Road, where his boxing life began, on the way to pick up some seed for his birds. With his son Roycen asleep in the backseat, we drove over in his large blue Toyota truck. Along the way, he pointed out his school and where various friends and relatives lived and worked around town.

As we got closer to his childhood home, he grew more distant and removed. Then a traffic light off in the distance had his attention.

"Daddy," Roycen, now awake, asked from the backseat. "What was your old job?"

"My old job ain't changed from my current job—I always been a fighter."

"You didn't have no real job before?"

"Boxing always been my job."

Roycen fell back asleep, and I asked his dad if he ever imagined having a "real" job. He smiled, saying, "Nope. This was it."

A few minutes later, he slapped me on the shoulder.

"You see that traffic light next to that old restaurant, Jimmy's Grill?" he asked.

"Yep."

"Jim Lampley vouched for you, so I'm gonna go all-in and show you something right now. I don't like to come around these parts much. Too many bad memories." He grew silent but put his foot down on the gas to accelerate for the light until we were passing traffic along the highway with disturbing ease.

We blew through an amber light at the intersection he'd singled out, and again he slapped me on the shoulder. We were still picking up speed. Jones looked completely relaxed everywhere except for his eyes, fixed in some haunted metaphysical stare across his whole life.

"Now listen," he said. "You keep an eye outside for just how much distance we're covering from here on in till we get back to my old man's house."

I looked over at the odometer under the wheel, but he immediately pointed me out the window to track the mileage via the woods and power lines racing by. After a couple of minutes, Jones braked hard before a turn on Barth Road and gunned it until we reached a gray cinder-block house. I looked at it while Jones stared sullenly straight ahead.

"You looking in the wrong place," he said. "That house ain't the one I grew up in. Mine was across the street." He pointed, and I turned to follow his finger and see a backyard of grass and dirt with hung laundry, a swing, some toys and a few basketballs lying around.

"They tore down our old place and put up something new. Don't think I'd be able to come back here if the old place was still standing. All these roads was dirt before. Not much paved. Changed a lot now. We used to fish and hunt deer in these woods growing up."

"That backyard is where you and your dad first started training?"

"Yup," he said, staring off. "And every single goddamned day I ran from right here all the way out to that traffic light and back. You seen how my knees give me trouble? Wonder why? And I wasn't out there running alone when I was a kid. My dad had older kids from the neighborhood out there with me, and if they beat me, then you know I had a good beatin' waiting for me when I got home."

"He had you out here running ten miles every day?"

"And sparring until I drop. Nothing but training. On my way up as a pro, they used to say I was the most gifted or talented athlete ever to fight. Bullshit! Most talented or gifted?" he glared at me, eyes burning. "Try hardest worker. No fighter in history ever worked harder to achieve their dream than me. Early days? Shit. I worked harder than any fighter in history. Period. End of story."

"And he'd still beat you anyway?"

"Kill 'im, you gonna go to jail," he said, without a trace of emotion in his voice. "You don't kill him, he's gonna end up tryin' to kill you. I grew up always knowing sooner or later I was gonna have to go all the way. When I got old enough—when he killed my dog—by that time, I knew the time had come."

"You ever wonder if your dad had posttraumatic stress disorder from what he saw in Vietnam?"

"Bullshit," Jones scoffed. "Bullshit. If he had PTSD, why was I the only one he inflicted that on? You tell me that. Why not nobody else?"

"It happened, but nothing like what he laid into me with practically every day."

I asked him if I could take a few photos of him in front of the house on the site of the one in which he grew up. "Sure," he said, getting out and inspecting some of the changes.

"You brought up my daddy fighting over in the jungle," Roy said. "My daddy went to Vietnam and then made sure I did too, growing up. He made damn sure."

"How did you survive this shit, Roy?"

"I thought about killing myself all the time. It wasn't like I didn't have access to guns. As I got older, when more people came around to the gym and see us train, he couldn't be as bad as he wanted to be. He had to be more careful in case somebody saw and reported that he was abusing kids. He couldn't be as open back when nobody could see.

"This is a big piece to what made me who I am. But I'm gonna take you to meet a bigger piece. My daddy trained me to be a champion, but his siblings, as much as my mama, looked after me as a human being. While I go play basketball I'm gonna drop you off with my uncle Freddie. Nobody on this earth knows me better than that man."

ROUND SIX

"RJJ" adorns the front gate leading down a steep hill to another of Jones's properties around Pensacola. He bought it soon after he won his first world title. Freddie Jones moved there soon after.

Before becoming part of his nephew's "supporting cast" on the way to boxing glory, Freddie worked at a local Olive Garden and did some landscaping. Though he's actually eight years younger than Roy, over the years, he's often been mistaken for his older brother or taken for his twin. Their physical resemblance is spooky—accentuated by similar broad builds, mustaches, and a shared preference for ball caps—but their characters, by all accounts, are worlds apart.

Freddie had cancer removed from part of his jaw and neck over a decade ago, and yet, soon after his nephew drove off for the naval base to play ball against kids half his age, Freddie wanted to go out for a pack of cigarettes.

"Some people say me and Big Roy are twins despite us being eight years apart," Freddie began. "Usually there's two personalities to every person out there, a good and a bad side. But with me and Big Roy, I think one of us personifies the good and the other personifies the bad side. That's what we probably represented to Little Roy from his point of view.

"I don't think he would have went as far as he did without that balance. He mighta slipped off without that. Any athlete as dedicated as Roy—and there ain't too many I'd put in that category—without that balance, pretty soon you're gonna read about 'em in the paper, you know what I mean?"

"Roy brought up murder and suicide an awful lot when he mentions growing up with his dad, and I didn't get the sense it was hyperbole."

"Little Roy cut off his dad at twenty-three," Freddie shrugged, "to break away from that cycle. I was sorta what you might call their conduit to one another. You remember when Toney was taunting Roy, sayin', 'I'm breakin' you up!' and Little Roy told him, 'I'm your huckleberry'? Well, Big Roy would be on the phone screaming at me two seconds later, 'Who is this guy to talk to him like that? Tell Little Roy to knock this motherfucker's head off!'"

Soon the subject turns to Roy continuing his career at his advanced age. I ask Freddie if he ever thought Little Roy would still be at it, pushing forty-seven next January and still fighting.

"Truthfully," Freddie shrugs. "I thought he'd done enough after the heavyweight title and would move on. But if he's still enjoying it, who's to say he should have to stop? It's always been his decision to make."

"Do you ever wish he'd stop?"

Freddie looked at me hard and reached into his pack for another cigarette. "What I think doesn't matter beyond what I've always tried to do with Little Roy. I was always there to make my nephew the best nephew he could be. I'm not here to exemplify doubt. I don't feel I have that right. I'm here to support in every way I can. I'm not here to deter; I'm here to support."

I shrugged. "It's a cruel game."

"He knows he can't do this forever. Sooner or later, it's gonna end. You can only keep going for a certain length of time. He's typical of most athletes in that he doesn't wanna think when the end is gonna happen. But sooner or later, it's gonna happen to you. That's just the cycle of life.

"He's got so much to live for. He's got kids, his wife . . . pretty soon grandkids. When God says, 'Roy, you went as far as you can, son. Sit down.' I think he's gonna sit down. You can't put this ugly part of life off forever. It's comin'.

"He's probably struggling with it in his mind right now. Fighting is all he knows. I know he don't wanna never come up lame like them other folks I'm sure he's seen come before."

ROUND SEVEN

The following afternoon, Jones picked me up in his blue truck and took me over to the naval base to watch him play his daily game of basketball.

On the way over to the basketball court, we stopped for gas, picked up some more seed for his birds, and passed through the naval checkpoint. Every time Jones has to get out of his truck or even roll down the window, someone recognizes him and greets him warmly. He's gracious and appreciative with anyone he encounters.

His degree of fame in his hometown never seems intrusive for him, and with almost every interaction he delights in putting a smile on people's faces and generally shares a laugh before carrying on his way. But I never had the sense that he was putting on the charm—no celebrity boilerplate. His decency shone through. It's hard to spend any time with him and not have him grow on you.

Jones, four months shy of his forty-seventh birthday, jogged up and down the basketball court on the knees of a seventy-five-year-old construction worker against hyper-athletic youthful military cadets. It was the only basketball court I've ever seen that abutted a wing of the gym reserved for boxing equipment.

While a heavy bag swayed and someone feebly took a few swings at a speed bag, Jones was spotting up for threes and taking his time getting back on defense.

Mostly, he played the game cautiously and intelligently, never overextending himself or risking injury. His knees progressively got worse and more painful. Then a game would get close, and his competitiveness would get the best of him.

His team two points down, I watched him drive through the lane for a layup. The next time down the court, he winced in agony, spinning off a defender for a jump shot for the win. The shot rainbowed down for a swish, and Jones had his jackpot moment. He commenced a Zorro signature with his shooting hand and looked over to the bleachers. "You saw it! Don't pretend like you didn't!"

ROUND EIGHT

The drive over to Big Roy's house was tense and quiet.

Roy Jones Jr. has never minced words when talking about the open wound of his childhood in Pensacola and the "torture chamber" passageway out in the sticks to becoming a man: kill or be killed. Beyond the sanctuary of the ring and raising his beloved roosters, the constant companion of Jones's journey was death—his own or his father's. The switchblade he carried throughout his youth was for protection against his own blood, driven into his father's heart in endless bitter fantasies.

With an almost Dickensian devotion to abuse, humiliation, and torment, his father made sure that before Little Roy entered his teens he was driven to the brink of murder or suicide, often on a daily basis, while being reared to be the greatest fighter who ever lived. By fiendish design, no opponent would ever be more feared than his own father.

Jones confirms that he hasn't had a conversation with his father in over a decade. He says he doesn't worry about missing a chance to make up with Big Roy before he's gone. He says Big Roy isn't worth hating. He says he wouldn't feel "a damn thing" if Big Roy were to pass away. Yet, Jones bought and still pays taxes on Big Roy's house. The Bentley and Rolls-Royce in the driveway? Little Roy bought those, too.

"Where does your dad stack up next to the other famous father-son dads?" I wonder out loud. "I guess I'm thinking of Joe Jackson or Floyd Mayweather Sr."

"My daddy is one of the most brilliant people I ever met," he said, shaking his head. "I'll say that flat out. But listen, Floyd and his daddy make good reality TV. Their deal—for cameras or not—helped sell fights on 24/7. Good for them. Michael and Joe had a TV movie selling their deal as the American Dream. They couldn't make nothin' about me and my daddy if even half of it was true."

Roy reached over with his forearm and showed me some scars. "You imagine doin' that to a little boy? And what I ever do wrong to deserve gettin' whooped the way he done?"

ROUND NINE

A few minutes later, our tires crackled over some pebbles in the dirt as we pulled up in front of a decaying, otherwise plain house with some caged farm animals dozing while others wandered around the yard. The aging, slightly rusting Bentley and Rolls-Royce, mud smeared on their hubcaps, were in the driveway, clashing surreally with the gravel under their tires and an assortment of propped rakes and shovels nearby.

"Hey!" Jones hollered toward the house.

"Hey yourself!" someone growled from inside.

When Big Roy emerged from the back door, he avoided any recognition of his son and glared exclusively at me. Like an old grizzly bear, he lumbered over carefully on his own pair of shaky knees and never broke eye contact.

"Who's this, Roy?" Big Roy asked. Seemingly by instinct, he exerted zero effort to look at his son who, in turn, was looking anywhere but in his father's direction during this exchange.

"This here's a reporter doing a profile on me."

"Yeah?" Big Roy bellowed, reaching up with his index finger to scrape something from his teeth. As he opened his mouth, he exposed only a few badly neglected teeth surrounded by darkness.

"Yeah," said his son.

"OK, then," said Big Roy.

And with that, Little Roy nodded either at a power line or a shingle on a neighbor's house or the sound of a distant train—for all I could tell, that's as close as he wanted to come to actually acknowledging his dad—and turned back for the solace of his truck and immediate departure. I chased after him, but without turning around, he held up his hand to address my concern.

He asked his father to drop me off at the hotel after we were done, and instructed me to then come find him later to talk.

Door slammed. Engine turned. Tires peeled. The father-and-son reunion from hell had concluded.

"Well," said the sixty-nine-year-old Big Roy, straining to smile hospitably. "I gotta pick up my little boy from school. Why don't you hop in my car, and I can drop you off after I pick up the last of my Mohicans."

As the Bentley engine purred, I asked when he and his son had parted ways.

"That's a funny way to put it. We don't interact, but he's still my son," he said. "I told him that, 'Ain't nothing you can do. Ain't nothing I can do. I'm always gonna be your father. What you gonna do with your life is strictly your business.' He couldn't be no bigger screw-up than me.

"But I didn't raise him to be me; I raised him to be better. If somehow you unsatisfied with that when you get old enough to understand that? That's on you. First thing you gotta understand? Boxing was never my idea for what I wanted him to do. It was his dream; it wasn't my dream."

Big Roy's Bentley pulled up into a queue of other parents picking up their kids from elementary school. When his son—maybe a year older than Little Roy's youngest—jumped in the car, he patted my headrest.

"Who dis?"

"Your brother brought him over," Big Roy said, making a little mocking sound in his throat and looking over at me. "What else you wanna ask?"

"You worried your son is fighting too long?"

"Like a lot of folks, I think he shoulda quit too. But if that's what he wanna do? Well, that's his decision. He seems to have all his facilities. The press getting on him about that is gonna do nothing but encourage him to keep going to prove something."

"What could he possibly have left to prove?" I asked.

"I guess, in my belief, he understands he didn't accomplish everything he should've."

"What didn't he accomplish?" I asked.

"It ain't so much money. You can't take that with you. But, you know, legacy? That go with you. That's the reason they name high schools, stadiums—whatever—after you gone.

"Abraham Lincoln? He ain't dead. He's still everywhere you look. You wanna be renowned? It ain't about money; it's about legacy. My son wants to be remembered when he gone. He don't wanna die. When he ceases to exist, he wants to know and feel, there gonna be streets named after him and buildings."

But is it dangerous to still be chasing that?

"The way certain things happened, turn of events, there's an imbalance there," he explained. "Whatever he did, it doesn't add up to a high enough mention. He just figures that he never fulfilled the potential of his talent and ability. You don't detect that in him?"

"He's still going." I shrugged. "So I guess he isn't finished, and something's missing. I don't really see how the cruiserweight title would solve it."

"I want things to turn out well for him because he's my kid. I love him."

"You're proud of him?"

"I'm proud of his success, and I'm even proud of his mistakes. I wish he'd have done some differently, but he's his own man. I always raised him to be that way. Father Time is always gonna be there, and you can't buck him neither. I just wish he'd decide to make up his mind to do it before that decision is made for him."

Big Roy stopped to get his son a Happy Meal from a McDonald's. A minute later, he turned off the highway and pulled into my motel parking lot.

"Here we are," Big Roy announced. "Nice talkin' to you."

ROUND TEN

On the last night I spent with Roy Jones Jr., we were driving back from a sports bar after watching a football game with his son, a cousin, and an old friend.

After asking about my impressions of his old man, he never again returned to watching the game. Suddenly, behind his eyes was the brave and wounded ten-year-old boy self, operating like a ventriloquist with the still-tormented forty-six-year-old man.

For an hour, he tore into his old man with a vengeance I'd never seen him unleash on an opponent throughout his career.

"I got holes," he cried. "My children know I got holes. My wife knows I got holes. But I ain't no liar. Ain't he exactly what I told you he was?" He punctuated each grievance with a backhand against my shoulder and, after roughly a hundred, finally became conscious of it and apologized.

He calmed down enough to inquire about the last story I'd worked on before flying out to Pensacola. I told him it was about Spain's relationship to bullfighting.

His eyes lit up: "I'd love bullfighting. Always wanted to see one. That's something I gotta see. Who's the Ali of bullfighting?"

"A matador named Juan Belmonte."

"He get gored pretty bad?"

"His critics said that the only thing he didn't do inside a bullring was die in one. He did everything else."

"How'd he end up?" Jones Jr. asked eagerly.

"He came out of retirement a few times. He lived hard, but he got old. Developed a heart condition and lung cancer. His doctors told him if he wanted to prolong the inevitable, he couldn't smoke, drink, fuck, or ride horses anymore."

"What he do?"

"He had his horse brought over to his house, some cigars, couple bottles of his favorite wine, and two of the best-looking prostitutes from a Seville brothel sent to meet him at a cottage he rode over to. The next morning, he blew his head off."

Jones laughed. "I wouldn't blown my damn head off," he said, smiling mischievously. "Why blow your head off? I'd have had that day over and over again until I finally died. My old barber, they told him if he kept drinking, he was gonna die. He said, 'OK. But I'm not gonna stop drinking.' So he kept drinking until he died. But you know what he told me? He said, 'I gotta die of something.'"

CONTRIBUTORS

ROBERT ANASI is the author of *The Gloves: A Boxing Chronicle* and *The Last Bohemia: Scenes from Life in Williamsburg, Brooklyn.* His journalism, interviews, and reviews have appeared in the *New York Times,* the *Times Literary Supplement, Virginia Quarterly Review,* the *New York Observer, Salon,* and *Publishers Weekly.* He received his PhD from the University of California, Irvine, where he was both a Schaeffer and Chancellor's Club Fellow. He is also a founding editor of the literary journal *Entasis.*

BRIN-JONATHAN BUTLER has written for *SBnation, ESPN Magazine, Harper's,* the *Paris Review, Esquire, Salon,* and *Vice.* He published his second book with Picador USA in 2015, a memoir of his time in Cuba: *The Domino Diaries: My Decade Boxing with Olympic Champions and Chasing Hemingway's Ghost in the Last Days of Castro's Cuba.*

DONOVAN CRAIG lives in Georgia with his wife and their two children. He has covered combat sports on four continents and to this day is the only journalist to cover a mixed martial arts competition in an active warzone—in Mosul, Iraq, in 2008. When he sold stocks, he once talked a preacher into mortgaging his house to cover a margin call. Today he abhors all lies. Jack Dempsey is still his hero.

SARAH DEMING'S essays about boxing, booze, and sex have appeared in the *Threepenny Review, Penthouse Forum,* the *Washington Post,* the

Guardian, and *Stiff Jab.* She is the author of the children's novel *Iris, Messenger,* ghostwriter of several erotic novels, and researcher for the ultramarathon memoir *Eat and Run.* Sarah won a Pushcart Prize, a MacDowell Fellowship, and around half of her amateur fights. She coaches at Atlas Cops and Kids, a free youth boxing gym in Brooklyn.

MICHAEL EZRA has been in post-prime decline since 1979, when he won the spelling bee and made the all-star team. These days he works as a college professor and is the author of *Muhammad Ali: The Making of an Icon* and the editor of the *Journal of Civil and Human Rights.* He lives in California with his wife, daughter, and cat.

CHARLES FARRELL has spent his professional life moving between music and boxing, with occasional detours. He has managed five world champions, and played and recorded with many of the musicians he most admires—Ornette Coleman, Evan Parker, and Jim Schapperoew among them.

RAFAEL GARCIA was born in Nuevo Laredo, Mexico. He became a fan of the sweet science at age seven while watching Julio Cesar Chavez versus Meldrick Taylor. He has covered dozens of live cards throughout the United States and Canada and writes exclusively for *The Fight City.* He obtained his master's degree from Concordia University in Montreal, where he currently lives with his girlfriend and baby daughter.

GORDON MARINO is professor of philosophy and director of the Hong Kierkegaard Library at St. Olaf College, Northfield, Minnesota. He is the boxing writer for the *Wall Street Journal* and a regular contributor to *The Ring.* The former head coach of boxing at Virginia Military Institute, Marino has been training fighters since 1994.

LOUIS MOORE is associate professor of history at Grand Valley State University, where he teaches African American history, civil rights, sports, and US history. His research and writing examine interconnections between race, gender, and sports. He is finishing *Beyond the Battle Royal*, a book about boxing, black manhood, and race in America from 1880 to 1915 and is also under contract to write a book about the black athlete and the civil rights movement.

GARY LEE MOSER, who was instantly and totally captured by the classic middleweight battle between Nino Benvenuti and Luis Rodriguez in 1969, has amassed a prodigious personal library of boxing memorabilia that has fostered his abiding interest in the analysis of career records, with particular appreciation for sustained excellence over the merely meteoric. A retired corporate accountant, he is a stock day trader and continues a quest to run the Boston Marathon despite the lasting effects of a car crash in 1987.

HAMILTON NOLAN has written for *Gawker* since 2008 and covers boxing for *Deadspin* and HBO. He lives in Brooklyn.

GABE OPPENHEIM has written two books, one of which examines the lives of boxers in the hard-knocks city of Philadelphia. His articles and essays—on boxing, on Cuba, on postage in the Himalayas—have appeared in the *Washington Post*, *Rolling Stone*, *Vice*, and other outlets. He writes and lives in New York and is currently at work on a forthcoming novel set in the pulpy yakuza underworld of 1960s Tokyo.

CARLO ROTELLA'S books include *October Cities*, *Good with Their Hands*, *Cut Time*, and *Playing in Time*. He is a regular contributor to the *New York Times Magazine*, and his work has also appeared in the *New Yorker*, *Harper's*, *Slate*, the *Boston Globe*, *The Believer*, and *The Best American Essays*. A recipient of a Guggenheim fellowship, the Whiting Writers Award, and the L. L. Winship/PEN New England Award, he is director of American Studies at Boston College.

SAM SHERIDAN washed dishes on the USNS *Able* after high school, and from there it was a short step to Harvard University. Sam has worked as a professional sailor, a wild-land firefighter with the Gila Hotshots, a ranch-hand on the largest cattle ranch in Montana, and a construction worker at the South Pole Station in Antarctica. He's the author of *A Fighter's Heart*, *The Fighter's Mind*, and *The Disaster Diaries*.

CARL WEINGARTEN is an American music producer, slide guitarist, photographer, writer, and film collector. As a teenager studying filmmaking, he was inspired by the excitement surrounding the first Muhammad Ali–Joe Frazier fight and soon became an avid boxing enthusiast. His passion for boxing history includes a lifelong pursuit and study of historic fight films. He has consulted for and provided footage to *Sports Illustrated*, ESPN, documentaries, and public schools. He lives in the San Francisco Bay Area.